Silas White Leonard

New Christian Psalmist

A Collection of Psalms, Hymns, and Spiritual Songs, with Appropriate...

Silas White Leonard

New Christian Psalmist
A Collection of Psalms, Hymns, and Spiritual Songs, with Appropriate...

ISBN/EAN: 9783337041847

Printed in Europe, USA, Canada, Australia, Japan

Cover: Foto ©Thomas Meinert / pixelio.de

More available books at **www.hansebooks.com**

CHRISTIAN PSALMIST:

A COLLECTION OF

Psalms, Hymns, and Spiritual Songs,

WITH APPROPRIATE MUSIC, ORIGINAL AND SELECTED,

SUITABLE FOR

Family and Congregational Worship,

SINGING CLASSES AND SUNDAY-SCHOOLS.

COMPILED AND ARRANGED BY

SILAS W. LEONARD,

AUTHOR OF THE "CHRISTIAN PSALMIST," "CHRISTIAN VOCALIST," "NUMERAL SINGER," "S. S. HYMN BOOK," "TEMPERANCE SONGSTER," ETC., ETC.

. SECOND EDITION.

CINCINNATI:
R. W. CARROLL & CO., PUBLISHERS,
117 WEST FOURTH STREET,
1871.

Entered according to Act of Congress, in the year 1870,

BY R. W. CARROLL & CO.,

In the Office of the Librarian of Congress, at Washington.

ELECTROTYPED AT THE FRANKLIN TYPE FOUNDRY, CINCINNATI.

INTRODUCTORY NOTE.

As the author of "THE NEW CHRISTIAN PSALMIST" died before a Preface was written for his book, I have been requested by the Publishers to write an Introductory Note. This I do with the more pleasure, because I believe the book which he has prepared is a good one, and will meet a public want.

The popularity of the old "CHRISTIAN PSALMIST," by the same author, was unprecedented—560,000 copies having been sold since its first publication. That work is now out of print, and this is designed to take its place.

While the new book will contain many of the same features, and much of the same matter, it is, in my judgment, far superior in almost all respects to the old edition. It contains a larger per cent. of the old *standard* tunes, a better selection of hymns, and is published in both round notes and figure-faced notes, so that purchasers can order either edition they may desire.

The "NEW CHRISTIAN PSALMIST" will carry with it a melancholy interest to those who have become familiar with the name of its lamented author. He had just put the last pages into the hands of the Publishers when he was called home to join in the new song which, we are assured, the redeemed of God are permitted to sing when they have passed from the toils and struggles of the present life. Let us hope that this, his last work, may prove to be his best, and that it will contribute to the joy of thousands of hearts in the sweet service of sacred song.

ISAAC ERRETT.

CINCINNATI, December 5, 1870.

THE
NEW CHRISTIAN PSALMIST.

DEVOTION. L. M.

1 *Praise to God.* L. M.

ALL-POWERFUL, self-existent God,
Who all creation does sustain!
Thou wast, and art, and art to come,
And everlasting is thy reign.

2 Fixed and eternal as thy days,
Each glorious attribute divine,
Through ages infinite, shall still
With undimished luster shine.

3 Fountain of being! source of good!
Immutable dost thou remain;
Nor can the shadow of a change
Obscure the glories of thy reign.

4 Earth may with all her powers dissolve,
If such the great Creator's will:
But thou forever art the same;
"I am" is thy memorial still.

2 *Power of God.* L. M.

ETERNAL Power! whose high abode
Becomes the grandeur of a God;
Infinite lengths beyond the bounds
Where stars revolve their little rounds.

2 Thee, while the first archangel sings,
He hides his face behind his wings;
And ranks of shining thrones around
Fall worshiping, and spread the ground.

3 Lord, what shall earth and ashes do?
We would adore our Maker too;
From sin and dust to thee we cry,
The Great, the Holy, and the High.

4 Earth from afar hath heard thy fame,
And worms have learned to lisp thy name,
But, oh! the glories of thy mind
Leave all our soaring thoughts behind.

5 God is in heaven, and men below;
Be short our tunes, our words be few;
A solemn reverence checks our songs,
And praise sits silent on our tongues.

3 *God, the Helper.* L. M.

MY Helper, God! I bless his name,
The same his power, his grace the same,
The tokens of his friendly care
Open, and crown, and close the year.

2 I 'mid ten thousand dangers stand,
Supported by his guardian hand;
And see, when I survey my ways,
Ten thousand monuments of praise.

3 Thus far his arm has led me on;
Thus far I make his mercy known;
And, while I tread this desert land,
New blessings shall new songs demand.

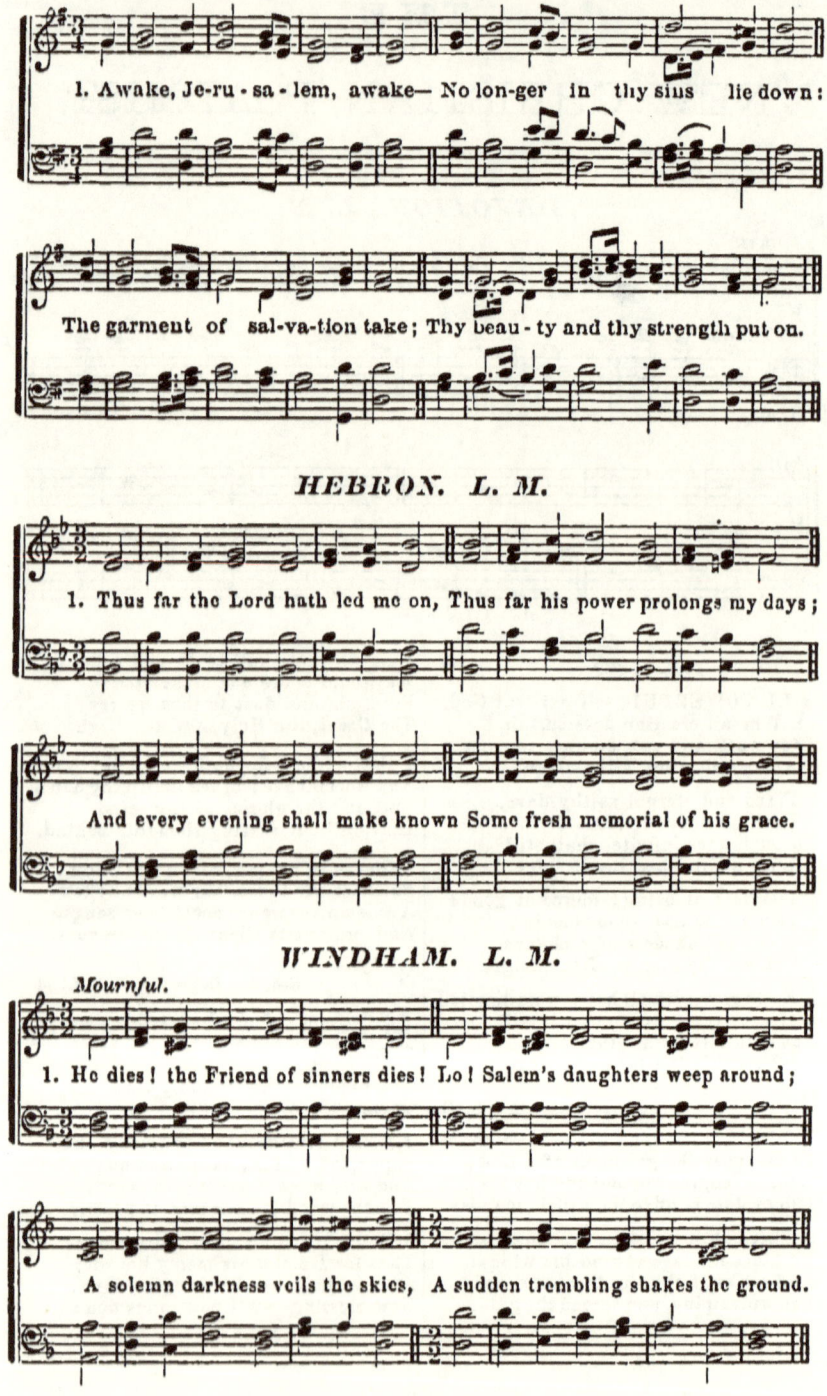

PRAISE TO GOD.

4 *Put on thy beautiful garments, O Jerusalem.* L. M.

AWAKE, Jerusalem, awake!
No longer in thy sins lie down:
The garment of salvation take:
Thy beauty and thy strength put on.

2 Shake off the dust that binds thy sight,
And hides the promise from thine eyes;
Arise, and struggle into light;
The great Deliv'rer calls, Arise!

3 Shake off the bands of sad despair;
Zion, assert thy liberty;
Look up, thy broken heart prepare,
And God shall set the captive free.

4 Vessels of mercy, sons of grace,
Be purged from every sinful stain;
Be like your Lord, his word embrace,
Nor bear his hallow'd name in vain.

5 *Great is the Lord.* L. M.

PRAISE ye the Lord! 'tis good to raise
Our hearts and voices in his praise:
His nature and his works invite
To make this duty our delight.

2 Great is the Lord! and great his might,
And all his glories infinite:
His wisdom vast, and knows no bound,
A deep where all our tho'ts are drowned.

3 He loves the meek, rewards the just,
Humbles the wicked in the dust,
Melts and subdues the stubborn soul,
And makes the broken spirit whole.

4 His saints are precious in his sight;
He views his children with delight;
He sees their hope, he knows their fear,
Approves, and loves his image there.

6 *Evening hymn.* L. M.

THUS far the Lord hath led me on,
Thus far his power prolongs my days;
And every evening shall make known
Some fresh memorial of his grace.

2 Much of my time has run to waste,
And I, perhaps, am near my home;
But he forgives my follies past;
He gives me strength for days to come.

3 I lay my body down to sleep;
Peace is the pillow for my head;
While well-appointed angels keep
Their watchful stations round my bed.

4 Faith in his name forbids my fear;
Oh, may thy presence ne'er depart!
And in thy morning make me hear
Thy loving-kindness in my heart.

5 And when the night of death shall come,
Still may I trust almighty love—
The love which triumphs o'er the tomb,
And leads to perfect bliss above.

7 *"How unsearchable are thy judgments."* L. M.

LORD, my weak thought in vain would climb
To search the starry vault profound;
In vain would wing her flight sublime,
To find creation's utmost bound.

2 But weaker yet that tho't must prove,
To search thy great eternal plan—
Thy sovereign counsels, born of love
Long ages ere the world began.

3 When my dim reason would demand
Why that, or this, thou dost ordain,
By some vast deep I seem to stand,
Whose secrets I must ask in vain.

4 When doubts disturb my troubled breast,
And all is dark as night to me,
Here, as on solid rock, I rest;
That so it seemeth good to thee.

5 Be this my joy, that evermore
Thou rulest all things at thy will:
Thy sovereign wisdom I adore,
And calmly, sweetly, trust thee still.

8 *Eternity of God.* L. M.

ERE mountains reared their forms sublime,
Or heaven and earth in order stood,
Before the birth of ancient time,
From everlasting thou art God.

2 A thousand ages, in their flight,
With thee are as a fleeting day;
Past, present, future, at thy sight
At once their various scenes display.

3 But our brief life's a shadowy dream,
A passing thought, that soon is o'er,
That fades with morning's earliest beam,
And fills the musing mind no more.

4 To us, O Lord, the wisdom give
Each passing moment so to spend,
That we at length may with thee live,
Where life and bliss shall never end.

9 *The all-seeing God.* L. M.

LORD, thou hast searched and seen me through;
Thine eye commands with piercing view
My rising and my resting hours,
My heart and flesh with all their powers.

2 My thoughts, before they are my own,
Are to my God distinctly known;
He knows the words I mean to speak
Ere from my opening lips they break.

3 Within thy circling power I stand;
On every side I find thy hand:
Awake, asleep, at home, abroad,
I am surrounded still with God.

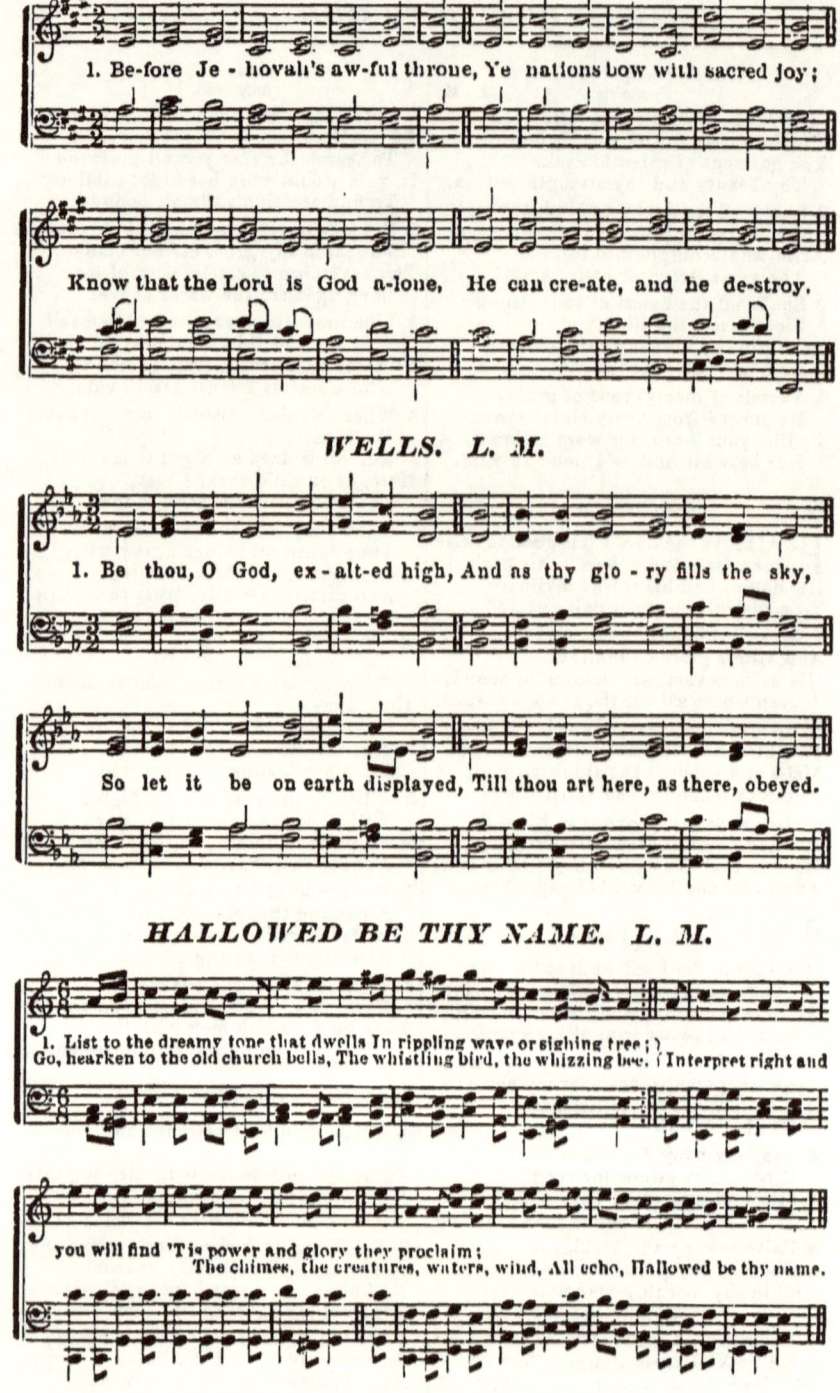

10   Praise.   L. M.

BE thou, O God, exalted high,
   And as thy glory fills the sky,
So let it be on earth displayed,
Till thou art here, as there, obeyed.

2 O God, my heart is fixed; 'tis bent,
Its thankful tribute to present;
And, with my heart, my voice I'll raise
To thee, my God, in songs of praise.

3 Thy praises, Lord, I will resound
To all the listening nations round;
Thy mercy highest heaven transcends;
Thy truth beyond the clouds extends.

4 Be thou, O God, exalted high,
And as thy glory fills the sky,
So let it be on earth displayed,
Till thou art here, as there, obeyed.

11   Praise.   L. M.

BEFORE Jehovah's awful throne,
   Ye nations bow with sacred joy;
Know that the Lord is God alone,
He can create and he destroy.

2 His sovereign power, without our aid,
Made us of clay and formed us men;
And when, like wandering sheep, we strayed,
He brought us to his fold again.

3 We'll crowd thy gates with thankful songs;
High as the heavens our voices raise;
And earth, with her ten thousand tongues,
Shall fill thy courts with sounding praise.

4 Wide as the world is thy command,
Vast as eternity thy love;
Firm as a rock thy truth shall stand,
When rolling years have ceased to move.

12   Hallowed be thy Name.   L. M.

LIST to the dreamy tone that dwells
   In rippling wave or sighing tree;
Go, hearken to the old church bells,
The whistling bird, the whizzing bee.
Interpret right, and you will find
   'Tis power and glory they proclaim;
The chimes, the creatures, waters, wind,
   All echo, Hallowed be thy name.

2 The pilgrim journeys till he bleeds,
To gain the altar of his sires;
The hermit pores above his beads
With zeal that never wanes or tires:
But holiest rite or longest prayer
That art can yield or wisdom frame,
What better import can it bear [name?"
Than, "Father, hallowed be thy

3 Or nature, or the Bible, read, [still;
Those precious words you'll find there
We trace them in the flowering mead,
We hear them in the flowing rill.
One chorus hails the great Supreme;
Each varied breathing tells the same;
The strains may differ, but the theme
Is, "Father, hallowed be thy name."

13   Praise.   L. M.

WITH Israel's God who can compare?
   Or who, like Israel, happy are?
Oh, people saved by the Lord,
He is our shield and great reward.

2 Upheld by everlasting arms,
We are secure from foes and harms!
In vain their plots and false their boasts—
Our refuge is the Lord of hosts.

14   All thy works praise thee.   L. M.

NATURE, with all her powers, shall
   God the Creator, and the King; [sing
Nor air, nor earth, nor skies, nor seas,
Deny the tribute of their praise.

2 Begin to make his glories known,
Ye seraphs, who sit near his throne;
Tune high your harps, and spread the
To the creation's utmost bound. [sound

3 Thus let our flaming zeal employ
Our loftiest thoughts and fondest songs;
Nations, pronounce with warmest joy
Hosannas, from ten thousand tongues.

4 Yet, mighty God, our feeble frame
Attempts in vain to reach thy name;
The strongest notes that angels raise
Faint in the worship and the praise.

15   He raiseth the stormy wind.   L. M.

GLORY to thee, whose powerful word
   Bids the tempestuous wind arise;
Glory to thee, the sovereign Lord
Of air and earth, and seas and skies.

2 Let air, and earth, and skies obey,
And seas thy awful will perform;
From them we learn to own thy sway,
And shout to meet the gathering storm.

3 What though the floods lift up their voice;
Thou hearest, Lord, our silent cry;
They can not damp thy children's joys,
Or shake the soul, while God is nigh.

4 Roar on, ye waves! our souls defy
Your roaring to disturb their rest;
In vain to impair the calm ye try—
The calm in a believer's breast.

BRIDGEWATER. L. M.

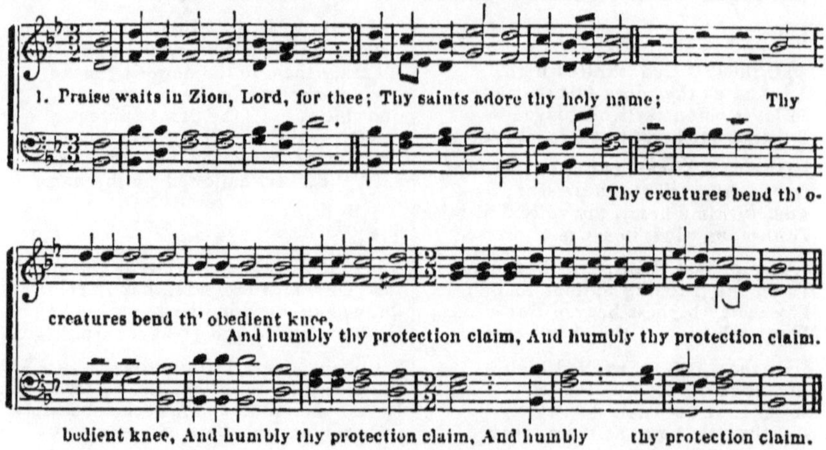

1. Praise waits in Zion, Lord, for thee; Thy saints adore thy holy name; Thy
Thy creatures bend th' o-
creatures bend th' obedient knee,
And humbly thy protection claim, And humbly thy protection claim.
bedient knee, And humbly thy protection claim, And humbly thy protection claim.

LUTON. L. M.

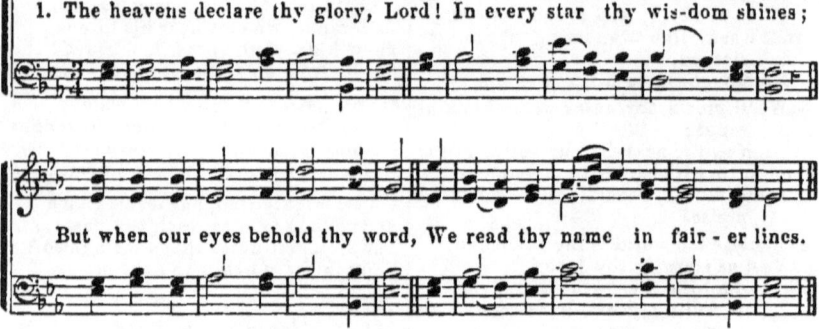

1. The heavens declare thy glory, Lord! In every star thy wis-dom shines;
But when our eyes behold thy word, We read thy name in fair - er lines.

CHESTER. L. M.

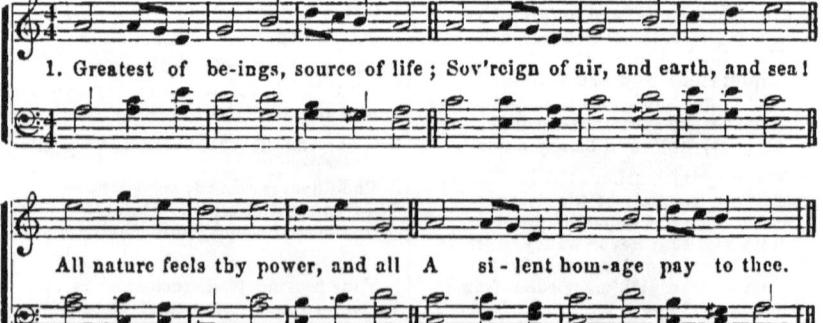

1. Greatest of be-ings, source of life; Sov'reign of air, and earth, and sea!
All nature feels thy power, and all A si - lent hom-age pay to thee.

16   *The Lord Reigneth.*   L. M.

GIVE thanks to God, he reigns above,
  Kind are his thoughts, his name is
His mercy ages past have known, [love;
  And ages long to come shall own.

2 He feeds and clothes us all the day;
He guides our footsteps in the way,
And guards us with a powerful hand,
And brings us to the heavenly land.

3 Oh, let the saints with joy record,
The truth and goodness of the Lord;
How great his works! how kind his ways!
Let every tongue pronounce his praise!

17   *Praise waits in Zion.*   L. M.

PRAISE waits in Zion, Lord, for thee;
  Thy saints adore thy holy name;
Thy creatures bend th' obedient knee,
And humbly thy protection claim.

2 Thy hand has raised us from the dust;
  The breath of life thy Spirit gave;
Where, but in thee, can mortals trust?
Who, but our God, has power to save?

3 Eternal source of truth and light,
To thee we look, on thee we call;
Lord, we are nothing in thy sight,
But thou to us art all in all.

4 Still may thy children in thy word,
  Their common trust and refuge see;
Oh, bind us to each other, Lord,
By one pure tie—the love of thee.

5 So shall our sun of hope arise,
With brighter still, and brighter rays,
Till thou shalt bless our longing eyes,
With beams of everlasting days.

18   *The works and word of God.*   L. M.

THE heavens declare thy glory, Lord!
  In every star thy wisdom shines;
But when our eyes behold thy word,
We read thy name in fairer lines.

2 The rolling sun, the changing light,
  And nights and days thy power confess,
But the blest volume thou hast writ
Reveals thy justice and thy grace.

3 Sun, moon, and stars convey thy praise
Round the whole earth, and never
So when thy truth began its race, [stand;
It touched and glanced on every land.

4 Nor shall thy spreading gospel rest
Till thro' the world thy truth has run;
Till Christ has all the nations blest
That see the light, or feel the sun.

5 Great Sun of Righteousness! arise;
Bless the dark world with heavenly
  light;
Thy gospel makes the simple wise,
Thy laws are pure, thy judgments right.

6 Thy noblest wonders here we view,
  In souls renewed, and sins forgiven;
Lord! cleanse my sins, my soul renew,
And make thy word my guide to
  heaven.

19   *He is clothed with majesty.*   L. M.

JEHOVAH reigns: he dwells in light,
  Arrayed with majesty and might;
The world, created by his hands,
Still on its firm foundation stands.

2 But ere this spacious world was made,
Or had its first foundation laid,
His throne eternal ages stood,
Himself the ever-living God.

3 Forever shall his throne endure;
His promise stands forever sure;
And everlasting holiness
Becomes the dwellings of his grace.

20   *Thy saints shall bless thee.*   L. M.

GREATEST of beings, source of life;
  Sov'reign of air, and earth, and sea!
All nature feels thy power, and all
A silent homage pay to thee.

2 Waked by thy hand, the morning sun
Pours forth to thee its earlier rays,
And spreads thy glories as it climbs;
While raptured worlds look up and
  praise.

3 The moon, to the deep shades of night,
Speaks the mild luster of thy name;
While all the stars, that cheer the scene,
Thee, the great Lord of light, proclaim.

4 And groves, and vales, and rocks, and
And every flower, and every tree, [hills,
Ten thousand creatures, warm with life,
Have each a grateful song for thee.

21   *Praise of God due from man.*   L. M.

THERE seems a voice in every gale,
  A tongue in every opening flower,
Which tells, O Lord! the wondrous tale
Of thy indulgence, love, and power.

2 The birds that rise on soaring wing
Appear to hymn their Maker's praise,
And all the mingling sounds of spring
To thee a general pæan raise.

3 And shall my voice, great God, alone
Be mute 'midst nature's loud acclaim?
No; let my heart with answering tone
Breathe forth in praise thy holy name.

4 And nature's debt is small to mine;
Thou bad'st her being bounded be,
But—matchless proof of love divine—
Thou gav'st immortal life to me.

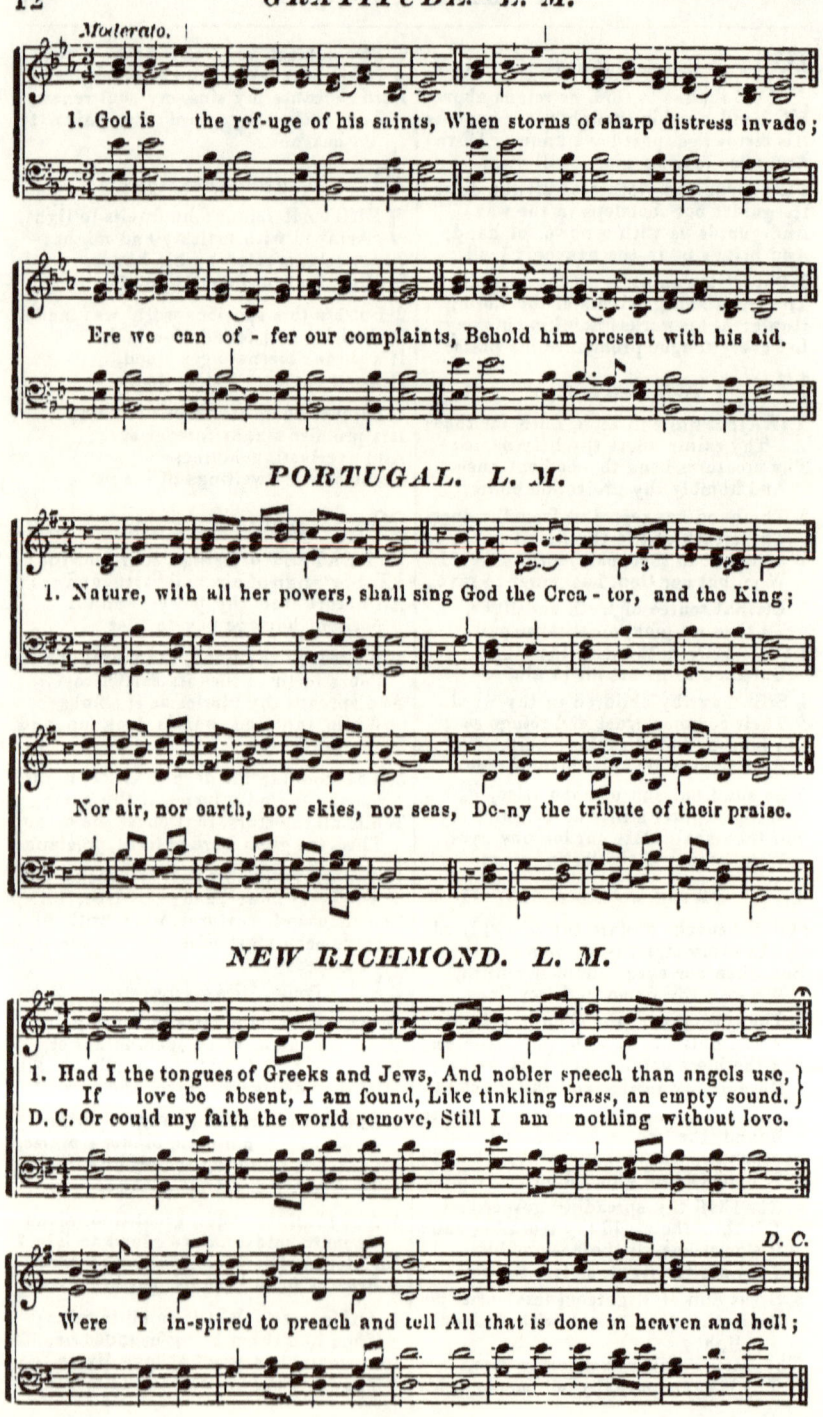

22 God is our refuge. L. M.

GOD is the refuge of his saints,
When storms of sharp distress invade;
Ere we can offer our complaints,
Behold him present with his aid.

2 Loud may the troubled ocean roar;
In sacred peace our souls abide;
While every nation, every shore,
Trembles, and dreads the swelling tide.

3 Zion enjoys her Monarch's love,
Secure against a threatening hour;
Nor can her firm foundation move,
Built on his truth and armed with power.

23 Give cheerfully. L. M.

COME, let us, with a joyful heart,
In this blest labor share a part;
Not prayers alone, but off'rings bring,
To aid the triumphs of our King.

2 Our hearts exult in songs of praise,
In hope to see the latter days;
Oh, may we not forget to prove '
By generous deeds how much we love.

3 Where'er his hand has spread the skies,
His bounty every need supplies;
Shall we not imitate his grace,
And fill with gifts this favoring place?

4 A generous heart the Lord approves,
A liberal hand our Savior loves;
Come, then, you saints, approve his will,
And let your gifts his treas'ry fill.

24 Creation and redemption. L. M.

GIVE to our God immortal praise;
Mercy and truth are all his ways:
Wonders of grace to God belong;
Repeat his mercies in your song.

2 Give to the Lord of lords renown,
The King of kings with glory crown:
His mercies ever shall endure,
When lords and kings are known no more.

3 He built the earth, he spread the sky,
And fixed the starry lights on high;
Wonders of grace to God belong;
Repeat his mercies in your song.

4 He fills the sun with morning light,
He bids the moon direct the night;
His mercies ever shall endure, [more.
When suns and moons shall shine no

5 He sent his Son with power to save
From guilt and darkness, and the grave:
Wonders of grace to God belong;
Repeat his mercies in your song.

6 Through this vain world he guides our
And leads us to his heavenly seat; [feet,
His mercies ever shall endure,
When this vain world shall be no more.

25 The more excellent way. L. M.

HAD I the tongues of Greeks and Jews,
And nobler speech than angels use,
If love be absent, I am found,
Like tinkling brass, an empty sound.

2 Those joys which earth can not afford,
We'll seek in fellowship to prove,
Joined in one spirit to our Lord,
Together bound by mutual love.

3 And while we pass this vale of tears
We'll make our joys and sorrows known;
We'll share each other's hopes and fears,
And count a brother's cares our own.

4 Once more our welcome we repeat,
Receive assurance of our love;
Oh, may we all together meet
Around the throne of God above.

26 Contentment. L. M.

O LORD, how full of sweet content
My years of pilgrimage are spent!
Where'er I dwell, I dwell with thee,
In heaven, in earth, or on the sea.

2 To me remains nor place nor time;
My country is in every clime:
I can be calm and free from care
On any shore, since God is there.

3 While place I seek, or place I shun,
The soul finds happiness in none;
But with my God to guide my way,
'T is equal joy to go or stay.

27 Grace. L. M.

MY God, how excellent thy grace!
Whence all our hope and comfort
The sons of Adam, in distress, [springs;
Fly to the shadow of thy wings.

2 Life, like a fountain rich and free,
Springs from the presence of my Lord,
And in thy light our souls shall see
The glories promised in thy word.

28 Rocked in the cradle of the deep. L. M.

ROCKED in the cradle of the deep,
I lay me down in peace to sleep;
Secure I rest upon the wave,
For thou, O Lord! hast power to save.

2 I know thou wilt not slight my call!
For thou dost mark the sparrow's fall!
And calm and peaceful is my sleep,
Rocked in the cradle of the deep.

3 And such the trust that still were mine,
Though stormy winds swept o'er the brine,
Or though the tempest's fiery breath
Roused me from sleep to wreck and death.

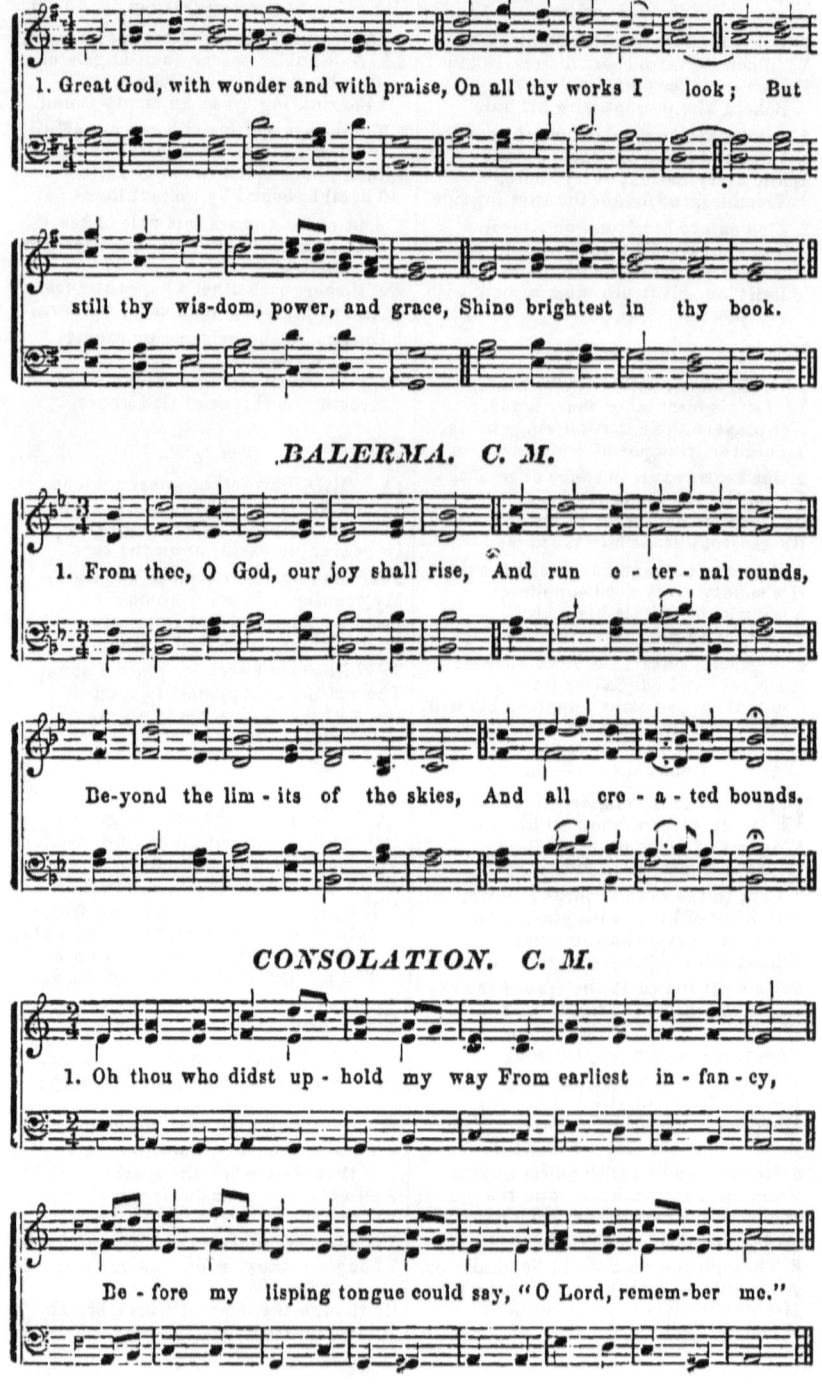

BALERMA. C. M.

CONSOLATION. C. M.

29 *The Bible.* C. M.

GREAT God, with wonder and with
  On all thy works I look; [praise,
But still thy wisdom, power, and grace,
  Shine brightest in thy book.

2 Here are my choicest treasures hid;
    Here my best comfort lies;
  Here my desires are satisfied,
    And here my hopes arise.

3 Lord, make me understand thy law;
    Show what my faults have been;
  And from thy gospel let me draw
    The pardon of my sin.

30 *The Infinite One.* C. M.

GREAT God, how infinite art thou!
  How frail and weak are we!
Let the whole race of creatures bow,
  And pay their praise to thee.

2 Thy throne eternal ages stood,
    Ere seas or stars were made;
  Thou art the everliving God,
    Were all the nations dead.

3 Eternity, with all its years,
    Stands present in thy view;
  To thee there's nothing old appears;
    Great God! there's nothing new.

4 Our lives through varying scenes are
    And vexed with trifling cares, [drawn,
  While thine eternal thought moves on
    Thine undisturbed affairs.

5 Great God, how infinite art thou!
    How frail and weak are we!
  Let the whole race of creatures bow,
    And pay their praise to thee.

31 *Immortality of the soul.* C. M.

FROM thee, O God, our joy shall rise,
  And run eternal rounds,
Beyond the limits of the skies,
  And all created bounds.

2 The holy triumphs of our souls
    Shall death itself outbrave,
  Leave dull mortality behind,
    And fly beyond the grave.

3 There, where our blessed Savior reigns,
    In heaven's unmeasured space,
  We'll spend a long eternity
    In pleasure and in praise.

4 Blest Savior, every smile of thine
    Shall fresh endearments bring,
  And thousand tastes of new delight
    From all thy graces spring.

5 Haste, our beloved, bear our souls
    Up to thy blest abode;
  Haste, for our spirits long to see
    Our Savior and our God.

32 *Compared with Christ.* C. M.

COMPARED with Christ, in all beside
  No comeliness I see;
The one thing needful, dearest Lord,
  Is to be one with thee.

2 The sense of thy expiring love
    Into my soul convey;
  Thyself bestow! for thee alone,
    My ALL in ALL I pray.

3 Less than thyself will not suffice
    My comfort to restore;
  More than thyself I can not crave;
    And thou canst give no more.

4 Whate'er consists not with thy love,
    Oh, teach me to resign;
  I'm rich to all th' intents of bliss
    If thou, O God, art mine.

33 *Lord, remember me.* C. M.

O THOU who didst uphold my way
    From earliest infancy,
  Before my lisping tongue could say,
    "O Lord, remember me!"

2 Still thro' the path of youth, my guide
    And my protector be;
  And when my feet would turn aside,
    "O Lord, remember me!"

3 And shouldst thou graciously ordain
    That manhood I should see,
  Oh, let me never live in vain;
    "O Lord, remember me!"

4 If thou shouldst pain or sickness send,
    From murm'ring keep me free;
  Or, if thy hand should riches lend,
    "O Lord, remember me!"

34 *Man frail—God eternal.* C. M.

O GOD, our help in ages past,
    Our hope for years to come,
  Our shelter from the stormy blast,
    And our eternal home.

2 Beneath the shadow of thy throne,
    Thy saints have dwelt secure;
  Sufficient is thy arm alone,
    And our defense is sure.

3 Before the hills in order stood,
    Or earth received her frame,
  From everlasting thou art God,
    To endless years the same.

4 A thousand ages in thy sight,
    Are like an evening gone:
  Short as the watch that ends the night,
    Before the rising sun.

5 The busy tribes of flesh and blood,
    With all their cares and fears,
  Are carried downward with the flood,
    And lost in following years.

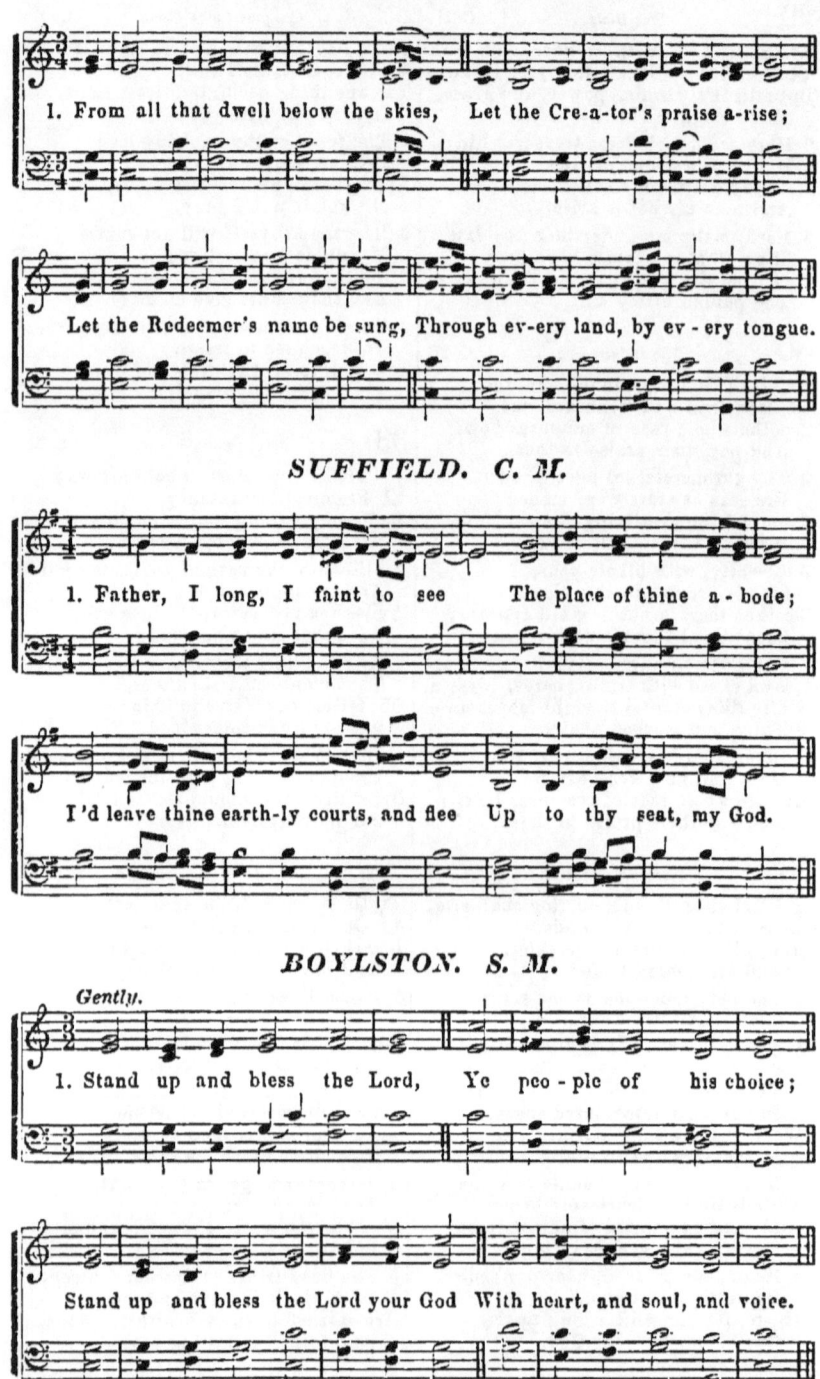

35 *Let every one that hath breath praise the Lord.* L. M.

FROM all that dwell below the skies,
  Let the Creator's praise arise;
Let the Redeemer's name be sung,
Through every land, by every tongue.

2 Eternal are thy mercies, Lord,
Eternal truth attends thy word; [shore,
Thy praise shall sound from shore to
Till suns shall rise and set no more.

36 *Great is the Lord, and greatly to be praised.* C. M.

FATHER, I long, I faint to see
  The place of thine abode;
I'd leave thine earthly courts, and flee
Up to thy seat, my God.

2 Here I behold thy distant face,
And 't is a pleasing sight;
But to abide in thine embrace
Is infinite delight.

3 There all the heavenly hosts are seen,
In shining ranks they move;
And drink immortal vigor in,
With wonder and with love.

4 There at thy feet with awful fear
Adoring armies fall;
With joy they shrink to nothing there,
Before th' Eternal All.

5 There I would vie with all the host
In duty and in bliss;
While less than nothing I could boast,
And vanity confess.

6 The more thy glories strike mine eyes
The humbler I shall lie;
While thus I sink, my joys shall rise
Immeasurably high.

37 *Bless the Lord, oh, my soul.* S. M.

STAND up and bless the Lord,
  Ye people of his choice;
Stand up and bless the Lord your God
With heart, and soul, and voice.

2 Though high above all praise,
Above all blessing high,
Who would not fear his holy name,
And laud, and magnify?

3 Oh! for the living flame,
From his own altar brought,
To touch our lips—our minds inspire,
And raise to heaven our thought.

4 God is our strength and song,
And his salvation ours;
Then be his love in Christ proclaimed,
With all our ransomed powers.

5 Stand up and bless the Lord,
The Lord your God adore;
Stand up and bless his glorious name
Henceforth for evermore.

38 *Thy will be done on earth as in heaven.* L. M.

OUR Father, God, who art in heaven,
  To thy great name be reverence given,
Thy peaceful kingdom wide extend,
And reign, O Lord, till time shall end.

2 Thy sacred will on earth be done,
As 't is by angels round thy throne;
And let us ev'ry day be fed,
With earthly and with heavenly bread.

3 Our sins forgive, and teach us thus
To pardon those who injure us;
Our shield in all temptations prove,
And every evil far remove.

4 Thine is the kingdom to control,
And thine the power to save the soul;
Great be the glory of thy reign,
Let every creature say, Amen.

39 *Praise ye the Lord.* S. M.

O LORD, our heavenly king,
  Thy name is all divine;
Thy glories round the earth are spread,
And o'er the heavens they shine.

2 When to thy works on high,
I raise my wondering eyes,
And see the moon, complete in light,
Adorn the darksome skies:

3 When I survey the stars,
And all their shining forms,
Lord, what is man, that worthless thing,
Akin to dust and worms?

4 Lord, what is worthless man,
That thou shouldst love him so?
Next to thine angels is he placed,
And lord of all below.

5 How rich thy bounties are!
How wondrous are thy ways!
That from the dust thy power should
A monument of praise. [frame

6 To God the Father sing
Hallelujah and praise:
To Christ our great and gracious King,
Your loudest anthems raise!

40 *Contrition.* S. M.

IS this the kind return?
  Are these the thanks we owe?
Thus to abuse eternal love,
Whence all our blessings flow?

2 Turn, turn us, mighty God,
And mold our souls afresh;
Break, sovereign grace, these hearts of
And give us hearts of flesh. [stone,

3 Let past ingratitude
Provoke our weeping eyes;
And hourly, as new mercies fall,
Let hourly thanks arise.

41 *I will praise Thee early.* C. M.

MY God was with me all the night,
 And gave me sweet repose;
His angels watched me while I slept,
 Or I had never rose.

2 Now, for the mercies of the night,
 My humble thanks I'll pay;
And unto God I'll dedicate
 The first fruits of the day.

3 In midst of dangers, fears, and deaths,
 Thy goodness I'll adore;
And praise thee for thy mercies past,
 And humbly hope for more.

4 My life, if thou preserve my life,
 Thy sacrifice shall be;
My death, when death shall be my lot,
 Shall join my soul to thee.

42 *He giveth his beloved sleep.* C. M.

DREAD Sovereign, let my evening
 Like holy incense rise;   [song
Assist the off'rings of my tongue
 To reach the lofty skies.

2 Through all the dangers of the day,
 Thy hand was still my guard;
And still to drive my wants away,
 Thy mercy stood prepared.

3 Sprinkled afresh with pard'ning blood,
 I lay me down to rest;
As in the embraces of my God,
 Or on my Savior's breast.

43 *Praise to Christ.* C. M.

HOSANNA to the Prince of Light,
 Who clothed himself in clay,
Entered the iron gates of death,
 And tore the bars away.

2 Death is no more the king of dread,
 Since our Immanuel rose;
He took the painful sting away,
 And spoiled our hellish foes.

3 See how the Conqueror mounts aloft,
 And to his Father flies,
With scars of honor in his flesh,
 And triumph in his eyes.

4 There our exalted Savior reigns,
 And scatters blessings down;
Our Jesus with his Father sits
 On the celestial throne.

5 Raise your devotion, mortal tongues,
 To reach his blest abode;
Sweet be the accents of your songs,
 To our incarnate God.

6 Bright angels, strike your loudest
 Your sweetest voices raise; [strings,
Let heaven, and all created things,
 Sound our Immanuel's praise.

44 *Prayer and praise to God.* C. M.

O GOD, with humble heart and voice,
 We now approach thy throne,
Released from every earthly thought,
 To worship thee alone.

2 Thy all-sustaining hand has kept
 Us safe since morning light,
And now we thy protection ask,
 To guard us through the night.

3 Oh, may our thankful songs to thee
 Like grateful incense rise,
And mingle with the praises which
 Are sung above the skies.

4 But when we lift the voice in prayer,
 With reverential fear,
Bow down from out thy high abode,
 And condescend to hear.

5 For oh, we come as children come,
 And ask thee to supply
Our hungry souls with living food,
 Which thou wilt ne'er deny.

6 But as the gentle dews descend,
 So may thy grace be given,
To cheer us in thy earthly courts,
 While on our way to heaven.

7 Oh, may our hearts all yield to thee,
 Our stormy passions cease,
As fall the waters of the deep,
 When thou commandest peace.

45 *Praise ye the Lord.* C. M.

GREAT God, where'er we pitch our
 Let us an altar raise;   [tent,
And there, with humble frame, present
 Our sacrifice of praise.

2 To thee we give our health and strength,
 While health and strength shall last;
For future mercies humbly trust,
 Nor e'er forget the past.

46 *Praise to God.* S. M.

YOUR harps, ye trembling saints,
 Down from the willows take;
Loud to the praise of love divine,
 Bid every strain awake.

2 His grace shall to the end,
 Stronger and brighter shine;
Nor present things, nor things to come,
 Shall mar his love divine.

3 The glorious time will come,
 When all shall plainly see,
And know, ev'n as we now are known,
 Throughout eternity.

4 Lord, search and know our hearts,
 Oh, make our souls sincere:
Bid all hypocrisy depart,
 And keep our conscience clear.

47 *I was brought low, and he helped me.* L. M.

I WILL extol thee, Lord, on high:
  At thy command diseases fly;
Who, but a God can speak and save
From the dark borders of the grave?

2 Thine anger but a moment stays,
Thy love is life and length of days:
Though grief and tears the night employ,
The morning star restores our joy.

48 *The Lord will strengthen him, etc.* C. M.

WHEN languor and disease invade
  This trembling house of clay,
'Tis sweet to look beyond my pains
And long to fly away:

2 Sweet to look inward, and attend
The whispers of his love;
Sweet to look upward to the place
Where Jesus pleads above.

3 Sweet to look back, and see my name
In life's fair book set down;
Sweet to look forward, and behold
Eternal joys my own.

4 Sweet to rejoice in lively hope,
That when my change shall come,
Angels shall hover round my bed,
And waft my spirit home.

5 Sweet in his faithfulness to rest,
Whose love can never end;
Sweet on his covenant of grace
For all things to depend.

6 If such the sweetness of the streams,
What must the fountain be,
Where saints and angels draw their bliss
Immediately from thee!

7 Oh may the unction of these truths
Forever with me stay;
Till, from her sin-worn cage dismiss'd,
My spirit flies away.

49 *Entire submission.* C. M.

AND can my heart aspire so high,
  To say—"My Father God?"
Lord, at thy feet I long to lie,
And learn to kiss the rod.

2 I would submit to all thy will,
For thou art good and wise;
Let every anxious thought be still,
Nor one faint murmur rise.

3 Thy love can cheer the darksome gloom,
And bid me wait serene; [gloom,
Till hopes and joys immortal bloom,
And brighten all the scene.

4 My Father! Oh permit my heart
To plead her humble claim;
And ask the bliss those words impart,
In my Redeemer's name.

50 *The sorrows of death compassed me.* C. M.

MY God, thy service well demands
  The remnant of my days:
Why was this fleeting breath renew'd,
But to renew thy praise?

2 Thine arms of everlasting love
Did this weak frame sustain;
When life was hov'ring o'er the grave,
And nature sunk with pain.

3 Thou, when the pains of death were
Didst chase the fears of hell, [felt,
And teach my pale and quiv'ring lips
Thy matchless grace to tell.

4 Calmly I bow'd my fainting head
On thy dear, faithful breast;
Pleas'd to obey my Father's call
To his eternal rest.

5 Into thy hands, my Savior God,
Did I my soul resign,
In firm dependence on that truth
Which made salvation mine.

6 Back from the borders of the grave,
At thy command I come,
Nor will I urge a speedier flight
To my celestial home.

51 *The refiner's fire.* L. M.

SAVIOR! though my rebellious will
  Has been, by thy blest power, re-
Yet in its secret workings still [newed;
How much remains to be subdued!

2 Oft I recall, with grief and shame,
How many years their course had run
Ere grace my murmuring heart o'ercame,
Ere I could say, "Thy will be done!"

3 At length thy patient, wondrous love,
Unchanging, tender, pitying, strong,
Availed that stony heart to move,
Which had rebelled, alas! so long,

4 Then was I taught by thee to say,
"Do with me what to thee seems best;
Give, take, whate'er thou wilt away,
Health, comfort, usefulness, or rest.

5 "Be my whole life in suffering spent,
But let me be in suffering thine;
Still, O my Lord, I am content, [mine."
Thou now hast made thy pleasure

52 *God only is my rock.* L. M.

MY spirit looks to God alone;
  My rock and refuge is his throne;
In all my fears, in all my straits,
My soul for his salvation waits.

2 Trust him, ye saints, in all your ways;
Pour out your hearts before his face;
When helpers fail and foes invade,
God is our all-sufficient aid.

53 *Remember me!* C. M.

O THOU from whom all goodness flows,
 I lift my soul to thee;
In all my sorrows, conflicts, woes,
 O Lord, remember me.

2 If, for thy sake, upon my name
 Reproach and shame shall be,
I'll hail reproach, and welcome shame;
 O Lord, remember me.

3 When worn with pain, disease and grief,
 This feeble body see;
Grant patience, rest, and kind relief;
 O Lord, remember me.

4 When, in the solemn hour of death,
 I wait thy just decree,
Be this the prayer of my last breath,
 O Lord, remember me.

5 And when before thy throne I stand,
 And lift my soul to thee,
Then, with the saints at thy right hand,
 O Lord, remember me.

54 *Heaven upon earth.* S. M.

MY God, my life, my love,
 To thee, to thee, I call:
I can not live if thou remove,
 For thou art all in all.

2 Thy shining grace can cheer
 This dungeon where I dwell:
'T is paradise when thou art here,
 If thou depart, 't is hell.

3 The smilings of thy face,
 How amiable they are!
'T is heaven to rest in thine embrace,
 And nowhere else but there.

4 To thee, and thee alone,
 The angels owe their bliss;
They sit around thy gracious throne,
 And dwell where Jesus is.

5 Not all the harps above
 Can make a heavenly place,
If God his residence remove,
 Or but conceal his face.

6 Nor earth, nor all the sky,
 Can one delight afford,
Nor yield one drop of real joy,
 Without thy presence, Lord.

7 Thou art the sea of love,
 Where all my pleasures roll:
The circle where my passions move,
 And center of my soul.

8 To thee my spirits fly,
 With infinite desire;
And yet how far from thee I lie!
 O Jesus, raise me higher.

55 *Bless, oh, my soul, the living God.* L. M.

BLESS, oh, my soul, the living God,
 Call home thy thoughts that rove
 abroad;
Let all the powers within me join,
In work and worship so divine.

2 Bless, oh, my soul, the God of grace,
 His favors claim thy highest praise;
Why should the wonders he has wrought
Be lost in silence and forgot.

3 The vices of the mind he heals,
 And cures the pain that nature feels,
Redeems the soul from death, and saves
Our wasting life from threatening graves.

4 Our youth decayed, his power repairs;
 His mercy crowns our growing years;
He satisfies our souls with good,
And fills our hopes with heavenly food.

56 *Reign in the Lord.* L. M.

YE nations round the earth, rejoice
 Before the Lord your Sovereign
 King;
Serve him with cheerful heart and voice;
 With all your tongues his glory sing.

2 The Lord is God, 't is he alone
 Doth life, and breath, and being give;
We are his work, and not our own,
 The sheep that on his pasture live.

3 Enter his gates with songs of joy;
 With praises to his courts repair;
And make it your divine employ
 To pay your thanks and honors there.

4 The Lord is good; the Lord is kind;
 Great is his grace, his mercy sure;
And all the race of man shall find
 His truth from age to age endure.

57 *The morning cometh.* C. M.

LIGHT of the lonely pilgrim's heart,
 Star of the coming day!
Arise, and with thy morning beams
 Chase all our griefs away!

2 Come, blessed Lord! let every shore
 And answering island sing
The praises of thy royal name,
 And own thee as their King.

3 Bid the whole earth, responsive now
 To the bright world above,
Break forth in sweetest strains of joy
 In memory of thy love.

4 Jesus! thy fair creation groans,
 The air, the earth, the sea,
In unison with all our hearts,
 And calls aloud for thee.

58 *The day of reckoning.* L. M.

THERE comes a day, a fearful day,
  When earth and heaven shall flee
    away.
Then, flaming on his great white throne,
Naught shall be seen but God alone;
The myriad crowds from every clime,
Shall gaze upon that throne sublime.
The great and small, the quick and dead,
Shall shout with joy, or quake with dread.

2 Oh! how shall I, a sinner born,
Lift up my head on that dread morn,
When glory, brightening to excess,
Proclaims the God of holiness?
The holy God, the lofty Lord,
Who, by his own omnific word,
Made thousand thousand worlds to be;
He speaks again, and lo! they flee.

3 When orbs on orbs affrighted fly,
In lawless terror through the sky;
When thrones and powers celestial fall
Before the glorious ALL IN ALL;
Oh! how shall I of baser birth,
A sinful man, a worm of earth,
Presume to meet the burning gaze
That wraps the heavens in sheets of
    blaze!

59 *The heavens declare thy glory.* L. M.

NATURE with all her power, shall sing
  Her great Creator, and her King:
Nor air, nor earth, nor skies, nor seas,
Deny the tribute of their praise.

2 Ye angels near his radiant throne,
Unite to make his glories known;
Attune your harps, and spread the sound
Throughout creation's utmost bound.

3 Oh may our grateful zeal employ
Each power of mind to hymns of joy;
And join, with heart-inspiring songs,
The anthems of angelic tongues.

4 Yet, gracious God, our feeble frame
Attempts in vain to reach thy name;
The highest notes that angels raise
Fall far below thy glorious praise.

60 *Just and true are thy ways.* C. M.

SINCE all the varying scenes of time
  God's watchful eye surveys,
Oh, who so wise to choose our lot,
  Or to appoint our ways!

2 Good when he gives—supremely good—
  Nor less when he denies;
E'en crosses, from his sov'reign hand,
  Are blessings in disguise.

3 Why should we doubt a Father's love,
  So constant and so kind?
To his unerring, gracious will
  Be every wish resign'd.

61 *Sanctify the Lord God in your hearts.* C. M.

WHILE thee I seek, protecting Power,
  Be my vain wishes stilled;
And may this consecrated hour
  With better hopes be filled.

2 Thy love the power of thought bestow-
  To thee my thoughts would soar; [ed;
Thy mercy o'er my life has flowed;
  That mercy I adore.

3 In each event of life, how clear
  Thy ruling hand I see!
Each blessing to my soul more dear,
  Because conferred by thee.

4 In every joy that crowns my days,
  In every pain I bear,
My heart shall find delight in praise,
  Or seek relief in prayer.

5 When gladness wings my favored hour,
  Thy love my thoughts shall fill;
Resigned, when storms of sorrow lower,
  My soul shall meet thy will.

6 My lifted eye, without a tear,
  The gathering storm shall see;
My steadfast heart shall banish fear;
  That heart shall rest on thee.

62 *Thy will be done.* C. M.

HOW sweet to be allowed to pray
  To God, the Holy One;
With filial love and trust to say,
  "O God, thy will be done."

2 We in these sacred words can find
  A cure for every ill;
They calm and soothe the troubled mind
  And bid all care be still.

3 Oh let that Will which gave me breath
  And an immortal soul,
In joy or grief, in life or death,
  My every wish control.

4 Oh, could my heart thus ever pray,
  Thus imitate thy Son!
Teach me, O God, with truth to say,
  Thy will, not mine, be done.

63 *Retirement and meditation.* C. M.

I LOVE to steal awhile away
  From every cumbering care,
And spend the hours of setting day
  In humble, grateful prayer.

2 I love in solitude to shed
  The penitential tear;
And all his promises to plead,
  Where none but God can hear.

3 I love to think on mercies past,
  And future good implore,
And all my cares and sorrows cast
  On him whom I adore.

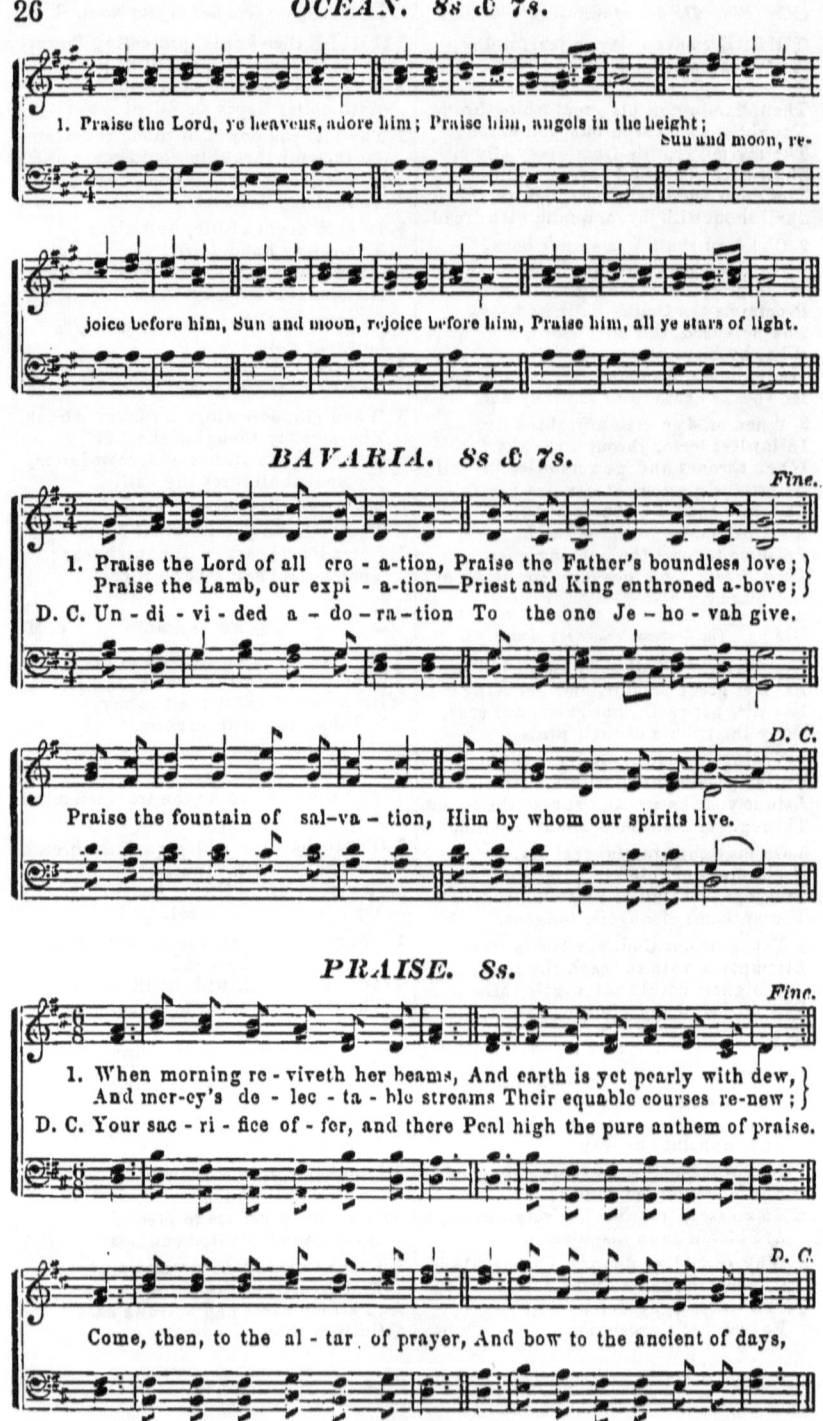

64 *Praise the Lord.* 8s & 7s.

PRAISE the Lord, ye heavens adore him,
  Praise him angels in the height.
Sun and moon rejoice before him,
  Praise him all ye stars of light.

2 Praise the Lord, for he hath spoken;
  Worlds his mighty voice obeyed;
Laws which never can be broken,
  For their guidance he hath made.

3 Praise the Lord, for he is glorious;
  Never shall his promise fail:
God doth make his saints victorious;
  Sin and death shall not prevail.

4 Praise the God of our salvation;
  Hosts on high his power proclaim;
Heaven and earth, and all creation,
  Praise and magnify his name.

65 *Greatness of God.* 8s & 7s.

GOD of all created wonder,
  God of countless orbs of light,
God of rain, and wind, and thunder,
  God of morning, noon, and night;
Blessed be thy name forever,
  Blessed be thy glorious reign;
Thy great system faileth never,
  All thy works in truth remain.

2 God of valley, plain, and mountain,
  God of garden, field, and wood;
God of river, stream, and fountain,
  God of all created good;
Thy great system faileth never,
  All thy works in truth remain;
Blessed be thy name forever,
  Blessed be thy glorious reign.

3 God of mercy, God of heaven,
  God of faith, and hope, and love,
Thankful are we that 't is given
  Us to have our hopes above.
Gracious Father, by thy Spirit
  And thy Word may we be led
Safely, until we inherit
  All that thou hast promised.

66 *Every tongue shall confess.*

COME, ye saints, come and adore Him,
  Fall before his glorious throne;
Angels prostrate fall before Him,
  Their Creator and our own.

2 Sinners, come and make confession,
  Of his high exalted name,
He was bruised for your transgressions,
  To redeem your souls he came.

3 All on earth and all in heaven,
  Join to chant a solemn song:
Unto Jesus should be given,
  Praises that to Him belong.

67 *"I will praise Thee right early.* 8s.

WHEN morning reviveth her beams,
  And earth is yet pearly with dew,
And mercy's delectable streams,
  Their equable courses renew;
Come then to the altar of prayer,
  And bow to the ancient of days,
Your sacrifice offer, and there
  Peal high the pure anthem of praise.

2 The God of the seasons adore,
  When spring breathes her earliest
When winter reluctant is o'er, [breeze,
  And smile all the rivers and trees;
When summer, in showers and gales,
  Her merciful mission fulfills;
When plenty matures in the vales
  And joy speaks aloud from the hills.

3 When autumn is sober and sere,
  And pours out her plentiful store,
Oh then, as declineth the year,
  The God of abundance adore;
When winter obscureth the sky,
  And vapory turbulence blows,
Forbid that devotion should die,
  Or freeze with the frosts and the snows.

4 At home with thy kindred and friends,
  Alone, or with strangers abroad,
Whatever kind Providence sends,
  Oh call on the name of thy God:
When sickness at last is thy lot,
  And death hastens on in the gloom,
The monarch of terrors fear not,
  For Jesus has conquered the tomb.

68 *God is love.* 8s & 7s.

WHEN the orb of morn enlightens
  Hill and mountain, mead and dell,
When the dim horizon brightens,
  And the serried clouds dispel,
And the sunflower eastward bending,
  Its fidelity to prove,
Be thy gratitude ascending
  Unto Him whose name is love.

2 When the vesper star is beaming
  In the coronet of even,
And the lake and river gleaming
  With the ruddy hues of heaven;
When a thousand notes are blending,
  In the forest and the grove,
Be thy gratitude ascending
  Unto Him whose name is love.

3 When the stars appear in millions
  In the portals of the west,
Bright bespangling the pavilions
  Where the blessed are at rest;
When the milky way is glowing
  In the cope of heaven above,
Let thy gratitude be flowing
  Unto Him whose name is love.

PRAISE TO GOD.

69 *Let all the angels of God worship Him.* C. M.

ALL hail the power of Jesus' name!
  Let angels prostrate fall:
Bring forth the royal diadem,
  And crown him Lord of all.

2 Crown him, you martyrs of our God,
    Who from his altar call:
  Extol the stem of Jesse's rod,
    And crown him Lord of all.

3 Ye chosen seed of Israel's race,
    A remnant weak and small,
  Hail him who saves you by his grace,
    And crown him Lord of all.

4 You Gentile sinners, ne'er forget
    The wormwood and the gall;
  Go, spread your trophies at his feet,
    And crown him Lord of all.

5 Babes, men, and sires, who know his love,
    Who feel your sin and thrall,
  Now join with all the hosts above,
    And crown him Lord of all.

6 Let every kindred, every tribe,
    On this terrestrial ball,
  To him all majesty ascribe,
    And crown him Lord of all.

7 Oh, that with yonder sacred throng,
    We at his feet may fall!
  We 'll join the everlasting song,
    And crown him Lord of all.

70 *All things are yours.* C. M.

SINCE God is mine, then present things
  And things to come are mine;
Yea, Christ, his word, and spirit, too,
  And glory all divine.

2 Since he is mine, then from his love
    He every trouble sends;
  All things are working for my good,
    And bliss his rod attends.

3 Since he is mine, I need not fear
    The rage of earth and hell;
  He will support my feeble power,
    Their utmost force repel.

4 Since he is mine, let friends forsake,
    Let wealth and honors flee:
  Sure, he who giveth me himself,
    Is more than these to me.

5 Since he is mine, I 'll boldly pass
    Through death's dark, lonely vale:
  He is my comfort and my stay,
    When heart and flesh shall fail.

6 And now, O Lord, since thou art mine,
    What can I wish beside?
  My soul shall at the fountain live,
    When all the streams are dried.

71 *Holy is his name.* C. M.

HOLY and reverend is the name
  Of our eternal King;
"Thrice holy Lord," the angels cry—
  Thrice holy let us sing.

2 The deepest reverence of the mind
    Is due unto the Lord,
  And he by all about him should
    With reverence be adored.

3 With sacred awe pronounce his name,
    Whom words nor thoughts can reach:
  A contrite heart shall please him more
    Than noblest forms of speech.

4 Thou holy God preserve our souls
    From all pollution free;
  The pure in heart are thy delight,
    And they thy face shall see.

72 *The sacred day.* C. M.

WITH joy we hail the sacred day
  Which God has called his own;
With joy the summons we obey
  To worship at his throne.

2 Thy tabernacles, Lord, how fair!
    Where willing votaries throng,
  To breathe the humble, fervent prayer,
    And pour the choral song.

3 Savior of men, oh deign to dwell
    Within thy church below;
  Make her in holiness excel,
    With pure devotion glow.

4 Let peace within her walls be found —
    Let all her sons unite
  To spread with grateful zeal around
    Her clear and shining light.

5 Great God, we hail the sacred day
    Which thou hast called thine own;
  With joy the summons we obey
    To worship at thy throne.

73 *The Lord reigneth.* C. M.

KEEP silence—all created things,
  And wait your Maker's nod,
My soul stands trembling while she sings
  The honors of her God.

2 Life, death, and hell, and worlds un-
    Hang on his firm decree;   [known
  He sits on an eternal throne,
    Supremely high is he.

3 His providence unfolds his book,
    And makes his counsels shine,
  Each opening leaf—and every stroke
    Fulfill some deep design.

4 In thy fair book of life and grace,
    Oh may I find my name
  Recorded in some humble place,
    Beneath the Lord, the Lamb.

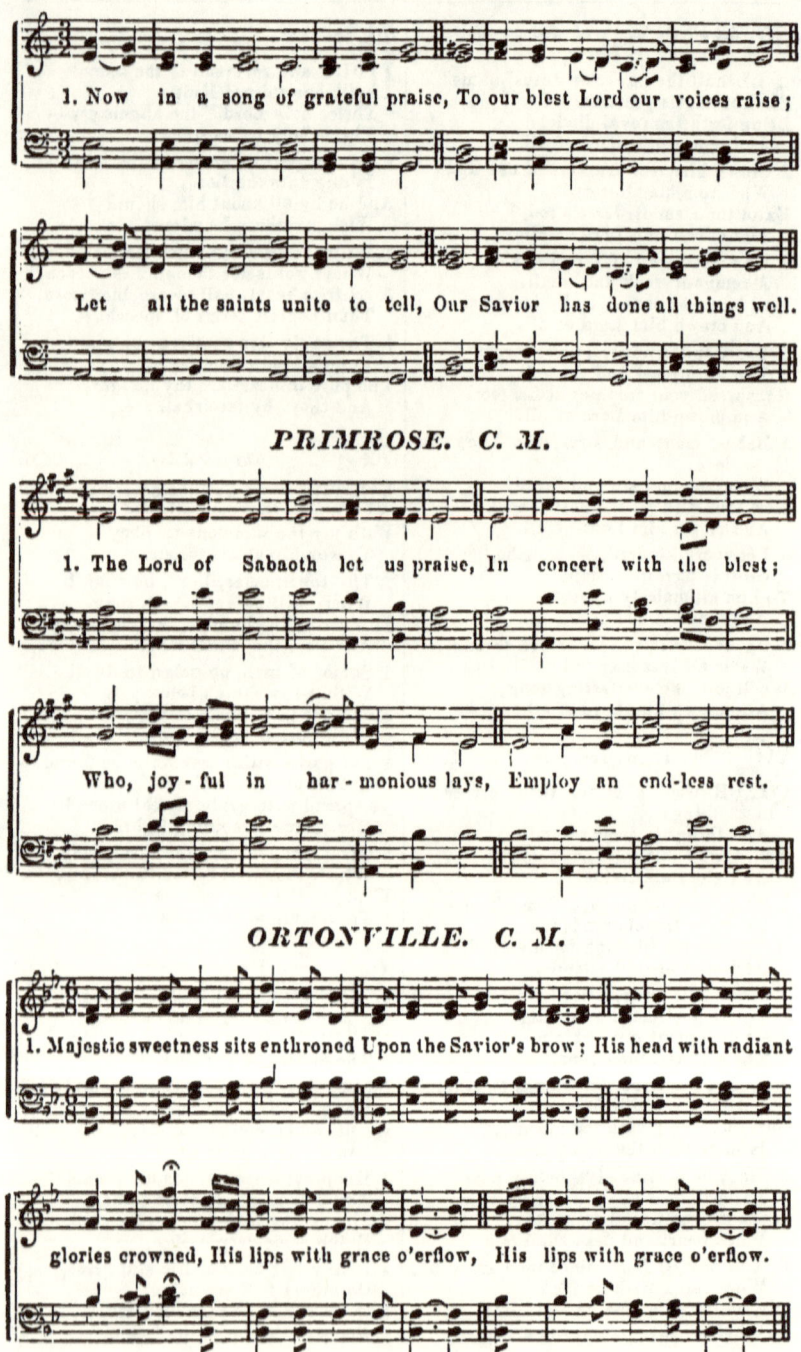

74. Praise to Christ. L. M.

NOW in a song of grateful praise,
  To our blest Lord our voices raise;
Let all the saints unite to tell
Our Savior has done all things well.

2 All worlds his glorious power confess,
  His wisdom all his works express;
But, oh, his love, what tongue can tell
Our Savior has done all things well.

3 We spurned his grace, we broke his laws,
  But yet he undertook our cause,
To save our ruined souls from hell;
Our Savior has done all things well.

4 And now our souls have known his love,
  What mercy has he made us prove!
His mercy doth all praise excel;
Our Savior has done all things well.

5 Soon shall we pass the vale of death,
  And in his arms resign our breath;
And then our happy souls shall tell
Our Savior has done all things well.

75. Sing Praises. C. M.

THE Lord of Sabbaoth let us praise,
  In concert with the blest,
Who, joyful in harmonious lays,
  Employ an endless rest.

2 Thus, Lord, while we remember thee,
  We blessed and pious grow;
By hymns of praise we learn to be
  Triumphant here below.

3 On this glad day a brighter scene
  Of glory was displayed,
By Him, th' eternal Word, than when
  This universe was made.

4 He rises, who mankind has bought
  With grief and pain extreme:
'T was great to speak the world from
'T was greater to redeem. [naught;

76. Let us go up to the house of the Lord. C. M.

WITHIN thy house, O Lord our God,
  In glory now appear:
Make us the place of thine abode,
  And shed thy brightness here.

2 While we thy mercy-seat surround,
  Thy spirit, Lord, impart,
And let thy word's all-cheering sound,
  With power reach every heart.

3 Here let the blind their sight obtain;
  Here give the mourners rest;
Let Jesus here triumphant reign,
  Enthroned in every breast.

4 Here let the voice of sacred joy
  And humble prayer arise,
Till higher strains our tongues employ,
  In realms beyond the skies.

77. Chief among ten thousand. C. M.

MAJESTIC sweetness sits enthroned
  Upon the Savior's brow;
His head with radiant glories crowned,
  His lips with grace o'erflow.

2 No mortal can with him compare
  Among the sons of men;
Fairer is he, than all the fair
  Who fill the heavenly train.

3 He saw me plunged in deep distress,
  And flew to my relief;
For me he bore the shameful cross,
  And carried all my grief.

4 To him I owe my life and breath,
  And all the joys I have;
He makes me triumph over death,
  And saves me from the grave.

5 To heaven, the place of his abode,
  He brings my weary feet;
Shows me the glories of my God,
  And makes my joys complete.

6 Since from thy bounty I receive
  Such proofs of love divine,
Had I a thousand hearts to give,
  Lord! they should all be thine.

78. The chief corner-stone. C. M.

BEHOLD the sure foundation-stone
  Which God in Zion lays,
To build our heavenly hopes upon,
  And his eternal praise.

2 Chosen of God, to sinners dear,
  Let saints adore thy name;
They trust their whole salvation here,
  Nor shall they suffer shame.

3 The foolish builders, scribes, and priest
  Reject it with disdain;
Yet on this rock the church shall rest,
  And envy rage in vain.

4 What though the gates of hell with-
  Yet must this building rise; [stood;
'T is thine own work, almighty God,
  And wondrous in our eyes.

79. Prayer. C. M.

AGAIN, indulgent Lord, return
  With sweet and quickening grace,
To cheer and warm our sluggish souls,
  And speed us in our race.

2 Awake our love, our faith, our hope,
  For fortitude and joy;
Vain world begone—let things above
  Our happy thoughts employ.

3 Instruct our minds, our souls subdue,
  To heaven our passions raise,
And let our life forever be
  Devoted to thy praise.

80   *Christ is born in Bethlehem.*   7s.

SONGS of praise awoke the morn,
   When the Prince of Peace was born;
Songs of praise arose, when he
   Captive led captivity.

2 Heaven and earth must pass away,
Songs of praise shall crown that day ;
God will make new heavens and earth,
Songs of praise shall hail their birth.

3 And will man alone be dumb,
Till that glorious kingdom come?
No; the church delights to raise
Psalms, and hymns, and songs of praise.

4 Saints below, with heart and voice,
Still in songs of praise rejoice ;
Learning here, by faith and love,
Songs of praise to sing above.

5 Borne upon the latest breath,
Songs of praise shall conquer death ;
Then, amidst eternal joy,
Songs of praise their powers employ.

81   *Love to the Savior.*   7s.

HARK, my soul—it is the Lord!
   'T is thy Savior, hear his word:
Jesus speaks, he speaks to thee!
"Say, poor sinner, lov'st thou me?

2 "I delivered thee when bound,
And, when bleeding, heal'd thy wound;
Sought thee wand'ring, set thee right,
Turn'd thy darkness into light.

3 "Can a mother's tender care
Cease toward the child she bare?
Yes, she may forgetful be,
Yet will I remember thee.

4 "Mine is an unchanging love,
Higher than the heights above,
Deeper than the depths beneath,
Free and faithful, strong as death.

5 "Thou shalt see my glory soon,
When the work of faith is done,
Partner of my throne shall be :
Say, poor sinner, lov'st thou me?"

82   *Praise.*   7s.

HEAVENLY Father, sovereign Lord,
   Be thy glorious name adored!
Lord, thy mercies never fail,
Hail, celestial goodness, hail,

2 Though unworthy, Lord, thine ear,
Deign our humble songs to hear ;
Purer praise we hope to bring, .
When around thy throne we sing.

3 Then with angel harps again,
We will make a nobler strain ;
There in joyful songs of praise,
Our triumphant voices raise.

83   *Praise to Jesus.*   8s & 7s.

COME, thou Fount of every blessing,
   Tune my heart to sing thy grace:
Streams of mercy, never ceasing,
   Call for songs of loudest praise;
Teach me some melodious sonnet,
   Sung by flaming tongues above;
Praise the mount—I'm fixed upon it;
   Mount of thy redeeming love!

2 Here I'll raise my Ebenezer,
   Hither, by thy help, I'm come;
And I hope, by thy good pleasure,
   Safely to arrive at home.
Jesus sought me, when a stranger,
   Wand'ring from the fold of God!
He, to rescue me from danger,
   Interposed his precious blood!

3 Oh! to grace how great a debtor,
   Daily I'm constrained to be!
Let thy goodness, like a fetter,
   Bind my wand'ring heart to thee!
Prone to wander, Lord, I feel it ;
   Prone to leave the God I love—
Here's my heart, oh take and seal it
   Seal it for thy courts above.

84   *Prayer and praise.*   8s & 7s.

LOVE divine, all love excelling,
   Joy of heaven, to earth come down ;
Fix in us thy humble dwelling,
   All thy faithful mercies crown!
Jesus, thou art all compassion,
   Pure unbounded love thou art ;
Visit us with thy salvation ;
   Enter every trembling heart.

2 Breathe, oh breathe thy loving Spirit
   Into every troubled breast !
Let us all in thee inherit,
   Let us find that second rest.
Take away our bent to sinning,
   Alpha and Omega be,
End of faith, as its beginning,
   Set our hearts at liberty.

3 Come, almighty to deliver,
   Let us all thy life receive,
Suddenly return, and never,
   Never more thy temples leave:
Thee we would be always blessing ·
   Serve thee as thy hosts above ;
Pray, and praise thee, without ceasing,
   Glory in thy perfect love.

4 Finish, then, thy new creation,
   Pure and spotless let us be ;
Let us see thy great salvation,
   Perfectly restored in thee ;
Changed from glory into glory,
   Till in heaven we take our place,
Till we cast our crowns before thee,
   Lost in wonder, love, and praise.

ANTIOCH. C. M.

1. Joy to the world, the Lord is come! Let earth receive her King; Let ev'-ry heart prepare him room, And heav'n and nature sing, And heav'n and na-ture sing, And heav'n, And heav'n and nature sing.

EFFINGHAM. L. M.

1. I send the joys of earth a-way, A-way, ye tempters of the mind, False as the smooth, de-ceitful sea, And emp-ty as the whistling wind.

No. 900. 8s & 4.

1. My God, my Father, while I stray, Far from my home, on life's rough way,
Oh teach me from my heart to say, "Thy will be done!"

85   *Praise to Christ.*   C. M.

JOY to the world, the Lord is come,
   Let earth receive her King;
Let every heart prepare him room,
   And heaven and nature sing.

2 Joy to the earth—the Savior reigns,
   Let men their songs employ;
While fields and floods, rocks, hills, and
   Repeat the sounding joy.   [plains,

3 No more let sins and sorrows grow,
   Nor thorns infest the ground;
He comes to make his blessings flow,
   Far as the curse is found.

4 He rules the world with truth and grace,
   And makes the nations prove
The glories of his righteousness,
   And wonders of his love.

86   *Praise to God.*   L. M.

I SEND the joys of earth away;
   Away, ye tempters of the mind!
False as the smooth, deceitful sea,
   And empty as the whistling wind.

2 Your streams were floating me along
   Down to the gulf of black despair;
And while I listened to your song,
   Your streams have e'en conveyed me
      there.

3 Lord, I adore thy matchless grace
   That warned me of that dark abyss,
That drew me from those dangerous seas,
   And bade me seek superior bliss.

4 Now to the shining realms above,
   I stretch my hands, and glance mine
Oh! for the pinions of a dove,   [eyes;
   To bear me to the upper skies.

5 There, from the presence of my God,
   Oceans of endless pleasure roll;
There would I fix my last abode,
   And drown the sorrows of my soul.

87   *Thy will be done.*   8s & 4.

MY God, my Father, while I stray,
   Far from my home, on life's rough
Oh, teach me from my heart to say, [way,
   "Thy will be done."

2 What though in lonely grief I sigh
For friends beloved, no longer nigh?
Submissive still would I reply,
   "Thy will be done."

3 If thou shouldst call me to resign
What most I prize—it ne'er was mine;
I only yield thee what was thine:
   "Thy will be done."

4 If but my fainting heart be blest,
With thy sweet spirit for its guest,
My God, to thee I leave the rest:
   "Thy will be done."

88   *My trust is stayed on Thee.*   C. M.

BORNE o'er the ocean's stormy wave,
   The beacon's light appears,
When yawns the seaman's watery grave,
   And his lone bosom cheers.

2 Then, should the raging ocean foam,
   His heart shall dauntless prove,
To reach, secure, his cherished home,
   The haven of his love.

3 So, when the soul is wrapt in gloom,
   To worldly grief a prey,
Thy beams, blest hope, beyond the tomb,
   Illume the pilgrim's way.

4 They point to that serene abode
   Where holy faith shall rest,
Protected by the sufferer's God,
   And be forever blest.

5 Oh, still, though sorrow's rayless night
   O'ershade our worldly way,
May pure religion's holy light
   Shine with o'erpowering ray.

89   *Good news.*   C. M.

MORTALS, awake, with angels join,
   And chant the solemn lay,
Joy, love, and gratitude combine,
   To hail th' auspicious day.

2 In heaven the rapturous song began,
   And sweet seraphic fire
Through all the shining regions ran,
   And strung and tuned the lyre.

3 Swift through the vast expanse it flew,
   And loud the echo rolled;
The theme, the song, the joy was new,
   'T was more than heaven could hold.

4 Down through the portals of the sky
   The impetuous torrent ran;
And angels flew with eager joy,
   To bear the news to man.

5 With joy the chorus we'll repeat,
   "Glory to God on high!
Good will and peace are now complete,
   Jesus was born to die."

90   *The Lord's day.*   C. M.

HAIL the blest day the Lord has made.
   This glorious day of rest:
Unto our God be honors paid;
   Let love fill every breast.

2 Let saints rejoice in Christ their King,
   Their Savior, Brother, Friend;
Loud let the swelling anthems ring;
   His kingdom ne'er shall end.

PRAISE TO CHRIST. 37

91 *How amiable are thy tabernacles.* S. M.

I LOVE thy kingdom, Lord,
    The house of thine abode,
The church our blest Redeemer saved,
    With his own precious blood:
I love thy church, O God!
    Her walls before thee stand,
Dear as the apple of thine eye,
    And graven on thy hand.

2 For her my tears shall fall,
    For her my prayers ascend;
To her my cares and toils be given,
    Till toils and cares shall end:
Beyond my highest joy
    I prize her heavenly ways,
Her sweet communion, solemn vows,
    Her hymns of love and praise.

3 Jesus, thou friend divine,
    Our Savior, and our King,
Thy hand from every snare and foe
    Shall great deliverance bring.
Sure as thy truth shall last,
    To Zion shall be given
The brightest glories earth can yield,
    And brighter bliss of heaven.

92 *Prayer.* C. M.

LET not despair, nor fell revenge,
    Be to my bosom known,
Oh give me tears for others' woes,
    And patience for my own.

2 Feed me, O Lord, with needful food,
    I ask not wealth or fame;
But give me eyes to view thy works,
    A heart to praise thy name.

3 Oh may my days obscurely pass,
    Without remorse or care;
And let me for my parting hour,
    From day to day prepare.

93 *Praise to Christ.* C. M.

THE Savior risen to-day we praise,
    In concert with the blest;
For now we see his work complete,
    And enter into rest.

2 On this first day a brighter scene
    Of glory was displayed
By the creating Word, than when
    The universe was made.

3 He rises who mankind has bought,
    With grief and pain extreme;
'Twas great to speak the world from
    'Twas greater to redeem.   [naught,

4 How vain the stone, the watch, the
    Naught can forbid his rise;   [seal;
'Tis he who shuts the gates of hell,
    And opens paradise.

94 *Christ died for our sins.* C. M.

FOR me, oh did my Savior bleed,
    And did my Sovereign die,
Would he devote that sacred head
    For such a worm as I!

2 Was it for crimes that I have done
    He groaned upon the tree?
Amazing pity, grace unknown,
    And love beyond degree.

3 Well might the sun in darkness hide,
    And shut his glories in,
When Christ, the Lord, was crucified
    For man, the rebel's sin.

4 Thus might I hide my blushing face
    While his dear cross appears;
Dissolve my heart in thankfulness,
    And melt my eyes to tears.

5 But tears of grief can ne'er repay
    The debt of love I owe;
Here, Lord, I give myself away,
    'Tis all that I can do.

95 *Rejoicing.* S. M.

COME you that love the Lord,
    And let your joys be known;
Join in a song of sweet accord,
    And thus surround the throne.
The sorrows of the mind
    Be banished from this place!
Religion never was designed
    To make our pleasures less.

2 Let those refuse to sing
    Who never knew our God,
But children of the heavenly King
    May speak their joys abroad.
The God that rules on high,
    And thunders when he please,
That rides upon the stormy sky,
    And calms the roaring seas.

3 This mighty God is ours,
    Our Father and our love;
He will send down his heavenly powers
    To carry us above.
There shall we see his face,
    And never, never sin;
There, from the rivers of his grace,
    Drink endless pleasures in.

4 Yes, and before we rise
    To that immortal state,
The thoughts of such amazing bliss
    Shall constant joys create.
The men of grace have found
    Glory begun below;
Celestial fruits, on earthly ground,
    From faith and hope may grow.

96. Resurrection and ascension of Christ. 7s.

ANGELS! roll the rock away,
Death! yield up thy mighty prey
See! the Savior leaves the tomb,
Glowing with immortal bloom.

2 Hark! the wondering angels raise
Louder notes of joyful praise;
Let the earth's remotest bound
Echo with the blissful sound.

3 Now, ye saints, lift up your eyes,
See him high in glory rise!
Hosts of angels, on the road,
Hail him—the incarnate God.

4 Heaven unfolds its portals wide,
See the Conqueror through them ride!
King of glory! mount thy throne—
Boundless empire is thine own.

5 Praise him, ye celestial choirs!
Tune, and sweep your golden lyres;
Raise, oh earth! your noblest songs,
From ten thousand thousand tongues.

97. Praise to Christ. L. M.

COME all who would to glory go,
And leave this world of sin and woe,
Renounce your sins without delay,
Believe, and you shall win the day.

Chorus.

Happy day, happy day,
When Jesus washed my sins away;
He taught me how to watch and pray,
And live rejoicing every day.

2 Oh, do not tarry longer here,
You're sure to die in dark despair,
I'll show to you a better way,
In which you're sure to win the day.

3 And when you reach the realms above,
Where all is harmony and love,
There you shall join the heavenly lay,
And shout and sing I've won the day.

98. Spirits in bright array. 7s.

WHO are these in bright array,
This exulting, happy throng,
Round the altar night and day,
Hymning one triumphant song?
"Worthy is the Lamb once slain,
Blessing, honor, glory, power,
Wisdom, riches, to obtain,
New dominion every hour."

2 These through fiery trials trod;
These from great afflictions came;
Now, before the throne of God,
Sealed with his almighty name:
Clad in raiment pure and white,
Victor palms in every hand;
Through their great Redeemer's might,
More than conquerors they stand.

99. Christ's invitation. 7s.

WHAT could your Redeemer do
More than he has done for you!
To procure your peace with God,
Could he more than shed his blood?
After all this flow of love,
All his drawings from above,
Why will you your Lord deny?
Why will you resolve to die?

2 Turn, he cries, oh sinner, turn,
By his love your God makes known.
He would have you turn and live,
He would all the world receive.
If your death were his delight
Would he thus to life invite?
Would he ask, beseech, and cry,
Why will you resolve to die?

3 Sinners turn while God is near,
Do not think him insincere;
Now, e'en now, your Savior stands,
All day long he spreads his hands:
Cries, "You will not happy be,
No, you will not come to me;
Me, who life to none deny,
Why will you resolve to die?"

4 Can you doubt if God is love,
That to all his bowels move?
Will you not his Word receive?
Will you not his oath believe?
See the suffering Lord appears,
Jesus weeps—believe his tears;
Mingled with his blood they cry,
"Why will you resolve to die?"

100. Happy day. L. M.

OH happy day, that fixed my choice
On thee, my Savior and my God!
Well may this glowing heart rejoice,
And tell its raptures all abroad.

Chorus.

Happy day, happy day,
When Jesus washed my sins away;
He taught me how to watch and pray,
And live rejoicing every day.

2 Oh happy bond, that seals my vows
To him who merits all my love!
Let cheerful anthems fill his house,
While to that sacred shrine I move.

3 'Tis done—the great transaction's done;
I am my Lord's, and he is mine;
He drew me, and I followed on,
Charmed to confess the voice divine.

4 Now rest, my long divided heart!
Fixed on this blissful center rest;
Here have I found a nobler part,
Here heavenly pleasures fill my breast.

LENOX. 6s & 8s.

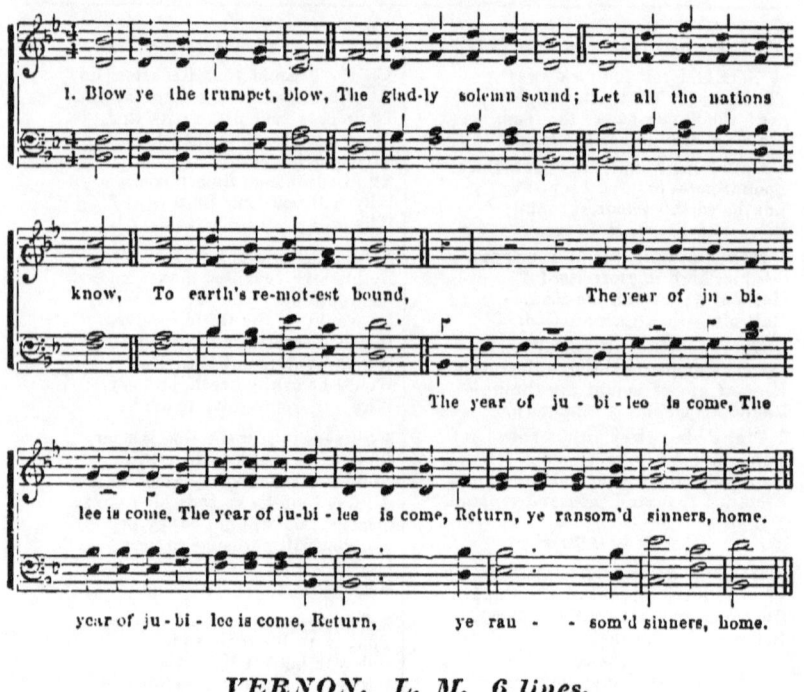

VERNON. L. M. 6 lines.

No. 800. H. M.

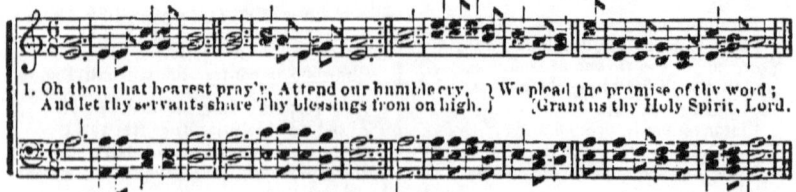

101   *The Gospel.*   6s & 8s.

BLOW ye the trumpet, blow,
  The gladly solemn sound,
Let all the nations know,
  To earth's remotest bound!
Chorus.
The year of jubilee is come,
The year of jubilee is come,
Return ye ransomed sinners home.

2 Extol the Lamb of God,
   The sin-atoning Lamb;
Redemption by his blood
   Through all the world proclaim.

3 Jesus, our great High Priest,
   Propitiation made;
You weary spirits rest,
   You mournful souls be glad:

4 You slaves of sin and hell,
   Your liberty receive,
And safe in Jesus dwell,
   And blessed in Jesus live.

5 You bankrupt debtors, know
   The wondrous grace of heaven,
Though sums immense you owe,
   A free discharge is given.

102   "*I will not leave you comfortless.*"   L. M.

JESUS, thou source of calm repose,
  All fullness dwells in thee divine;
Our strength to quell the proudest foes;
  Our light, in deepest gloom to shine:
Thou art our fortress, strength, and tower,
Our trust, and portion, evermore.

2 Jesus, our Comforter, thou art;
  Our rest in toil, our ease in pain;
The balm to heal each broken heart,
  In storms our peace, in loss our gain;
Our joy, beneath the worldling's frown;
In shame our glory and our crown.

3 In want our plentiful supply;
  In weakness, our almighty power;
In bonds, our perfect liberty;
  Our refuge in temptation's hour;
Our comfort, 'midst all grief and thrall;
Our life in death; our all in all.

103   "*He will give the Holy Spirit.*"   H. M.

OH thou that hearest prayer,
  Attend our humble cry,
And let thy servants share
  Thy blessings from on high.
We plead the promise of thy word;
Grant us thy Holy Spirit, Lord.

2 If earthly parents hear
  Their children when they cry—
If they, with love sincere,
  Their varied wants supply;
Much more wilt thou thy love display,
And answer when thy children pray.

104   *He leadeth me beside the still waters.*   L. M.

THE Lord my pasture shall prepare,
  And feed me with a shepherd's care;
His presence shall my wants supply,
And guard me with a watchful eye;
My noon-day walks he will attend,
And all my midnight hours defend.

2 When in the sultry glebe I faint,
Or on the thirsty mountain pant,
To fertile vales and dewy meads
My weary, wandering steps he leads;
Where peaceful rivers, soft and slow,
Amid the verdant landscapes flow.

3 Though in a bare and rugged way,
Through devious, lonely wilds I stray,
Thy presence shall my pain beguile;
The barren wilderness shall smile,
With sudden greens and herbage crowned,
And streams shall murmur all around.

4 Though in the paths of death I tread,
With gloomy horrors overspread,
My steadfast heart shall fear no ill,
For thou, O Lord! art with me still;
Thy friendly rod shall give me aid,
And guide me through the dreadful shade.

105   *The Bible.*   6s & 8s.

THROUGH tribulation deep
  The way to glory is;
This stormy course I keep
  On the tempestuous seas: [driven,
By winds and waves I'm tossed and
Freighted with grace, and bound for heav'n.

2 The Bible is my chart—
  By it the seas I know;
I can not with it part—
  It rocks and sands doth show.
It is my chart and compass, too,
Whose needle points forever true.

3 'Ere I reach heaven's coast,
  I must a gulf pass through,
Which gloomy proves to most,
  For all this passage go;
But all death's waves can't me o'erwhelm,
If God himself is at the helm.

106   *Worship.*   6s & 8s.

KIND Lord, before thy face
  Again with joy we bow;
For all the gifts and grace,
  Thou dost on us bestow,
Our tongues would all thy love proclaim,
And chant the honors of thy name.

2 Here, in thine earthly house,
  Once more with joy we meet;
Here pay our holy vows,
  And feel our union sweet;
For this our tongues thy love proclaim,
And chant the honors of thy name.

107 *The resurrection.* 8s.

THE angels that watched round the tomb,
Where, low the Redeemer was laid,
When deep in mortality's gloom,
He hid for a season his head;

2 Have witnessed his rising, and swept
The chords with the triumphs of joy,
That veiled their face while he slept,
And ceased their sweet harps to employ.

3 You saints who once languished below,
But long since have entered your rest,
I pant to be glorified, too,
To lean on Immanuel's breast!

4 The grave in which Jesus was laid,
Has buried my guilt and my fears;
And while I contemplate its shade,
The light of his presence appears.

5 Oh sweet is the season of rest,
When life's weary journey is done!
The blush that spreads over its west,
The last lingering ray of its sun!

6 Though dreary the empire of night,
I soon shall emerge from its gloom,
And see immortality's light
Arise on the shades of the tomb.

7 Then welcome the last rending sighs,
When these aching heart-strings shall break;
When death shall extinguish these eyes,
And moisten with dew the pale cheek.

108 *"He sweat, as it were, great drops of blood."*

NIGHT with ebon pinion,
Brooded o'er the vale;
All around was silent,
Save the night-wind's wail;
When Christ, the man of sorrows,
In sweat, and tears, and blood,
Prostrate in the garden,
Raised his voice to God.

2 Smitten for offenses
Which were not his own,
He for our transgressions,
Had to weep alone;
No friend with words of comfort
Nor hand of help was there,
When the meek and lowly
Bowed himself in prayer.

3 Abba, Father! Father!
If, indeed, it may,
Let this cup of anguish
Pass from me away!
Yet, if it must be suffered
By me, thine only Son,
Abba, Father! Father!
Let thy will be done.

109 *Death and resurrection of Christ.* L. M.

HE dies, the friend of sinners dies!
Lo! Salem's daughters weep around;
A solemn darkness veils the skies,
A sudden trembling shakes the ground.

2 Here's love and grief beyond degree,
The Lord of glory dies for men!
But, lo! what sudden joys we see!
Jesus the dead revives again!

3 The rising Lord forsakes the tomb!
(The tomb in vain forbids his rise!)
Cherubic legions guard him home,
And shout him welcome to the skies.

4 Break off your tears, you saints, and tell
How high our great Deliv'rer reigns;
Sing how He spoiled the hosts of hell,
And led the monster death in chains.

110 *Blot out my transgressions.* L. M.

OH thou that hear'st when sinners cry,
Though all my sins before thee lie,
Behold me not with angry look,
But blot their memory from thy book.

2 Create my nature pure within,
And form my soul averse to sin;
Let thy good spirit ne'er depart,
Nor hide thy presence from my heart.

3 I can not live without thy light,
Cast out and banished from thy sight;
Thy holy joys, my God, restore,
And guard me that I fall no more.

4 Though I have grieved thy Spirit,
His help and comfort still afford; [Lord,
And let a sinner seek thy throne,
To plead the merits of his Son.

111 *The resurrection.*

BEHOLD, the bright morning appears,
And Jesus revives from the grave!
His rising removes all our fears,
And shows that he's mighty to save.

2 How strong were his tears and his cries;
The worth of his blood, how divine!
How perfect is his sacrifice,
Who rose, though he suffered for sin!

3 The man that was crowned with thorns,
The man that on Calvary died,
The man that bore scourging and thorns,
Whom sinners agreed to deride—

4 Now blessed forever is made,
And life has rewarded his pain;
Now glory has crowned his head; [slain.
Heaven sings to the Lamb that was

5 Believing we share in his joy;
By faith we partake in his rest;
With this we can cheerfully die,
For with him we hope to be blessed.

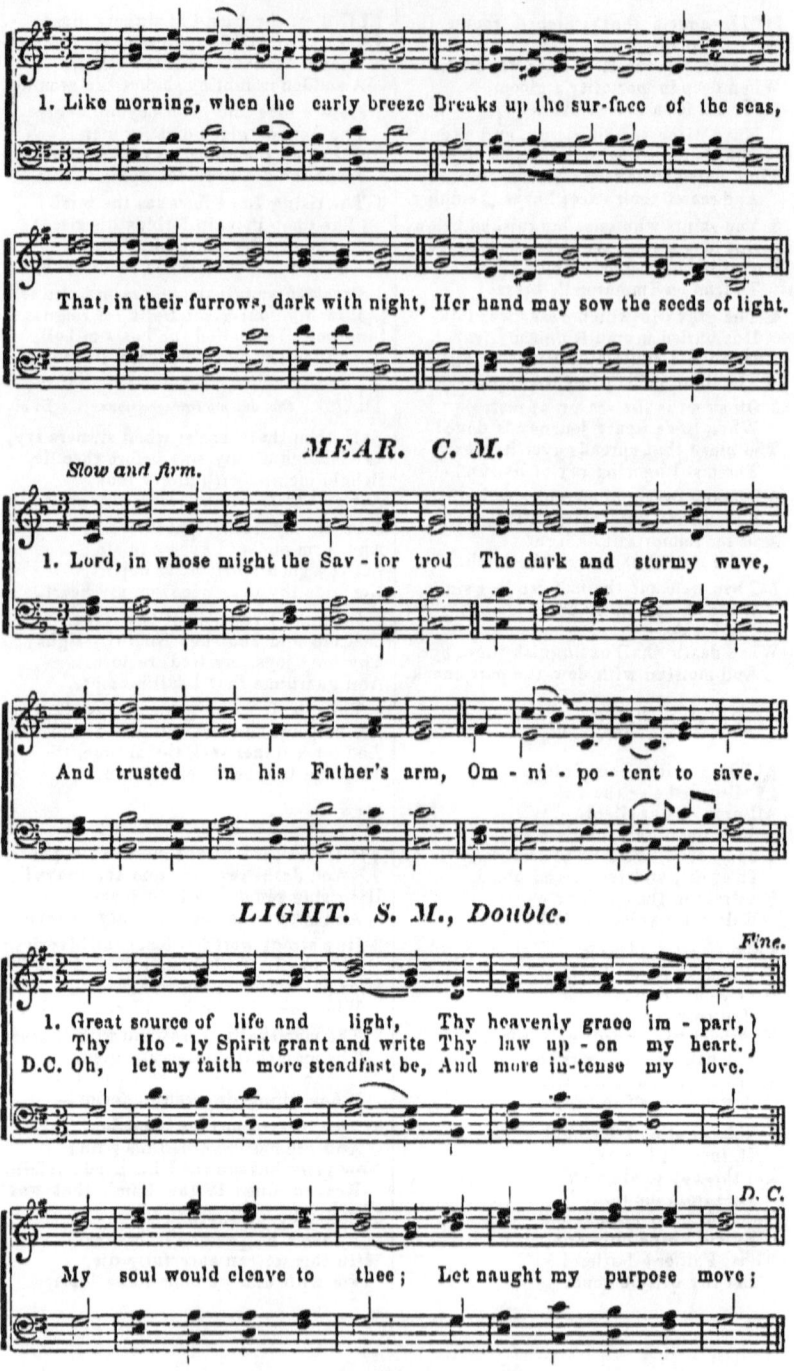

112 *Thou hath he quickened.* L. M.

LIKE morning—when her early breeze
Breaks up the surface of the seas,
That, in their furrows, dark with night,
Her hand may sow the seeds of light—

2 Thy grace can send its breathings o'er
The spirit dark and lost before;
And, freshening all its depths, prepare
For truth divine to enter there.

3 Till David touched his sacred lyre,
In silence lay the unbreathing wire;
But when he swept its chords along,
Then angels stooped to hear the song.

4 So sleeps the soul, till thou, O Lord,
Shall deign to touch its lifeless chord;
Till waked by thee, its breath shall rise
In music worthy of the skies.

113 *I will write my law in their hearts.* S. M.

GREAT source of life and light!
Thy heavenly grace impart,
Thy Holy Spirit grant, and write
Thy law upon my heart;
My soul would cleave to thee;
Let naught my purpose move:
Oh, let my faith more steadfast be,
And more intense my love!

2 Long as my trials last,
Long as the cross I bear,
Oh, let my soul on thee be cast
In confidence and prayer!
Conduct me to the shore
Of everlasting peace,
Where storm and tempest rise no more,
Where sin and sorrow cease.

114 *Praise to Christ.* C. M.

BEHOLD the glories of the Lamb,
Amidst his Father's throne,
Prepare new honors for his name,
And songs before unknown.

2 Let elders worship at his feet,
The church adore around,
With vials full of odors sweet,
And harps of sweeter sound.

3 Now to the Lamb that once was slain,
Be endless blessings paid;
Salvation, glory, joy, remain
Forever on thy head.

4 Thou hast redeemed our souls with
Hast set the prisoners free, [blood,
Hast made us kings and priests to God,
And we shall reign with thee.

5 All hail! thou only glorious Lord!
By all the sons of men
Be thou eternally adored,
Amen, Amen, Amen.

115 *Peace in the storm.* C. M.

LORD, in whose might the Savior trod
The dark and stormy wave,
And trusted in his Father's arm,
Omnipotent to save.

2 When thickly round our footsteps rise
The floods and storms of life,
Grant us thy Spirit, Lord, to still
The dark and fearful strife.

3 Strong in our trust, on thee reposed,
The ocean path we'll dare,
Though waves around us rage and foam,
Since thou art present there.

116 *The Spirit of God dwelleth within you.* C. M.

LORD, let thy Spirit penetrate
This heart and soul of mine;
And my whole being with thy grace
Pervade, oh life divine!

2 As this clear air surrounds the earth,
Thy grace around me roll:
As the fresh light pervades the air,
So pierce and fill my soul.

3 As from these clouds drops down in love
The precious summer rain,
So from thyself pour down the flood
That freshens all again.

4 As these fair flowers exhale their scent
In gladness at our feet,
So from thyself let fragrance breathe,
More heavenly and more sweet.

5 Thus life within our lifeless hearts,
Shall make its glad abode;
And we shall shine in beauteous light,
Filled with the light of God.

117 *The gift of the Holy Spirit.* L. M.

O LORD! and shall thy Spirit rest
In such a wretched heart as mine!
Unworthy dwelling! glorious guest!
Favor astonishing, divine!

2 When sin prevails, and gloomy fear,
And hope almost expires in night,
Lord, can thy Spirit then be here,
Great Spring of comfort, life and light?

3 Sure the blest Comforter is nigh!
'T is he sustains my fainting heart;
Else would my hopes forever die,
And every cheering ray depart.

4 When some kind promise glads my soul,
Do I not find his healing voice
The tempest of my fears control,
And bid my drooping powers rejoice?

5 Let thy kind Spirit in my heart
Forever dwell, O God of love!
And light and heavenly peace impart—
Sweet earnest of the joys above.

118 *Praise to the Lord.* 8s, 7s & 4s.

LORD, to us thy word is precious
  Thy redeeming love we sing;
Thou art ever, ever gracious,
  Mediator, Priest, and King:
    May thy people
Evermore thy glory sing.

2 May we feel thy full salvation,
  In thy grace forever grow;
And may every tribe and nation,
  Thy redemption fully know:
    That thy glory
All the earth may overflow.

119 *Hail, sacred truth.* C. M.

HAIL, sacred truth! whose piercing
  Dispel the shades of night, [rays,
Diffusing o'er the mental world
  The healing beams of light.

2 Thy word, O Lord, with friendly aid,
  Restores our wandering feet,
Converts the sorrows of the mind,
  To joys divinely sweet.

3 Oh, send thy light and truth abroad,
  In all their radiant blaze;
And bid th' admiring world adore
  The glories of thy grace.

120 *Faith in Christ.* S. M.

QUICK as the spark inspires
  This mortal flesh of ours,
So quick the word of Jesus fires
  The soul's immortal powers.

2 He speaks—our spirits wake
  Astonished and renewed,
And mounting up, his grace partake,
  With strength divine endued.

3 We walk, we run, we fly,
  Along the heavenly way,
'Scaped from the jaws of death, on high
  We seek a brighter day.

121 *The law of the Lord is perfect.* S. M.

O LORD, thy perfect word
  Directs our steps aright;
Nor can all other books afford
  Such profit or delight.

2 Celestial light it sheds
  To cheer this vale below;
To distant lands its glory spreads,
  And streams of mercy flow.

3 True wisdom it imparts;
  Commands our hope and fear:
Oh, may we hide it in our hearts,
  And feel its influence there.

122 *The Bible.* C. M.

FATHER of mercies, in thy word,
  What endless glory shines!
Forever be thy name adored,
  For these celestial lines!

2 Here may the wretched sons of want
  Exhaustless riches find;
Riches above what earth can grant,
  And lasting as the mind.

3 Here the fair tree of knowledge grows,
  And yields a rich repast;
Sublimer sweets than nature knows,
  Invite the longing taste.

4 Here springs of consolation rise,
  To cheer the fainting mind,
And thirsty souls receive supplies,
  And sweet refreshment find.

5 Oh may these heavenly pages be
  My ever dear delight;
And still new beauties may I see,
  And still increasing light.

123 *The books of nature and scripture.* S. M.

BEHOLD! the lofty sky
  Declares its maker, God;
And all his starry works, on high,
  Proclaim his power abroad.

2 The darkness and the light
  Still keep their course the same;
While night to day, and day to night,
  Divinely teach his name.

3 In every different land
  Their general voice is known;
They show the wonders of his hand,
  And orders of his throne.

4 Ye Christian lands! rejoice;
  Here he reveals his word;
We are not left to nature's voice,
  To bid us know the Lord.

124 *Rejoice in God's Word.* C. M.

LORD, I have made thy word my choice,
  My lasting heritage;
This shall my noblest powers rejoice,
  My warmest thoughts engage.

2 I'll read the hist'ries of thy love,
  And keep thy laws in sight,
While through the promises I rove,
  With ever fresh delight.

3 'Tis a broad land of wealth unknown,
  Where springs of life arise;
Seeds of immortal bliss are sown,
  And hidden glory lies—

4 The best relief that mourners have,
  It makes our sorrows blest;
Our fairest hope beyond the grave,
  And our eternal rest.

125   *Good news.*   L. M.

THE God who dwells above the skies
   Abominates and hates all lies;
Unrighteousness will not conceal,
But will all wickedness reveal.

2 Ye sinful ones, then turn to God,
   And cleanse your souls in Jesus' blood;
Go be baptized without delay,
And then your Savior's voice obey.

3 See! from his hands, his feet, his side,
   How richly flows the healing tide;
And he hath said, "Whoever will
May drink the living waters still."

4 Then, sinner, come without delay,
   Your Savior's gracious call obey,
His yoke upon you come and take,
The burden light to you He'll make.

126   *Peace and love.*   L. M.

AND is the gospel peace and love?
   Such let our conversation be:
The serpent blended with the dove—
Wisdom and meek simplicity.

2 Whene'er the angry passions rise,
   And tempt our thoughts and tongues to
To Jesus let us lift our eyes,   [strife,
Bright pattern of the Christian life.

3 Oh how benevolent and kind!
   How mild! how ready to forgive!
Be this the temper of our mind,
And this the rule by which we live.

4 To do his heavenly Father's will,
   Was his employment and delight;
Humility, and love, and zeal,
Shone through his life divinely bright.

5 Dispensing good where'er he came,
   The labors of his life were love—
Oh! if we love the Savior's name,
Let his divine example move.

127   *By grace are ye saved.*   S. M.

GRACE! 't is a charming sound,
   Harmonious to the ear;
Heav'n with the echo shall resound,
   And all the earth shall hear.

2 Grace first contriv'd the way
   To save rebellious man;
And all the steps that grace display,
   Which drew the wond'rous plan.

3 Grace led our wand'ring feet
   To tread the heav'nly road;
And new supplies each hour we meet,
   While pressing on to God.

4 Grace all the work shall crown
   Through everlasting days;
It lays in heav'n the topmost stone,
   And well deserves our praise.

128   *Triumph of the gospel.*   7s & 6s.

THE morning light is breaking,
   The darkness disappears,
The sons of earth are waking,
   To penitential tears;
Each breeze that sweeps the ocean,
   Brings tidings from afar,
Of nations in commotion,
   Prepared for Zion's war.

2 Rich dews of grace come o'er us,
   In many a gentle shower,
And brighter scenes before us,
   Are opening every hour;
Each cry to heaven going,
   Abundant answers brings,
And heavenly gales are blowing,
   With peace upon their wings.

3 See heathen nations bending
   Before the God we love,
And thousand hearts ascending,
   In gratitude above;
While sinners now confessing,
   The gospel call obey,
And seek the Savior's blessing
   A nation in a day.

4 Blest river of salvation,
   Pursue thy onward way,
Flow thou to every nation,
   Nor in thy richness stay;
Stay not, till all the lowly
   Triumphant reach their home;
Stay not, till all the holy
   Proclaim the Lord has come.

129   *The gospel banner.*   7s & 6s.

NOW be the gospel banner
   In every hand unfurled;
And be the shout hosanna,
   Re-echoed through the world;
Till every isle and nation,
   Till every tribe and tongue,
Receive the great salvation,
   And join the happy throng.

2 What, though the embattled legions
   Of earth and hell combine?
His arm throughout their regions
   Shall soon resplendent shine:
Ride on, O Lord, victorious!
   Immanuel, Prince of Peace!
Thy triumph shall be glorious;
   Thy empire shall increase.

3 Yes, thou shalt reign forever,
   O Jesus, King of kings!
Thy light, thy love, thy favor,
   Each ransomed captive sings:
The isles for thee are waiting,
   The deserts learn thy praise,
The hills and valleys greeting,
   The song responsive raise.

130 *The evidence of things not seen.* C. M.

FAITH is the brightest evidence
  Of things beyond our sight;
It pierces through the veil of sense,
  And dwells in heavenly light.

2 It sets time past in present view,
  Brings distant prospects home,
Of things a thousand years ago,
  Or thousand years to come.

3 By faith we know the world was made
  By God's almighty word;
By faith we know the earth shall fade,
  And be again restored.

4 Abram obeyed the Lord's command,
  From his own country driven;
By faith he sought a promised land,
  And found his rest in heaven.

5 Thus through life's pilgrimage we stray,
  The promise in our eye;
By faith we walk the narrow way,
  That leads to joys on high.

131 *Not seeing, yet believing.* 8s & 4.

WHERE countless throngs in spirit one,
    Forever glorious as the sun.
Shall live, when time has ceased to run,
    There is my home.

2 Where peace and love the air perfume,
  Where an eternal summer's bloom,
And joy and gladness banish gloom—
    There is my home.

3 Where streams of crystal onward flow,
  Where streets of gold in splendor glow,
And fadeless flowers in beauty grow—
    There is my home.

4 Where lips shall never breathe farewell,
  Nor tears the parting anguish tell,
Where friends united ever dwell—
    There is my home.

5 Where, seated on the eternal throne,
  He shall his faithful followers own,
With gracious smile; in heaven alone—
    There is my home!

132 *We walk by faith, not by sight.* L. M.

BY faith in Christ I walk with God
  With heaven, my journey's end in
Supported by his staff and rod,   [view,
  My road is safe and pleasant, too.

2 I travel through a desert wide,
  Where many round me blindly stray!
But he vouchsafes to be my guide,
  And keeps me in the narrow way.

3 Though snares and dangers throng my
              path,
  And earth and hell my course with-
I triumph over all by faith,   [stand;
  Guarded by his almighty hand.

133 *Faith.* C. M.

FAITH adds new charms to earthly
  And saves me from its snares; [bliss,
Its aid in every duty brings,
  And softens all my cares.

2 Extinguishes the thirst of sin,
  And lights the sacred fire
Of love to God and heavenly things,
  And feeds the pure desire.

3 The wounded conscience knows its
    The healing balm to give; [power,
That balm the saddest heart can cheer,
  And make the dying live.

4 Wide it unveils celestial worlds,
  Where deathless pleasures reign,
And bids me seek my portion there,
  Nor bids me seek in vain.

5 Shows me the precious promise sealed
  With the Redeemer's blood,
And helps my feeble hope to rest
  Upon a faithful God.

134 *Strong in faith.* C. M.

OH, for a faith that will not shrink,
   Though pressed by many a foe;
That will not tremble on the brink
  Of poverty or woe.

2 That will not murmur nor complain
  Beneath the chastening rod;
But in the hour of grief or pain
  Can lean upon its God.

3 A faith that shines more bright and
  When tempests rage without; [clear
That when in danger knows no fear,
  In darkness feels no doubt:

4 That bears unmoved the world's dread
  Nor heeds its scornful smile; [frown,
That sin's wild ocean can not drown,
  Nor its soft arts beguile.

135 *Lord, I believe.* P. C. M.

JUST as I am—without one plea,
  But that thy blood was shed for me,
And that thou bidst me come to thee—
  Oh Lamb of God, I come!

2 Just as I am—and waiting not
  To rid my soul of one dark blot,
To thee, whose blood can cleanse each spot,
  Oh Lamb of God, I come!

3 Just as I am—thou wilt receive,
  Wilt welcome, pardon, cleanse, relieve,
Because thy promise I believe—
  Oh Lamb of God, I come!

4 Just as I am—thy love unknown
  Has broken every barrier down;
Now to be thine, yea, thine alone,
  Oh Lamb of God, I come!

136
Penitence. P. M. 7s, 6s & 8s.

JESUS, let thy pitying eye,
  Call back a wandering sheep,
False to thee, like Peter,—
  I would fain, like Peter, weep.
Let me be by grace restored,
  On me be all long-suffering shown;
Turn and look upon me, Lord,
  And break my heart of stone.

2 Savior, Prince, enthroned above,
    Salvation to impart,
  Give me, through thy dying love,
    The humble, contrite heart—
  Give, what I have long implored,
    A portion of thy love unknown,
  Turn and look upon me, Lord,
    And break my heart of stone.

3 See me, Savior, from above,
    Nor suffer me to die;
  Life, and happiness, and love,
    Drop from thy gracious eye;
  Speak the reconciling word,
    And let thy mercy melt me down;
  Turn, and look upon me, Lord,
    And break my heart of stone.

137
Longing for heaven. 11s.

OH! who would remain in this prison
      of clay,   [away—
When friends and companions are hasting
Away to the climes of the blessed and free,
Where death never comes, and where pure
      spirits be.

2 Oh! could we but go with the friends
      that we love,
  And taste their enjoyments in glory above;
  No more would we fancy this desert below,
  Where tears of deep anguish so frequently
      flow.

3 Ye comrades of youth, and ye friends
      of ripe years,   [my tears?
  Oh! when shall I join you? when banish
  When shall the dull days of mortality
      cease?   [peace?
  Oh! when shall I live with my Savior in

138
Radiance. S. M.

SWEET is the friendly voice
  Which speaks of life and peace:
Which bids the penitent rejoice,
  And sin and sorrow cease.

2 No balm on earth like this
    Can cheer the contrite heart;
  No flattering dreams of earthly bliss
    Such pure delight impart.

3 Still merciful and kind,
    Thy mercy, Lord, reveal;
  The broken heart thy love can bind,
    The wounded spirit heal.

139
Hinder me not. S. M.

AH! whither should I go,
  Burdened, and sick, and faint?
To whom should I my trouble show
  And pour out my complaint?

2 My Savior bids me come,
    Ah! why do I delay?
  He calls the weary sinner home,
    And yet from him I stay?

3 What is it keeps me back
    From which I will not part?
  Which will not let the Savior take
    Possession of my heart?

4 Jesus, the hinderance show
    Which I have feared to see;
  And let me now consent to know
    What keeps me back from thee?

140
Reformation. 12s.

YOU may sing of the beauty of moun-
      tain and dale,
Of the silvery streamlet and flowers of the
      vale;
But the place most delightful this earth
      can afford,
Is the place of devotion—the house of the
      Lord.

2 You may boast of the sweetness of
      day's early dawn—
  Of the sky's softening graces when day is
      just gone;
  But there's no other season or time can
      compare
  With the hour of devotion—the season of
      prayer.

3 You may value the friendships of youth
      and of age,
  And select for your comrades the noble
      and sage;
  But the friends that most cheer me on
      life's rugged road,
  Are the friends of my Master—the chil-
      dren of God.

4 You may talk of your prospects, of
      fame, or of wealth,
  And the hopes that oft flatter the fav'rites
      of health;
  But the hope of bright glory—of heavenly
      bliss,
  Take away every other, and give me but
      this.

5 Ever hail, blessed temple, abode of my
      Lord!
  I will turn to thee often, to hear from his
      word;
  I will walk to the altar with those that I
      love,
  And delight in the prospects revealed
      from above.

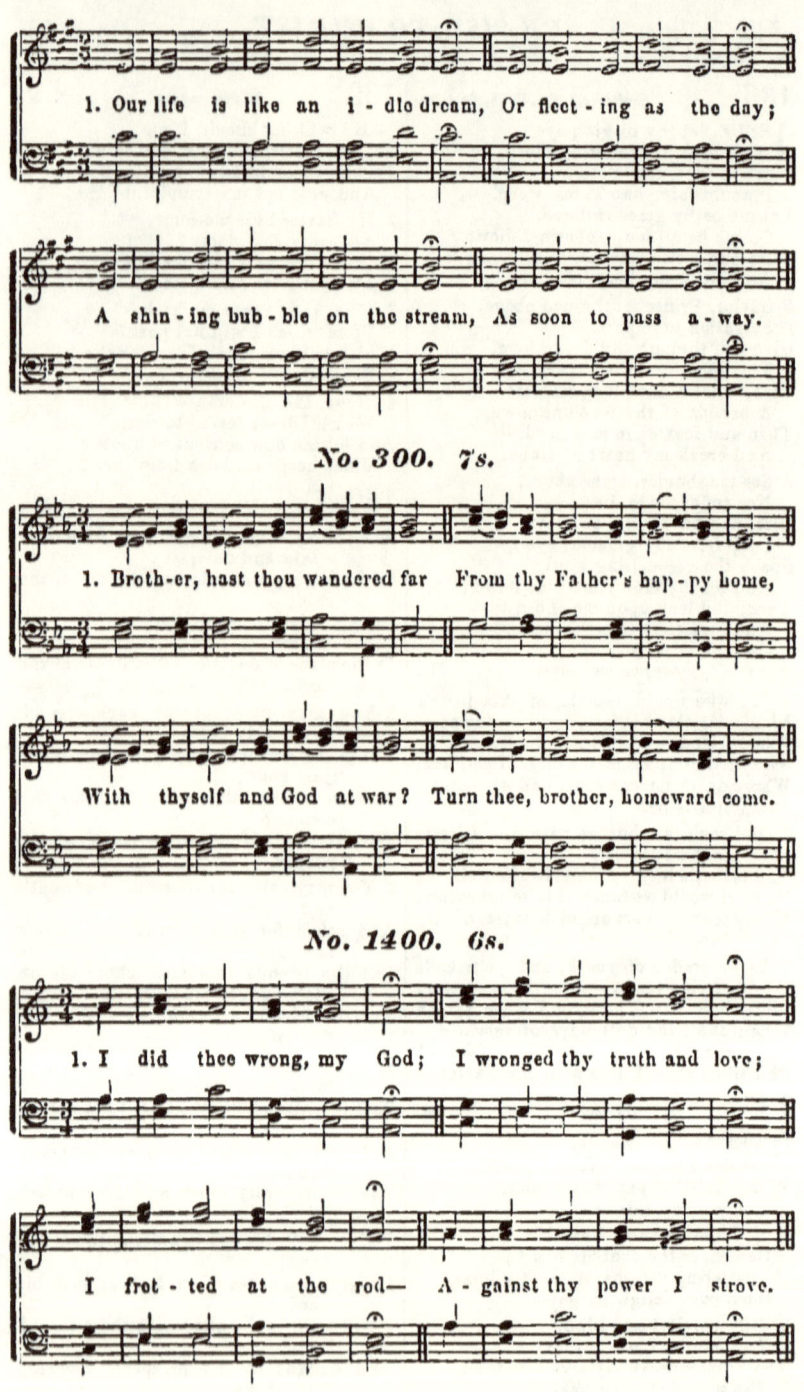

141 Simplicity. C. M.

OUR life is like an idle dream,
  Or fleeting as the day;
A shining bubble on the stream,
  As soon to pass away.

2 If life's so brief, why then prepare,
  For all the joys it brings;
Or give one thought of anxious care,
  To mere terrestrial things?

3 No more to trifling toys of time,
  Let precious hours be given,
But live to God a life sublime,
  And wear a crown in heaven.

142 Changed—from glory to glory. Cn.

I DID thee wrong, my God;
  I wronged thy truth and love;
I fretted at the rod—
  Against thy power I strove.

2 Come nearer, nearer still;
  Let not thy light depart;
Bend, break this stubborn will;
  Dissolve this iron heart!

3 Less wayward let me be,
  More pliable and mild;
In glad simplicity
  More like a trustful child.

4 Less, less of self each day,
  And more, my God, of thee;
Oh, keep me in the way,
  However rough it be.

5 Less of the flesh each day,
  Less of the world and sin:
More of thy Son, I pray,
  More of thyself within.

6 More molded to thy will,
  Lord, let thy servant be;
Higher and higher still,
  More, and still more, like thee!

143 Overcoming. C. M.

KIND Father, look with pity now
  On one by sin defiled;
While at the mercy-seat I bow,
  Oh bless thy erring child.

2 My struggles, Lord, to do thy will,
  How poor and weak they are!
But thou art gracious to me still,
  Then hear my humble prayer.

3 Let love upon my broken heart
  Pour out its healing balm;
Bid all my trembling fears depart—
  My troubled spirit calm.

4 And now my hope new courage takes,
  My faith grows strong and sure;
The cloud from off my vision breaks,
  Again my heart is pure.

5 My soul mounts up on wings of light,
  And soars to climes above,
The regions where all things are bright,
  The home of Peace and Love.

6 There, soon I'll sing of love divine,
  With all the ransomed throng,
There, Jesus shall be ever mine,
  His love my endless song.

144 The prodigal invited. 7s.

BROTHER, hast thou wandered far
  From thy Father's happy home,
With thyself and God at war?
  Turn thee, brother; homeward come.

2 Hast thou wasted all the powers
  God for noble uses gave?
Squandered life's most golden hours?
  Turn thee, brother; God can save.

3 He can heal thy bitterest wound,
  He thy gentlest prayer can hear:
Seek him, for he may be found;
  Call upon him, he is near.

145 If we confess our sins. 7s.

GOD of mercy! God of love!
  Hear our sad, repentant songs;
Listen to thy suppliant ones,
  Thou, to whom all grace belongs!

2 Deep regret for follies past,
  Talents wasted, time misspent;
Hearts debased by worldly cares,
  Thankless for the blessings lent;

3 Foolish fears and fond desires,
  Vain regrets for things as vain;
Lips too seldom taught to praise,
  Oft to murmur and complain;

4 These, and every secret fault,
  Filled with grief and shame we own;
Humbled at thy feet we bow,
  Seeking strength from thee alone.

5 God of mercy! God of love!
  Hear our sad, repentant songs;
Oh, restore thy suppliant ones,
  Thou to whom all grace belongs!

146 Confession. C. M.

THE sinner who confesseth me,
  I also will confess;
And, if obedient, he shall dwell
  Forever with the blest.

2 But every one that doth deny
  My name, shall surely be
Before the assembled universe
  Of God, denied by me.

3 Then, haste thee, and believe,
  Reform thee and confess;
Obey, and make the promises
  Your own, in righteousness.

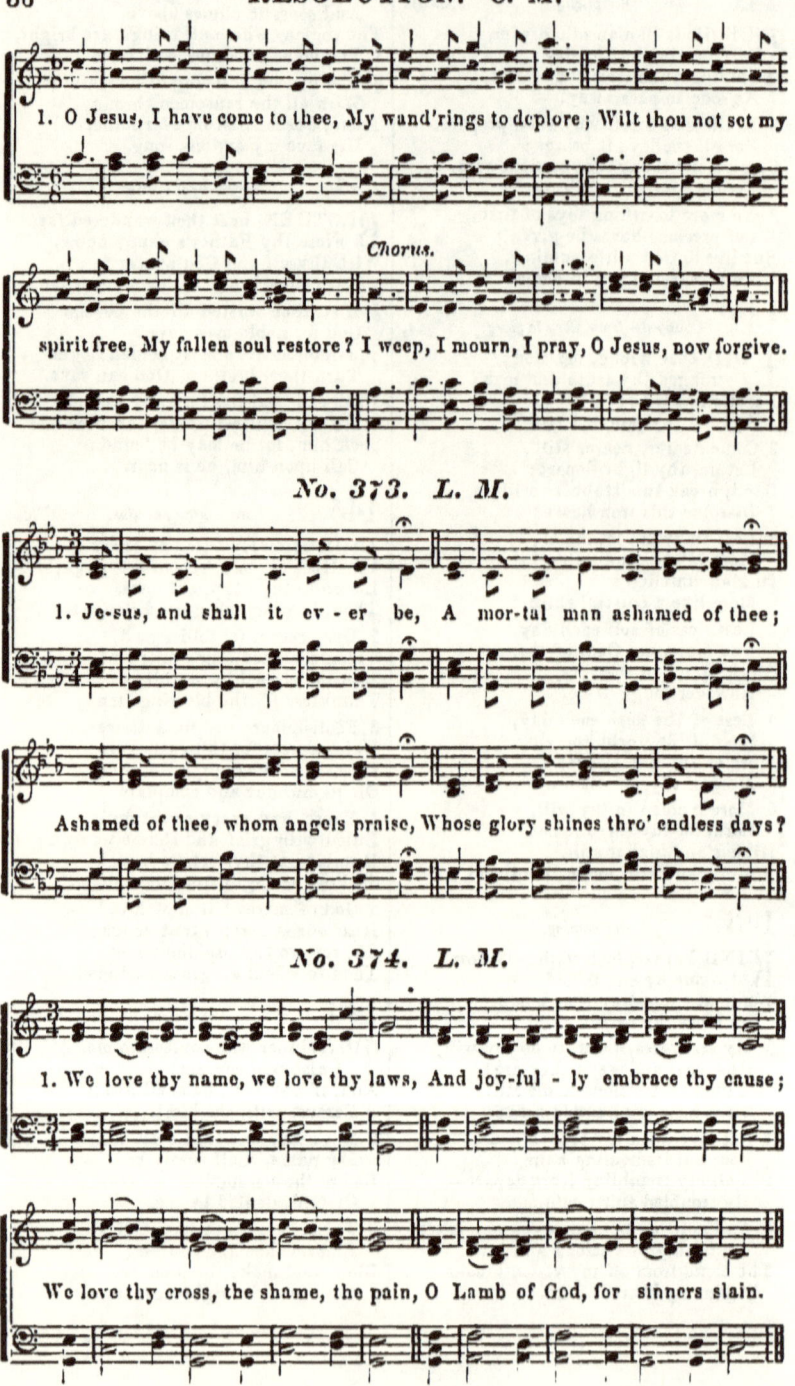

BAPTISM. 57

147 *Contrition.* C. M.

O JESUS, I have come to thee,
  My wanderings to deplore;
Wilt thou not set my spirit free,
  My fallen soul restore!

Chorus.

I weep, I mourn, I pray,
O Jesus now forgive.

2 My sins are more than I can bear,
  Oh speak them all forgiven:
My soul away from earth I tear,
  To seek a place in heaven.

3 Pity, O Lord, my helpless grief;
  My soul's deep anguish see;
And grant me now that sweet relief,
  Which none can give but thee.

4 Didst thou not die that I might live,
  Might live thy love to know?
Oh let me now thy love receive,
  And in thy favor grow.

148 *Baptism.* L. M.

'TWAS the commission of our Lord,
  "Go teach the nations and baptize;"
The nations have received the word,
  Since he ascended to the skies.

2 He sits upon th' eternal hills,
  With grace and pardon in his hands,
And sends his cov'nant with his seals,
  To bless the distant Pagan lands.

3 "Repent and be baptized," he saith,
  "For the remission of your sins,"
And thus our sense assists our faith,
  And shows us what the gospel means.

4 Our souls he washes in his blood,
  As water makes the body clean;
And the good Spirit from our God,
  Descends like purifying rain.

149 *Arise, and be baptized.* C. M.

IN all my Lord's appointed ways,
  My journey I'll pursue;
Hinder me not, ye much-lov'd saints,
  For I must go with you.

2 Through floods and flames, if Jesus lead,
  I'll follow where he goes;
I will arise and be baptized,
  Though earth and hell oppose.

3 Through duty and through trials, too,
  I'll go at his command;
Hinder me not, for I am bound
  To my Immanuel's land.

4 And when my Savior calls me home,
  Still this my cry shall be,
Hinder me not, come, welcome death,
  I'll gladly go with thee.

150 *Ashamed of Jesus.* L. M.

JESUS, and shall it ever be,
  A mortal man asham'd of thee;
Asham'd of thee, whom angels praise,
Whose glory shines through endless days.

2 Asham'd of Jesus! Sooner far
Let ev'ning blush to own a star!
He sheds the beams of light divine
O'er this benighted soul of mine.

3 Asham'd of Jesus! Just as soon
Let morning be asham'd of noon:
'T is midnight with my soul, till he,
Bright Morning Star, bid darkness flee.

4 Asham'd of Jesus! that dear friend,
On whom my hopes of heav'n depend!
No! when I blush, be this my shame,
That I no more revere his name.

5 Asham'd of Jesus! Yes, I may,
When I've no guilt to wash away,
No tear to wipe, no good to crave,
No fears to quell, no soul to save.

6 Till then—nor is my boasting vain—
Till then I'll boast a Savior slain!
And, oh! may this my glory be,
That Christ is not asham'd of me.

7 His institutions would I prize,
Take up my cross, the shame despise—
Dare to defend his noble cause,
And yield obedience to his laws.

151 *The spirit of obedience.* L. M.

WE love thy name, we love thy laws,
  And joyfully embrace thy cause;
We love thy cross, the shame, the pain,
Oh Lamb of God, for sinners slain.

2 We sink beneath the mystic flood;
Oh, bathe us in thy cleansing blood;
We die to sin, and seek a grave,
With thee, beneath the yielding wave.

3 And, as we rise, with thee to live,
Oh, let the Holy Spirit give
The sealing unction from above,
The breath of life, the fire of love.

152 *Duty.* C. M.

IN duties, and in sufferings, too,
  My Lord I fain would trace;
As he hath done so would I do,
  Sustained by heavenly grace.

2 Inflamed with zeal, 't was his delight,
  To do his Father's will;
May the same zeal my soul excite,
  His precepts to fulfill.

3 Meekness, humility, and love,
Through all his conduct shine,
Oh may my whole deportment prove
A copy, Lord, of thine.

153 Thy sins be forgiven thee. L. M.

OH! let me sing of sins forgiven,
  The tranquil triumph of my soul;
Oh! let me sing a song of heaven,
  While steams of living comfort roll.
Adieu to every earthly toy,
  For nobler objects I am bound;
Since not one single drop of joy,
  I ever yet from earth have found.

2 Its brightest beauties fade away,
  Its richest jewels are but dross;
Its honors scarcely live a day,
  And every gain has proved a loss.
But there's an honor that will live,
  A gem that never will decay;
There is a gain that can't deceive,
  And beauty fading not away.

3 This priceless boon I humbly claim,
  This speechless joy of sins forgiven;
The love of God, that, like a flame,
  Burns on, and lights the soul to heaven.
By faith I have this treasure found,
  And gaze with wonder and surprise,
While in this dark, enchanted ground,
  "The day-spring" opens from the skies.

4 My home is in the distance seen,
  And gales come soft from Canaan's shore,
Though dark the wilderness between,
  I have sweet hopes of getting o'er.
Oh! happiness, it is no dream,
  For glory's opened in my soul;
And love divine shall be my theme,
  Long as eternal ages roll!

154 Amazing grace. C. M.

AMAZING grace, how sweet the sound,
  That saved a wretch like me,
I once was lost, but now am found,
  Was blind, but now I see.

2 'T was grace that taught my heart to fear,
  And grace my fears relieved; [fear,
How precious did that grace appear,
  The hour I first believed!

3 Through many dangers, toils and snares,
  I have already come; [snares,
'T is grace has brought me safe thus far,
  And grace will lead me home.

4 The Lord has promised good to me,
  His word my hope secures;
He will my shield and portion be,
  As long as life endures.

5 Yes, when this flesh and heart shall fail,
  And mortal life shall cease, [fail,
I shall possess, within the vail,
  A life of joy and peace.

155 Home in heaven. C. M. D.

HOW happy every child of grace,
  Who knows his sins forgiven!
This world, he cries, is not my place,
  I seek a home in heaven;
Oh, what a blessed hope is ours,
  While here on earth we stay;
We more than taste the heavenly powers,
  And antedate that day.

2 A country far from mortal sight,
  Yet, oh! by faith, I see,
The land of rest, the saints' delight,
  The heaven prepared for me.
We feel the resurrection near,
  Our life in Christ concealed,
And with his glorious presence here,
  Our earthen vessels filled.

156 Blessed is the man whose sin is covered. L. M.

EARTH has a joy unknown in heav'n—
  The new-born joy of sins forgiv'n!
Tears of such pure and deep delight,
Oh angels! never dimm'd your sight.

2 You saw of old on chaos rise
The beauteous pillars of the skies;
You know where morn exulting springs,
And ev'ning folds her drooping wings.

3 Bright heralds of th' Eternal Will,
Abroad his errands you fulfill;
Or, throned in floods of beamy day,
Symphonious in his presence play.

4 Loud is the song—the heavenly plain
Is shaken with the choral strain;
And dying echoes floating far,
Draw music from each chiming star.

5 But I amid your choirs shall shine,
And all your knowledge shall be mine;
You on your harps must lean to hear
A secret chord that mine shall bear.

157 Pleasures of the cross. C. M.

COURAGE, my soul, thy heavy cross
  In every trial here,
Shall bear thee to thy heaven above,
  But shall not enter there.
The sighing ones that humbly seek,
  In sorrowing paths below,
Shall in eternity rejoice,
  Where endless comforts flow.

2 Soon will the toilsome strife be o'er,
  Of sublunary care,
And life's dull vanities no more
  This anxious breast ensnare.
Courage, my soul, on God rely,
  Deliv'rance soon will come,
A thousand ways has Providence
  To bring believers home.

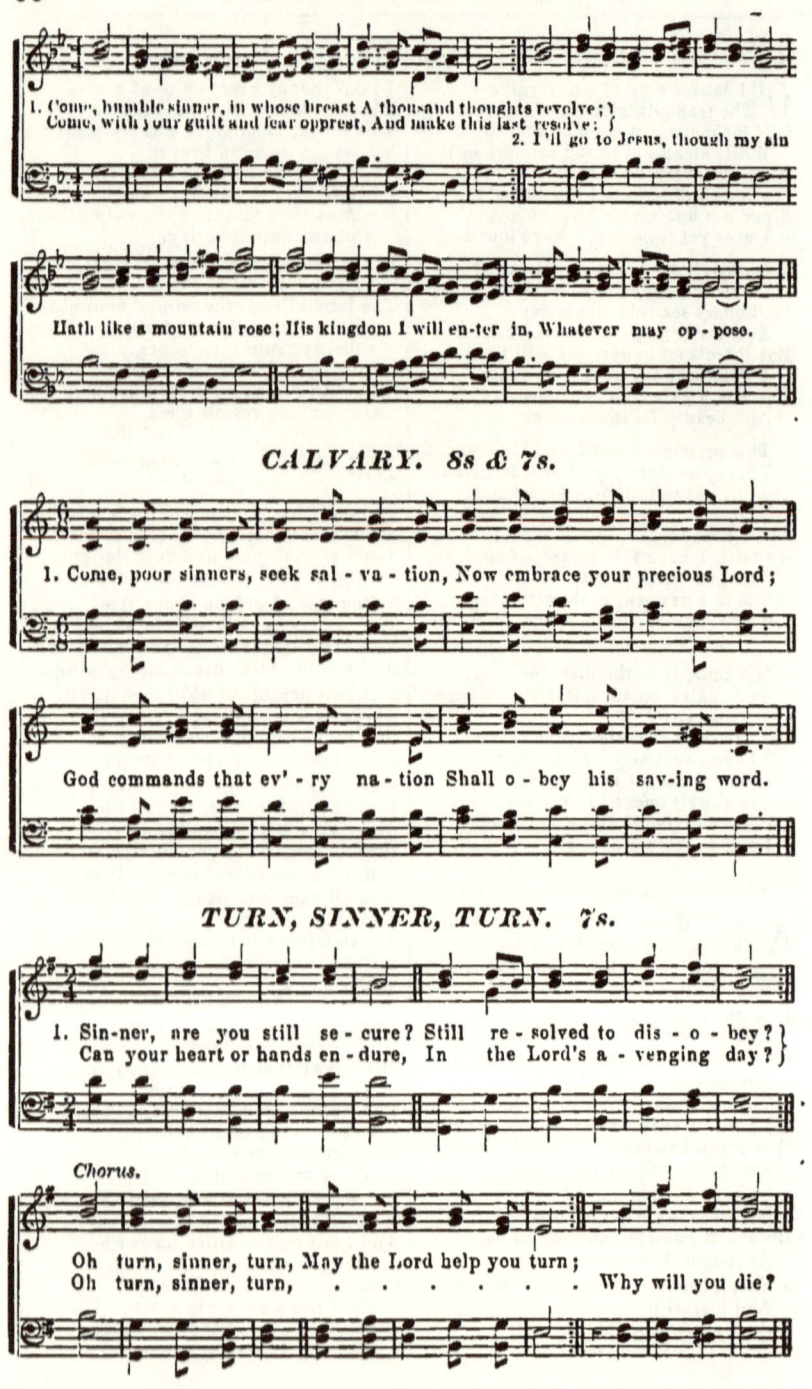

158   Come to Jesus.   C. M.

COME, humble sinner, in whose breast
A thousand thoughts revolve—
Come, with your guilt and fear opprest,
And make this last resolve:

2 I 'll go to Jesus, though my sin
Hath like a mountain rose;
His kingdom I will enter in,
Whatever may oppose;

3 Prostrate I 'll lie before his throne,
And there my guilt confess;
I 'll tell him I 'm a wretch undone,
Without his sovereign grace.

4 The Savior will admit my plea,
For he has bid me come;
Forthwith I 'll rise and to him flee,
For yet, he says, " there's room."

5 I can but perish if I go,
I am resolved to try;
For if I stay away, I know
I must forever die.

159   Invitation.   C. M.

COME to the glorious gospel-feast,
Ho! every one that will;
Oh come you starving souls and taste
Those joys that none can tell.

2 Arise you mortals that are sad,
And bordering on despair,
Lo! there is balm in Gilead,
And a Physician there.

3 Look to the Savior's bleeding side,
Behold the purple gore;
It was for wounded souls he died
The sin-sick to restore.

4 Behold him on the cursed tree,
With arms extended wide,
For sinners such as you and me,
The bleeding Savior died.

5 'T is finished, said his dying breath,
He conquered death and hell;
That rebels doomed to endless death,
Might in his bosom dwell.

6 Come, then, receive his grace, and tell
The wonders of his love;
Till we arrive with him to dwell,
In brighter worlds above.

7 No sin or foe shall there annoy,
Or wound our peaceful breast:
But boundless love, unmingled joy,
And everlasting rest.

Chorus.

When we've been there ten thousand
Bright shining as the sun;   [years,
We've no less days to sing his praise,
Then when we first begun.

160   Turn, sinner, turn.   7s.

SINNER, are you still secure?
Still resolved to disobey,
Can your heart or hands endure,
In the Lord's avenging day?

2 Who his advent may abide?
You that glory in your shame,
Can you find a place to hide,
When the world is wrapt in flame?

3 Hasten now, the time improve,
Listen to your Savior's voice;
Seek the things that are above,
Scorn the world's pretended joys.

Chorus.

Oh! turn, sinner, turn,
May the Lord help you, turn.
Oh! turn, sinner, turn,
Why will you die?

161   Seek salvation.   8s & 7s.

COME, poor sinners, seek salvation,
Now embrace your precious Lord:
God commands that every nation,
Shall obey his saving word.

2 Sinners, none but he can save us—
Fly, embrace your Savior's love,
He now breathes his Spirit in us;
Let his grace your bosom move.

162   Rely on the Lord.   7s.

THEY who on the Lord rely,
Safely dwell, though danger's nigh,
Lo! his sheltering wings are spread
O'er each faithful servant's head.

2 Vain temptation's wily snare;
Christians are Jehovah's care;
Harmless flies the shaft by day,
Or in darkness wings its way.

3 When they wake, or when they sleep,
Angel guards their vigils keep;
Death and danger may be near,
Faith and Love have naught to fear.

163   Haste, oh sinner.   7s.

HASTE, oh sinner—now be wise,
Stay not for to-morrow's sun;
Wisdom, if you still despise,
Harder is it to be won.

2 Haste—and mercy now implore,
Stay not for the morrow's sun;
Lest thy season should be o'er,
Ere this evening's stage be run.

3 Haste, oh sinner—now return;
Stay not for the morrow's sun,
Lest thy lamp should cease to burn,
Ere salvation's work is done.

164   *I'm on my journey home.*   L. M.

WE'RE traveling to our heav'nly home,
    Beyond the glittering starry skies,
Where nothing sinful e'er can come,
    Where angry passions never rise.
Chorus.
‖ : We're on our journey home
    To the New Jerusalem : ‖
So fare you well,
    ‖ : So fare you well : ‖
We are going home.

2 We're going to that holy land,
    By prophets and apostles sung,
To join the bright, angelic band—
    To sing with an immortal tongue.

3 Come, go with us, oh, sinner, come,
    And walk the straight and narrow
No longer in sin's mazes roam,   [way ;
    But seek the Lord without delay.

4 Like mists before the morning sun,
    Your days are swiftly floating by,
Your mortal race will soon be run,
    Then turn, oh turn you, ere you die.

165   *Mercy in Jesus's blood.*   8s, 7s & 4s.

COME, you sinners, come to Jesus ;
    Think upon your gracious Lord ;
He has pitied your condition,
    He has sent his gospel word ;
        Mercy calls you ;
Mercy flows in Jesus' blood.

2 Dearest Savior, help thy servant
    To proclaim thy wondrous love ;
Pour thy grace upon this people,
    That thy truth they may approve :
        Bless, oh bless them,
From thy shining courts above.

3 Now thy gracious word invites them
    To partake the gospel feast ;
Let thy Spirit sweetly draw them,
    Every soul be Jesus' guest :
        Oh, receive us !
Let us find thy promised rest.

166   *How swift is time.*   C. M.

REMARK, my soul, the narrow bounds
    Of the revolving year ;
How swift the weeks complete their
    rounds !
How short the months appear !

2 So fast eternity comes on,
    And that important day,
When all that mortal life has done,
    God's judgment shall survey.

3 Yet like an idle tale we pass
    The swift advancing year ;
And study artful ways t' increase
    The speed of its career.

167   *Passing away.*   C. M.

WE'RE passing from the earth away,
    As mists before the sun ;
Our eyes scarce open on the day,
    Before our race is run.
Chorus.
And, we're passing away,
    ‖ : We are passing away : ‖
To the great judgment day.

2 We're passing from the earth, as falls
    The grass before the blade ;
Our wealth, our fame, our honors, all
    Will soon be lowly laid.

3 " Our fathers, where are they ? and do
    The prophets live alway ? "
Ah, no ! how mournful 't is: how true ?
    They all have passed away.

4 We're passing from the earth, as flax
    Is by the fire consumed,
Or high, or low, death's scythe attacks,
    And brings all to the tomb.

5 We're passing down the stream of life,
    Swift as the weaver's thread ;
Soon there will be an end of strife,
    Soon we shall join the dead.

168   *Listen, sinner, to the message.*   8s, 7s & 4s.

SINNERS, will you scorn the message,
    Sent in mercy from above !
Every sentence—oh, how tender !
    Every line is full of love :
        Listen to it—
Every line is full of love.

2 Hear the heralds of the gospel,
    News from Zion's King proclaim,
" Pardon to each rebel sinner !
    Free forgiveness in his name."
        How important !
" Free forgiveness in his name."

3 Tempted souls, they bring you succor ;
    Fearful hearts, they quell your fears ;
And, with news of consolation,
    Chase away the falling tears.
        Tender heralds !
Chase away the falling tears.

4 False professors, groveling worldlings,
    Callous hearers of the word,
While the messengers address you,
    Take the warnings they afford ;
        We entreat you—
Take the warnings they afford.

5 Who hath our report believed ?
    Who received the joyful word ?
Who embraced the news of pardon,
    Offered to you by the Lord ?
        Can you slight it ?
Offered to you by the Lord ?

169   Come to Jesus.   8s, 7s & 4s.

COME, ye sinners, poor and needy,
   Weak and wounded, sick and sore,
Jesus ready stands to save you,
   Full of pity, love, and power:
      He is able,
He is willing—doubt no more.

2 Let not conscience make you linger,
   Nor of fitness fondly dream;
All the fitness he requireth,
   Is to feel your need of him:
      This he gives you;
'T is the Savior's rising beam.

3 Come, you weary, heavy laden,
   Bruised and mangled by the fall,
If you tarry till you're better,
   You will never come at all.
      Not the righteous—
Sinners, Jesus came to call.

4 Agonizing in the garden,
   Lo! your Savior prostrate lies,
On the bloody tree behold him,
   Hear him cry before he dies,
      "It is finished!"
Sinners, will not this suffice?

5 Lo! the rising Lord ascending
   To his Father and his God;
Venture on him, venture freely,
   Let no other trust intrude:
      None but Jesus
Can do helpless sinners good.

6 Saints and angels, joined in concert,
   Sing the praises of the Lamb,
While the blissful seats of heaven
   Sweetly echo to his name:
      Hallelujah!
Sinners, now his love proclaim.

170   Will you go?   8s & 6s.

WE'RE traveling home to heaven
      above,   [||: Will you go?: ||
To sing a Savior's dying love:
      Will you go? Will you go?
Our days of mourning past and gone,
Our sun shall there no more go down,
Our moon shall never be withdrawn.
      Will you go? Will you go?

2 We are going to walk the plains of light:
      Will you go? Will you go?
Where perfect day dispels the night:
      Will you go? Will you go?
The crown of life we all shall wear,
And palms of victory shall bear;
And heavenly joys forever share:
      Will you go? Will you go?

3 We are going to strike the golden lyre;
      Will you go? Will you go?
And sing with all the angels' choir;
      Will you go? Will you go?
We'll tell of God's redeeming grace;
We'll see our Savior's face to face;
And ever more proclaim his praise;
      Will you go? Will you go?

4 Oh could I hear some sinner say,
      I will go; I will go;
I'll start this moment on my way;
      I will go; I will go;
My old companions, fare you well;
I will not go with you to hell;
With my Redeemer I will dwell;
      Let me go—Let me go.

171   The youth's warning.   L. M.

YOUNG people all attention give,
   While I address you in God's name,
You who in sin and folly live,
   Come, hear the counsel of a friend.
I sought for bliss in glittering toys,
   I ranged the alluring scenes of vice,
But never found substantial joys,
   Until I heard my Savior's voice.

2 He spake, my sins at once forgiven,
   And washed my load of guilt away,
He gave me pardon, peace, and heaven,
   And thus I found the good old way;
And now with trembling sense I view,
   Huge billows roll beneath your feet,
For death eternal waits for you,
   And hell is moved your souls to meet.

3 Youth, like the spring, will soon be
      gone,
By fleeting time or conquering death;
Yon morning sun may set at noon,
   So transient is our mortal breath:
Your sparkling eyes and blooming cheeks
   Must wither like the blasted rose;
The coffin, earth, and winding sheet,
   Will soon your active limbs inclose.

4 Ye heedless ones that wildly stroll,
   The grave must soon become your bed,
Where silence reigns and vapors roll,
   In solemn silence round your head:
Your friends may pass that lonesome
      place,
And with a sigh move slowly on,
Still gazing on the spires of grass,
   With which your graves are over-
      grown.

5 But, oh! the soul where vengeance
      reigns,
It sinks with groans and ceaseless cries,
It rolls amidst the burning flames
   In endless woes and agonies:
There swallowed up in darkest night,
   Where devils howl, and thunders roar,
To rage in keen despair and guilt,
   When thousand thousand years are
      o'er.

172   *Sweet hour of prayer.*   L. M.

SWEET hour of prayer! sweet hour of
   prayer!
That calls me from a world of care,
And bids me at my Father's throne
Make all my wants and wishes known!
In seasons of distress and grief,
My soul has often found relief,
And oft escaped the tempter's snare,
By thy return, sweet hour of prayer.

2 Sweet hour of prayer! sweet hour of
   prayer!
The joy I feel, the bliss I share,
Of those whose auxious spirits burn
With strong desires for thy return.
With such I hasten to the place
Where God my Savior shows his face,
And gladly take my station there,
And wait for thee, sweet hour of prayer.

3 Sweet hour of prayer! sweet hour of
   prayer!
Thy wings shall my petition bear,
To him whose truth and faithfulness
Engage the waiting soul to bless;
And since he bids me seek his face,
Believe his word and trust his grace,
I'll cast on him my every care,
And wait for thee, sweet hour of prayer.

173   *All thy works praise thee.*   L. M.

THE turf shall be my fragrant shrine,
   My temple, Lord, that arch of thine,
My censor's breath, the mountain air,
And solitude shall hear my prayer.
My choir shall be the moonlit waves,
When murm'ring homeward to their
Or when the stillness of the sea, [caves,
E'en more than music breathes of thee.

2 I'll seek by day some glade unknown,
All light and silence like thy throne,
And the pale stars shall be at night
The only eyes that watch my rite.
Thy heaven, on which 't is bliss to look,
Shall be my pure and shining book;
Where I shall read in words of flame,
The glories of thy wondrous name.

174   *Prayer.*   L. M.

PRAYER is appointed to convey
   The blessings God designs to give;
Long as they live should Christians pray,
For only while they pray they live.

2 If pain afflict, or wrongs oppress;
If cares distract, or fears dismay;
If guilt deject; if sin distress;
In every case still watch and pray.

3 'T is prayer supports the soul that's
   weak;   [lame,
Though thought be broken, language
Pray if thou canst, or canst not speak,
But pray with faith in Jesus' name.

175   *Gracious.*   7s.

JESUS, lover of my soul!
   Let me to thy bosom fly.
While the billows near me roll,
   While the tempest still is high:
Hide me, oh my Savior, hide,
   Till the storm of life be past;
Safe into the haven guide,
   Oh! receive my soul at last.

2 Other refuge have I none—
   Hangs my helpless soul on thee;
Leave, oh! leave me not alone;
   Still support and comfort me.
All my trust on thee is stayed;
   All my help from thee I bring;
Cover my defenseless head
   With the shadow of thy wing.

3 Plenteous grace with thee is found;
   Grace to pardon all my sins;
Let the healing streams abound,
   Make and keep me pure within;
Thou of life the fountain art,
   Freely let me take of thee;
Spring thou up within my heart,
   Rise to all eternity.

176   *Prayer.*   C. M.

PRAYER is the soul's sincere desire,
   Unuttered or expressed,
The motion of a hidden fire,
   That trembles in the breast.

2 Prayer is the burden of a sigh,
   The falling of a tear,
The upward glancing of an eye;
   When none but God is near.

3 Prayer is the simplest form of speech
   That any lips can try—
Prayer the sublimest strains that reach
   The Majesty on high.

4 Prayer is the Christian's vital breath,
   The Christian's native air;
His watchword at the gate of death;
   He enters heaven with prayer.

5 Prayer is the contrite sinner's voice,
   Returning from his ways;
While angels in their songs rejoice,
   And say, Behold! he prays.

6 The saints in prayer appear as one,
   In word, in deed, in mind,
When with the Father and the Son
   Their fellowship they find.

7 Nor prayer is made on earth alone;
   The Holy Spirit pleads,
And Jesus on th' eternal throne,
   For sinners intercedes.

8 Oh! Thou, by whom we come to God,
   The Life, the Truth, the Way;
The path of prayer thyself hast trod,
   Lord, teach us how to pray.

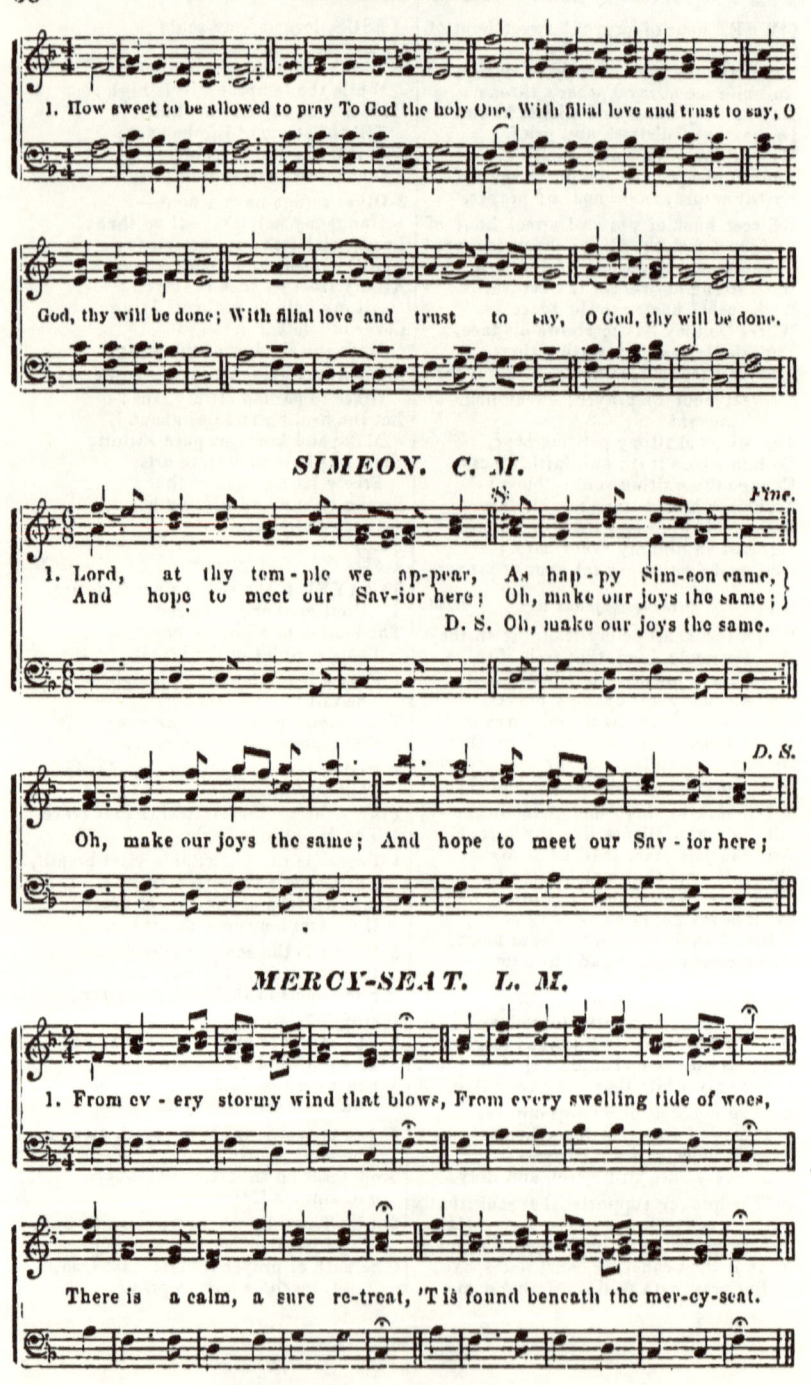

PRAYER.

177 *Thy will be done.* C. M.

HOW sweet to be allowed to pray
  To God the holy One,
With filial love and trust to say,
  O God, thy will be done.

2 We in these sacred words can find
  A cure for every ill,
They calm and soothe the troubled mind,
  And bid all care be still.

3 Oh let that will, which gave me breath,
  And an immortal soul,
In joy or grief, in life or death,
  My every wish control.

4 Oh could my heart thus ever pray,
  Thus imitate thy Son!
Teach me, O God, with truth to say,
  "Thy will, not mine, be done."

178 *Prayer and praise.* C. M.

LORD, at thy temple we appear,
  As happy Simeon came,
And hope to meet our Savior here;
  Oh, make our joys the same.

2 With what divine and vast delight,
  The good old man was filled,
When fondly, in his withered arms,
  He clasped the holy child.

3 Now I can leave this world, he cried,
  Behold thy servant dies;
I've seen thy great salvation, Lord,
  And close my peaceful eyes.

4 This is the light prepared to shine,
  Upon the Gentile lands!
Thine Israel's glory, and their hope,
  To break their slavish bands.

5 Jesus, the vision of thy face
  Has overpowering charms!
I shall not feel death's cold embrace,
  When dying in thy arms.

6 Then, while you hear my heart-strings break,
  How sweet my moment's roll;
A mortal paleness on my cheek,
  And glory in my soul!

179 *When prayer was wont to be made.* S. M.

HOW charming is the place,
  Where our Redeemer, Lord,
Unveils the glories of his face,
  According to his word.

2 Here, on the mercy-seat,
  With radiant glory crowned,
Our joyful eyes behold him sit,
  And smile on all around.

3 To him their prayers and cries
  Each contrite soul presents;
And while he hears their humble sighs,
  He grants them all their wants.

180 *The mercy-seat.* L. M.

FROM every stormy wind that blows,
  From every swelling tide of woes,
There is a calm, a sure retreat;
'T is found beneath the mercy-seat.

2 There is a place where Jesus sheds
  The oil of gladness on our heads;
A place than all besides more sweet—
It is the blood-bought mercy-seat.

3 There is a scene, where spirits blend,
  Where friend holds fellowship with friend;
Though sunder'd far, by faith they meet,
Around one common mercy-seat.

4 Ah! whither could we flee for aid,
  When tempted, desolate, dismay'd?
Or how the hosts of hell defeat,
Had suff'ring saints no mercy-seat.

5 There, there on eagle's wings we soar,
  And sin and sense molest no more;
And heaven comes down our souls to greet,
While glory crowns the mercy-seat.

181 *The mercy-seat.* C. M.

APPROACH, my soul, the mercy-seat,
  Where Jesus answers prayer;
There humbly fall before his feet,
  For none can perish there.

2 Thy promise is my only plea,
  With this I venture nigh;
Thou callest the burden'd soul to thee,
  And such, O Lord, am I.

3 Be thou my shield and hiding-place,
  That, shelter'd near thy side,
I may my fierce accuser face,
  And tell him thou hast died.

4 Oh, wondrous love! to bleed and die,
  To bear the cross and shame,
That guilty sinners, such as I,
  Might plead his gracious name.

182 *Christ's example.* S. M.

HOW sweet the melting lay
  Which breaks upon the ear,
When, at the hour of rising day,
  Christians unite in prayer!

2 The breezes waft their cries
  Up to Jehovah's throne;
He listens to their humble sighs,
  And sends his blessings down.

3 So Jesus rose to pray,
  Before the morning light—
Once on the chilling mount did stay,
  And wrestle all the night.

4 Glory to God on high,
  Who sends his blessing down,
To rescue souls condemned to die,
  And make his people one.

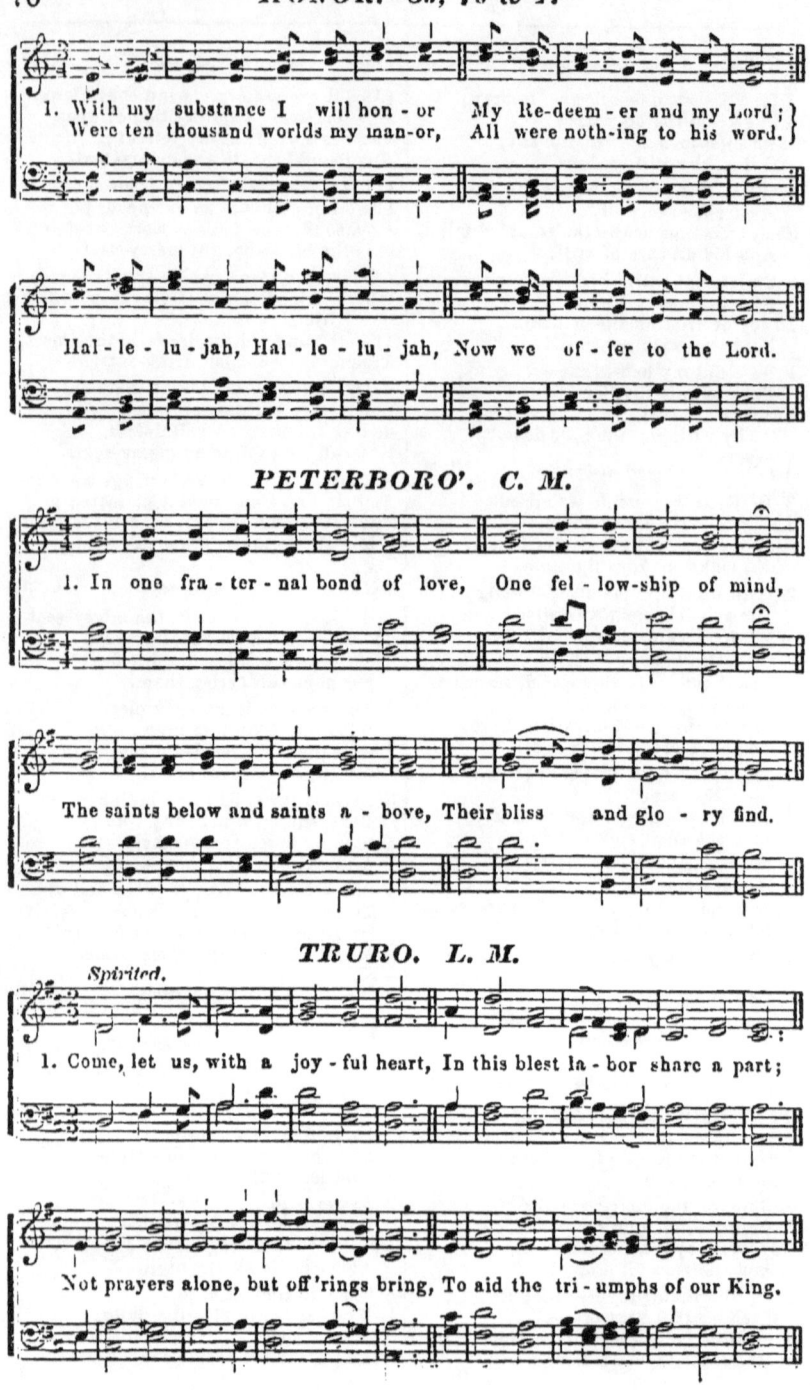

183   *The cattle on a thousand hills are his.*   8s, 7s & 4s.

WITH my substance I will honor
My Redeemer and my Lord;
Were ten thousand worlds my manor,
All were nothing to his word.
  Hallelujah—
Now we offer to the Lord.

2 While the heralds of salvation
His abounding grace proclaim,
Let his saints of every station
Gladly join to spread his fame.
  Hallelujah—
Gifts we offer to his name.

3 May his kingdom be promoted;
May the world the Savior know;
Be to him these gifts devoted,
For to him my all I owe.
  Hallelujah—
Run ye heralds to and fro.

4 Praise the Savior, all ye nations,
Praise him, all ye hosts above;
Shout with joyful acclamations,
His divine, victorious love.
  Hallelujah—
By this gift our love we 'll prove.

184   *See how these brethren love one another.*   C. M.

IN one fraternal bond of love,
  One fellowship of mind,
The saints below and saints above,
  Their bliss and glory find.

2 Here, in their house of pilgrimage,
  Thy statutes are their songs;
There, through one bright, eternal age,
  Thy praises they prolong.

3 Lord, may our union form a part
  Of that thrice happy whole;
Derive its pulse, from thee, the heart,
  Its life from thee, the soul.

185   *Of them first be a willing mind.*   L. M.

COME, let us with a joyful heart,
In this blest labor share a part;
Not prayers alone, but off'rings bring,
To aid the triumphs of our King.

2 Our hearts exult in songs of praise,
In hope to see the latter days;
Oh may we not forget to prove
By generous deeds how much we love.

3 Where'er his hand has spread the skies,
His bounty every need supplies;
Shall we not imitate his grace,
And fill with gifts this favoring place?

4 A generous heart the Lord approves,
A liberal hand our Savior loves;
Come, then, you saints, approve his will,
And let your gifts his treas'ry fill.

186   *We have fellowship, one with another.*   L. M.

HOW blest the sacred tie that binds,
In sweet communion, kindred minds!
How swift the heavenly course they run,
Whose hearts, whose faith, whose hopes,
  are one!

2 To each the soul of each how dear!
What tender love, what holy fear!
How doth the generous flame within
Refine from earth, and cleanse from sin!

3 Their streaming eyes together flow
For human guilt and mortal woe;
Their ardent prayers together rise
Like mingling flames in sacrifice.

4 Nor shall the glowing flame expire,
When dimly burns frail nature's fire;
Then shall they meet in realms above,
A heaven of joy, a heaven of love.

187   *Truly our fellowship is with the Father.*   C. M.

FROM all that's mortal, all that's vain,
  And from this earthly clod,
Arise, my soul, and strive to gain
  Some fellowship with God.

2 Say, what is there below the sky,
  Or all the paths thou 'st trod,
Can suit thy wishes or thy joys,
  Like fellowship with God?

3 Not life, nor all the toys of art,
  Nor pleasure's flowery road,
Can to my soul such bliss impart
  As fellowship with God.

4 Not health, nor friendship here below,
  Nor wealth, that golden load,
Can such delights and comforts show,
  As fellowship with God.

5 When I in love am made to bear
  Affliction's needful rod,
Light, sweet, and kind the strokes appear,
  Through fellowship with God.

6 And when the icy arms of death
  Shall chill my flowing blood,
With joy I 'll yield my latest breath,
  In fellowship with God.

188   *The poor ye have always with you.*   C. M.

HERE will we meet the Savior's poor,
  And fill their souls with bread;
The wretched stop at Jesus' door,
  And shall be largely fed.

2 Accept, O Lord, our prayers and vows;
  The offerings which we bring
Shall fill, like incense, all thy house,
  The palace of our King.

3 Thanks to thy great, thy glorious name,
  For all that we receive;
'T is meet that we should have the same,
  And all thy poor relieve.

189 *Love divine.* 8s & 6s.

OH love divine, how sweet thou art;
   When shall I find my willing heart
All taken up by thee?
I thirst, I faint, I die to prove
The greatness of redeeming love,
   The love of Christ to me.

2 Stronger his love than death or hell,
Its riches are unsearchable:
   The first-born sons of light
Desire in vain its depths to see;
They can not reach the mystery,
   The length, the breadth, and height.

3 God only knows the love of God;
Oh, that it now were shed abroad
   In this poor stony heart!
For love I sigh, for love I pine;
This only portion, Lord, be mine!
   Be mine this better part!

4 Oh, that I could forever sit
With Mary at the Master's feet!
   Be this my happy choice;
My only care, delight, and bliss,
My joy, my heaven on earth be this,
   To hear the Bridegroom's voice!

190 *Wondrous love.* C. M.

WHAT wondrous, mighty work is this,
   Unfolded by our Lord?
It gives our souls a taste for bliss,
   To read his holy word;   [bow'rs,"
'T was born in "Heaven's immortal
That blessed heaven above;
It gives us strength in lonely hours,
   And is the work of love.

2 We have received by this bright theme
   A hope of lasting life,
Beyond the shore of death's dark stream,
   Beyond this world of strife;
'T is far beyond the stars and sun,
   That blissful heaven above;
There we can dwell when time is done,
   By serving God in love.

3 'T was from that realm of love divine,
   That Jesus came to die;
As "God is love," let it combine
   To aid us home on high;
O'er all our race may it prevail,
   As it prevails above;
And they at death will not bewail,
   For they have lived in love.

4 'T is love unites God's church on earth,
   As it unites in heaven;
Then may we live to own his worth,
   And love the law he 's given!
Let every breast retain its joy,
   Till Jesus from above
Calls us where pain will ne'er annoy,
   Where all is peace and love.

191 *Love as brethren.* C. M.

HOW sweet, how heavenly is the sight
   When those who love the Lord,
With one another thus unite,
   And so fulfill the word!

2 Oh may we feel our brother's sigh,
   And with him bear a part:
May sorrows flow from eye to eye,
   And joy from heart to heart.

3 Free us from envy, scorn, and pride,
   Our wishes fix above;
May each his brother's failings hide,
   And show a brother's love.

4 Let love in one delightful stream,
   Through every bosom flow;
And union sweet, and dear esteem,
   In ev'ry action glow.

5 Love is the golden chain that binds
   The happy world above:
And he's an heir of heaven that finds
   His bosom glow with love.

192 *God's love.* C. M.

ALL nature feels attractive power,
   A strong, embracing force;
The drops that sparkle in the shower,
   The planets in their course.

2 Thus in the universe of mind
   Is felt the law of love;
The charity, both strong and kind,
   For all that live and move.

3 In this fine, sympathetic chain
   All creatures bear a part;
Their every pleasure, every pain,
   Linked to the feeling heart.

4 To earth below, from heaven above,
   The faith in Christ professed,
More clear reveals that God is love,
   And whom he loves is blest.

193 *The greatest of these is love.* C. M.

AMID the splendors of the sun,
   Great God! thy love appears,
In the soft radiance of the moon,
   Among a thousand stars.

2 Nature, through all her ample round,
   Thy boundless power proclaims;
And in melodious accents speaks
   The goodness of thy name.

3 Thy justice, holiness, and truth,
   Our solemn awe excite;
But the sweet charm of sovereign grace
   O'erpower us with delight.

4 Angels and men, the news proclaim,
   Through earth and heaven above,
The joyful, all-transporting news
   That God, the Lord, is love.

194 *Rest for the weary.* P. M.

IN the Christian's home in glory,
 There remains a land of rest,
There my Savior's gone before me,
 To fulfill my soul's request.

Chorus.

‖: There is rest for the weary: ‖
On the other side of Jordan,
In the sweet fields of Eden,
Where the tree of life is blooming,
 There is rest for you.

2 He is fitting up my mansion,
 Which eternally shall stand,
For my stay shall not be transient
 In that holy, happy land.

3 Pain nor sickness ne'er shall enter,
 Grief nor woe my lot shall share;
But in that celestial center,
 I a crown of life shall wear.

4 Death itself shall then be vanquished,
 And his sting shall be withdrawn;
Shout for gladness, oh, ye ransomed,
 Hail with joy the rising morn.

5 Sing, oh, sing, ye heirs of glory;
 Shout your triumph as you go;
Zion's gate will open for you,
 You shall find an entrance through.

195 *Comfort in God.* C. M.

DEAR refuge of my weary soul,
 On thee, when sorrows rise,
On thee, when waves of trouble roll,
 My fainting hope relies.

2 To thee I tell each rising grief,
 For thou alone canst heal;
Thy word can bring a sweet relief
 For every pain I feel.

3 But, oh, when gloomy doubts prevail,
 I fear to call thee mine;
The springs of comfort seem to fail,
 And all my hopes decline.

4 Yet, gracious God, where shall I flee?
 Thou art my only trust;
And still my soul would cleave to thee,
 Though prostrate in the dust.

196 *Joy in the conversion of sinners.* C. M.

OH, how the hearts of those revive,
 Who fear and love the Lord,
When sinners dead are made alive,
 By his all-quickening word.

2 The church of God their praises join,
 And of salvation sing;
They glorify the grace divine,
 Of their victorious King.

197 *Celebration.* P. M.

KNOW ye that better land,
 Where care's unknown?
Know ye that blessed band
 Around the throne?
There, there is happiness,
There streams of purest bliss;
There, there are rest and peace—
 There, there alone.

2 Yes, yes, we know that place,
 We know it well;
Eye hath not seen his face,
 Tongue can not tell:
There are the angels bright,
There saints enrob'd in white,
All, all are cloth'd in light—
 There, there they dwell.

3 Oh! we are weary here,
 A little band,
Yet soon in glory there
 We hope to stand;
Then let us haste away,
Speed o'er this world's dark way,
Unto that land of day—
 That better land.

4 Come! hasten that sweet day,
 Let time begone.
Come! Lord, make no delay,
 On thy white throne;
Thy face we wish to see
To dwell and reign with thee,
And, thine forever be—
 Thine, thine alone.

198 *Evening devotion.* C. M.

I LOVE to steal awhile away
 From every cumbering care,
And spend the hours of setting day
 In humble, grateful prayer.

2 I love in solitude to shed
 The penitential tear,
And all his promises to plead,
 Where none but God can hear.

3 I love to think on mercies past
 And future good implore,
And all my cares and sorrows cast,
 On him whom I adore.

4 I love by faith to take a view
 Of brighter scenes in heaven;
The prospect doth my strength renew,
 While here by tempest driven.

5 Thus when life's toilsome day is o'er,
 May its departing ray,
Be calm as this impressive hour,
 And lead to endless day.

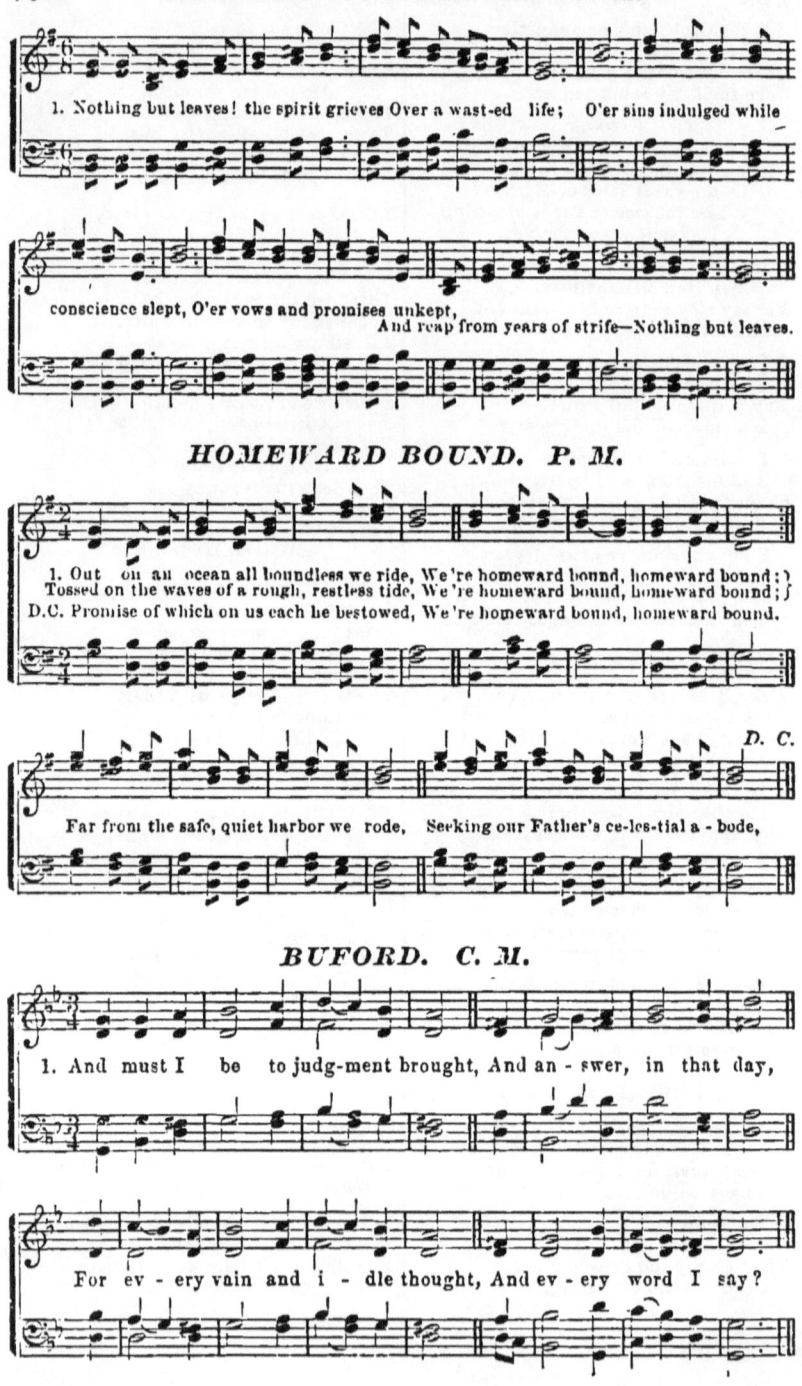

199. Nothing but leaves. P. M.

NOTHING but leaves! the spirit grieves
  Over a wasted life;
O'er sins indulged while conscience slept,
O'er vows and promises unkept,
And reap from years of strife—
  Nothing but leaves.

2 Nothing but leaves! no gathered sheaves
  Of life's fair ripening grain;
We sow our seeds, lo! tares and weeds,
Words, idle words for earnest deeds,
We reap with toil and pain—
  Nothing but leaves.

3 Nothing but leaves! sad memory weaves
  No vail to hide the past;
And as we trace our weary way,
Counting each lost and misspent day,
Sadly we find at last—
  Nothing but leaves.

4 Ah! who shall thus the Master meet,
  Bearing but withered leaves?
Ah! who shall at the Savior's feet,
Before the awful judgment-seat,
Lay down, for golden sheaves,
  Nothing but leaves?

200. Homeward bound. P. M.

OUT on an ocean all boundless we ride,
  We're homeward bound;
Tossed on the waves of a rough, restless tide,
  We're homeward bound;
Far from the safe, quiet harbor we rode,
Seeking our Father's celestial abode,
Promise of which on us each he bestowed,
  We're homeward bound.

2 Wildly the storm sweeps us on as it roars;
  We're homeward bound;
Look! yonder lie the bright heavenly shores,
  We're homeward bound;
Steady! oh pilot! stand firm at the wheel,
Steady, we soon shall outweather the gale,
Oh! how we fly 'neath the loud creaking sail,
  We're homeward bound.

3 We'll tell the world as we journey along,
  We're homeward bound;
Try to persuade them to enter our throng,
  We're homeward bound;
Come, trembling sinner, forlorn and oppressed,
Join in our number, oh come and be blest;
Journey with us to the mansion of rest,
  We're homeward bound.

4 Into the harbor of heaven we now glide,
  We're home at last;
Softly we drift on its bright silver tide,
  We're home at last;
Glory to God! all our dangers are o'er;
We stand secure on the glorified shore,
Glory to God! we will shout evermore,
  We're home at last.

201. I must go to the judgment. C. M.

AND must I be to judgment brought,
  And answer, in that day,
For every vain and idle thought,
  And every word I say?

2 Yes, every secret of my heart
  Shall shortly be made known,
And I receive my just desert
  For all that I have done.

3 How careful, then, ought I to live;
  With what religious fear;
Who such a strict account must give
  For my behavior here?

4 Thou mighty Judge of quick and dead,
  The watchful power bestow;
So shall I to my ways take heed,
  In all I speak or do.

202. A voice from the tomb. C. M.

HARK! from the tombs a doleful sound;
  My ears attend the cry—
"Ye living men, come view the ground
  Where you must shortly lie.

2 "Princes, this clay must be your bed,
  In spite of all your towers:
The tall, the wise, the reverend head,
  Must lie as low as ours."

3 Great God, is this our certain doom?
  And are we still secure?
Still walking downward to the tomb,
  And yet prepare no more?

4 Grant us the power of quickening grace,
  To fit our souls to fly;
Then, when we drop this dying flesh,
  We'll rise above the sky.

203. Time the period to prepare for eternity. C. M.

THEE we adore, Eternal Name,
  And humbly own to thee
How feeble is our mortal frame,
  What dying worms are we.

2 The year rolls round, and steals away
  The breath that first it gave;
Whate'er we do, where'er we be,
  We're traveling to the grave.

3 Great God, on what a slender thread
  Hang everlasting things!
The final state of all the dead
  Upon life's feeble strings!

4 Eternal joy, or endless woe,
  Attends on every breath;
And yet how unconcerned we go
  Upon the brink of death!

5 Awake, O Lord, our drowsy sense,
  To walk this dangerous road;
And if our souls are hurried hence,
  May they be found with God.

THE HEAVENLY REGION. 6s & 7s.

1. There's a re-gion a-bove, Free from sin and tempta-tion;
And a man-sion of love, For each heir of sal-va-tion; Then dis-
D. S. 'T will rise brighter to-morrow.

miss all thy fears, Weary pilgrim of sorrow; Though thy sun set in tears,

BREAST THE WAVE, CHRISTIAN. 5s & 6s.

1. Breast the wave, Christian, When it is strongest;
Watch for day, Christian, When the night's longest;

Onward and onward still, Be thine endeavor; The rest that remaineth Will be forever.

BALTIMORE. S. M.

1. Oh! sing to me of heaven, When I am called to die;
Chorus. There are no tears in heaven, Oh! there's no weep-ing there;

Sing songs of ho-ly ec-sta-sy, To waft my soul on high.
In heaven a-lone no sor-row's known! And there's no weeping there.

204 The region above. 6s & 7s.

THERE'S a region above,
  Free from sin and temptation,
And a mansion of love,
  For each heir of salvation.
Then dismiss all thy fears,
  Weary pilgrim of sorrow,
Tho' thy sun set in tears,
  'T will rise brighter to-morrow.

2 There our toils will be done,
  And free grace be our story,
God himself be our Sun,
  And our unsetting glory.
In that world of delight,
  Spring shall never be ended,
Nor shall shadows nor night,
  With its brightness be blended.

3 There shall friends no more part,
  Nor shall farewells be spoken,
There 'll be balm for the heart,
  That with anguish was broken.
From affliction set free,
  And from God ne'er to sever,
We his glory shall see,
  And enjoy him forever.

205 The land of promise. 6s & 7s, D.

SINNER, go: will you go
  To the highlands of heaven?
Where the storms never blow,
  And the long summer's given;
Where the bright, blooming flowers
  Are their odors emitting;
And the leaves of the bowers
  In the breezes are flitting.

2 Where the rich golden fruit
  Is in bright clusters pending,
And the deep laden boughs,
  Of life's fair tree are bending.
And where life's crystal stream
  Is unceasingly flowing,
And the verdure is green,
  And eternally growing.

3 Where the saints robed in white—
  Cleansed in life's flowing fountain;
Shining beauteous and bright,
  They inhabit the mountain.
Where no sin, nor dismay,
  Neither trouble nor sorrow,
Will be felt for a day,
  Nor be feared for the morrow.

4 He's prepared thee a home—
  Sinner, canst thou believe it?
And invites thee to come—
  Sinner, wilt thou receive it?
Oh, come, sinner, come,
  For the tide is receding,
And the Savior will soon,
  And forever, cease pleading.

206 Sing to me of heaven. S. M.

OH! sing to me of heaven,
  When I am called to die;
Sing songs of holy ecstasy,
  To waft my soul on high.

Chorus.
There are no tears in heaven,
  Oh! there's no weeping there;
In heaven alone, no sorrow's known!
  And there's no weeping there.

2 When cold and sluggish drops
  Roll off my marble brow,
Break forth in strains of joyfulness—
  Let heaven begin below.

3 When the last moment comes,
  Then watch my dying face,
And catch the bright seraphic gleam
  Which o'er my features pass.

4 Then to my raptured ears
  Let one sweet song be given—
Let music charm me last on earth,
  And greet me first in heaven.

5 Then close my sightless eyes,
  And lay me down to rest;
And clasp my pale and icy hands
  Across my peaceful breast.

6 Around my senseless clay
  Assemble those I love,
And sing of heaven, delightful heaven!
  My glorious home above.

207 Fight the fight of faith. 5s & 6s.

BREAST the wave, Christian,
  When it is strongest;
Watch for day, Christian,
  When the night's longest;
Onward and onward still,
  Be thine endeavor;
The rest that remaineth
  Will be forever.

2 Fight the fight, Christian,
  Jesus is o'er thee;
Run the race, Christian,
  Heaven is before thee.
He who hath promised,
  Faltereth never;
The love of eternity
  Flows on forever.

3 Lift the eye, Christian,
  Just as it closeth;
Raise the heart, Christian,
  Ere it reposeth;
Thee from the love of Christ
  Nothing shall sever;
Mount, when thy work is done,
  Praise him forever.

208 *A bruised reed he shall not break.* 11s.

TO the hall of that feast came the sinful
  and fair,
She heard, in the city, that Jesus was
  there;
Unheeding the splendor that blazed on
  the board,
She silently knelt at the feet of her Lord.

2 The hair on her forehead, so sad and so
  meek,
Hung dark on the blushes that glowed on
  her cheek;
And so sad and so lowly she knelt in her
  shame,
It seemed that her spirit had fled from
  her frame.

3 The frown and the murmur went round
  thro' them all,
That one so unhallowed should tread in
  the hall;
And some said the poor would be objects
  more meet
For the wealth of the perfume she showered
  on his feet.

4 She heard but her Savior—she spoke
  but in sighs,
She dared not look up to the heaven of his
  eyes;
And the hot tears gushed forth at each
  heave of her breast,
As her lips to his sandals she throbbingly
  pressed.

5 In the sky, after tempest, as shineth
  the bow,
In the glance of the sunbeam, as melteth
  the snow,
He looked on the lost one—her sins were
  forgiven,
And Mary went forth in the beauty of
  heaven!

209 *They played on harps of gold.* 8s & 7s, D.

HARK! ten thousand harps and voices
  Sound the note of praise above;
Jesus reigns, and heaven rejoices;
  Jesus reigns the God of love:
See, he sits on yonder throne,
Jesus rules the world alone.
  Hallelujah! Hallelujah! Hallelujah!
    Amen.

2 Jesus, hail, whose glory brightens
  All above, and gives it worth;
Lord of life, thy smile enlightens,
  Cheers and charms thy saints on earth.
When we think of love like thine,
Lord, we own it love divine.
  Hallelujah, etc.

3 King of glory, reign forever,
  Thine an everlasting crown;
Nothing from thy love shall sever
  Those whom thou hast made thine own;
Happy objects of thy grace,
Destined to behold thy face.
  Hallelujah, etc.

4 Savior, hasten thine appearing,
  Bring, oh bring the glorious day,
When, the awful summons hearing,
  Heaven and earth shall pass away,
Then with golden harps we'll sing,
Glory, glory, to our King.
  Hallelujah, etc.

210 *The night is far spent, etc.* 10s & 11s.

SOON and forever the breaking of day
  Shall chase all the night clouds of
    sorrow away;
Soon and forever we'll see as we're seen,
  And know the deep meaning of things
    that have been—
Where fightings without and conflicts
    within
Shall weary no more in the warfare with
    sin—
Where tears, and where fears, and where
    death shall be never,
Christians with Christ shall be soon and
    forever.

2 Soon and forever—such promise our
    trust—
Though ashes to ashes, and dust be to
    dust,
Soon and forever our union shall be
Made perfect, our glorious Redeemer, in
    thee;
When the cares and the sorrows of time
    shall be o'er,
Its pangs and its partings remembered no
    more;
Where life can not fail, and where death
    can not sever,
Christians with Christ shall be soon and
    forever.

3 Soon and forever the work shall be done,
  The warfare accomplished, the victory
    won—
Soon and forever the soldier lay down
  The sword for a harp, the cross for a
    crown—
Then droop not in sorrow, despond not in
    fear,
A glorious to-morrow is brightening and
    near,
When—blessed reward for each faithful
    endeavor—
Christians with Christ shall be soon and
    forever.

211
Sonnet. L. M.

WHEN for eternal worlds we steer,
 And seas are calm and skies are clear,
And faith in lively exercise,
And distant hills of Canaan rise,
 Chorus.
 My soul for joy she spreads her wings,
 And loud her lovely sonnet sings,
 Vain world adieu, vain world adieu;
 And loud her lovely sonnet sings,
  Vain world adieu.

2 With cheerful hopes her eyes explore
Each landmark on the distant shore,
The trees of life, the pastures green,
The golden streets, the crystal stream;
 Again for joy she spreads her wings,
 And loud her lovely sonnet sings, etc.

3 When nearer still she draws to land,
More eager all her powers expand,
With steady helm and free bent sail,
Her anchor drops within the vail.
 Oh then for joy she spreads her wings,
 And her celestial sonnet sings,
  On Canaan's shore, etc.

212
That they all may be one. 8s & 7s.

LET thy kingdom, blessed Savior,
 Come and bid our jarring cease;
Come, oh come, and reign forever—
 Lord of life, and Prince of Peace:
Visit now thy bleeding Zion,
 Lo! thy people mourn and weep;
Day and night thy flock is crying,
 Gracious Shepherd, feed thy sheep.

2 Some for Paul—some for Apollos;
 Some for Cephas—few agree
With thy holy word that calls us,
 Or resolve to follow thee:
Lord, in us there is no merit,
 At thy name our hearts do leap;
Guide us by thy Holy Spirit,
 Till in death our souls shall sleep.

3 Come, blest Lord, with courage arm us,
 Persecution rages here;
Naught, we know, can ever harm us,
 If our Shepherd be but near:
Glory, glory, be to Jesus!
 At his name our hearts do leap;
He both comforts us, and saves us;
 Gracious Shepherd, bless thy sheep.

213
Only waiting. 8s & 7s.

ONLY waiting till the shadows
 Are a little longer grown;
Only waiting till the glimmer
 Of the day's last beam is flown;
Till the night of earth is faded
 From the heart once full of day;
Till the stars of heaven are breaking
 Through the twilight soft and gray.

2 Only waiting till the reapers
 Have the last sheaf gathered home;
For the summer time is faded,
 And the autumn winds have come.
Quickly, reapers, gather quickly
 The last ripe hours of my heart,
For the bloom of life is withered,
 And I hasten to depart.

3 Only waiting till the shadows
 Are a little longer grown;
Only waiting till the glimmer
 Of the day's last beam is flown;
Then, from out the gathered darkness,
 Holy, deathless stars shall rise,
By whose light my soul shall gladly
 Tread its pathway to the skies.

214
And that rock was Christ. 7s & 6s.

ROCK of ages, cleft for me,
 Let me hide myself in thee;
Let the water and the blood,
 From thy riven side which flowed,
Be of sin the double cure;
 Cleanse me from its guilt and power.

2 Not the labor of my hands
 Can fulfill the law's demands;
Could my zeal no respite know,
 Could my tears forever flow,
All for sin could not atone;
 Thou must save, and thou alone.

3 Nothing in my hand I bring,
 Simply to thy cross I cling;
Naked, come to thee for dress;
 Helpless, look to thee for grace;
Foul, I to the fountain fly,
 Wash me, Savior, or I die.

4 While I draw this fleeting breath,
 When my heart-strings break in death,
When I soar to worlds unknown,
 See thee on thy judgment throne,
Rock of ages, cleft for me,
 Let me hide myself in thee.

215
Prayer for the unconverted.

SAVED ourselves by Jesus' blood,
 Let us now draw nigh to God;
Many round us blindly stray;
 Moved with pity, let us pray—
Pray that they who now are blind
 Soon the way of Truth may find.

2 Lord, awaken all around,
 Let them know the joyful sound;
Slaves to Satan heretofore,
 Let them now be slaves no more;
Lord, we turn our eyes to thee,
 Set the captive sinner free!

216 *We'll be there in a little while.* P. M.

WE have heard of that bright, that
 holy land,
We have heard and our hearts are glad,
For we are a lonely pilgrim band,
We are weary, and worn, and sad.
They tell us that pilgrims have a dwell-
 ing there,
No more are they homeless ones,
And they say that the goodly land is fair,
Where the fountain of life ever runs.

2 We have heard of the palms, the robes,
 the crowns,
Of that silvery band in white,
Of the city fair with its golden gates,
All radiant with heavenly light.
We have heard of the angels there, and
 saints,
With their golden harps, how they sing,
And the mount, with the fruitful tree of
 life,
And the leaves that healing bring.

3 There are beautiful birds in the bowers
 green,
Their songs are blithe and sweet,
Their warbling gushing ever new,
The angel harpers greet.
We'll be there, we'll be there in a little
 while,
And we'll join with the pure and blest;
We'll all have the palms, the robes, the
And we'll be forever at rest. [crowns,

217 *Shall we sing in heaven?* P. M.

SHALL we sing in heaven forever,
 Shall we sing?
Shall we sing in heaven forever,
 In that happy land?
Yes! oh, yes! in that land, that happy
 land,
They that meet shall sing forever,
Far beyond the rolling river,
Meet to sing, and love forever,
 In that happy land.

2 Shall we know each other ever,
 In that land?
Shall we know each other ever,
 In that happy land?
Yes! oh, yes, in that land, that happy
 land,
They that meet shall know each other,
Far beyond the rolling river, etc.

3 Shall we sing with holy angels,
 In that land?
Shall we sing with holy angels,
 In that happy land?
Yes! oh, yes! in that land, that happy
 land,
Saints and angels sing forever,
Far beyond the rolling river, etc.

4 Shall we rest from care and sorrow,
 In that land?
Shall we rest from care and sorrow,
 In that happy land?
Yes! oh, yes! in that land, that happy
 land,
They that meet shall rest forever,
Far beyond the rolling river, etc.

5 Shall we meet our dear, lost children,
 In that land?
Shall we meet our dear, lost children,
 In that happy land?
Yes! oh, yes! in that land, that happy
 land,
Children meet and sing forever,
Far beyond the rolling river, etc.

6 Shall we meet our Christian parents,
 In that land?
Shall we meet our Christian parents,
 In that happy land?
Yes! oh, yes! in that land, that happy
 land,
Parents and children meet together,
Far beyond the rolling river, etc.

7 Shall we meet our faithful teachers,
 In that land?
Shall we meet our faithful teachers,
 In that happy land?
Yes! oh, yes! in that land, that happy
 land,
Teachers and scholars meet together,
Far beyond the rolling river, etc.

8 Shall we know our blessed Savior,
 In that land?
Shall we know our blessed Savior,
 In that happy land?
Yes! oh, yes! in that land, that happy
 land,
We shall know our blessed Savior,
Far beyond the rolling river,
Love and serve him there forever,
 In that happy land.

218 *Christ's universal reign.* 7s, D.

HASTEN, Lord, the glorious time,
 When, beneath Messiah's sway,
Every nation, every clime,
 Shall the gospel call obey.

2 Mightiest kings his pow'r shall own;
 Heathen tribes his name adore;
Satan and his host o'erthrown,
 Bound in chains, shall hurt no more.

3 Then shall wars and tumult cease;
 Then be banished grief and pain;
Righteousness, and joy, and peace,
 Undisturbed shall ever reign.

4 Bless we, then, our gracious Lord;
 Ever praise his glorious name;
All his mighty acts record—
 All his wondrous works proclaim.

219 *Christ was born in Bethlehem.* 8s & 7s.

JESUS CHRIST, my Lord and Savior,
  Once became a child like me;
Oh, that in my whole behavior,
  He my pattern still may be.

2 If my feelings are not holy,
  Pride and passion dwell within;
But the Lord was meek and lowly,
  And was never known to sin.

3 While I 'm often vainly trying
  Some new pleasure to possess,
He was always self-denying—
  Patient in his worst distress.

4 Lord, assist a feeble creature,
  Guide me by thy word of truth;
Condescend to be my teacher
  Through my childhood and my youth.

220 *Sabbath-school celebration.* 7s & 6s.

TO thee, oh blessed Savior,
  Our grateful songs we raise;
Oh, tune our hearts and voices
  Thy holy name to praise;
'T is by thy sovereign mercy
  We're here allowed to meet;
To join with friends and teachers,
  Thy blessing to entreat.

2 Lord, guide and bless our teachers,
  Who labor for our good,
And may the holy Scriptures
  By us be understood;
Oh, may our hearts be given
  To thee, our glorious King;
That we may meet in heaven,
  Thy praises there to sing.

3 And may the precious gospel
  Be published all abroad,
Till the benighted heathen
  Shall know and serve the Lord;
Till o'er the wide creation
  The rays of truth shall shine,
And nations now in darkness
  Arise to light divine.

221 *If you love me keep my commandments.* 8s & 7s.

JESUS says that we must love him;
  Helpless as the lambs are we;
But he very kindly tells us,
  That our Shepherd he will be.

2 Heavenly Shepherd, please to watch us,
  Guard us both by night and day;
Pity show to little children,
  Who, like lambs, too often stray.

3 We are always prone to wander;
  Please to keep us from each snare;
Teach our infant hearts to praise thee,
  For thy kindness and thy care.

222 *All souls are mine.* C. M.

BY cool Siloam's shady rill,
  How sweet the lily grows!
How sweet the breath beneath the hill
  Of Sharon's dewy rose.

2 Lo! such a child, whose early feet,
  The paths of peace have trod,
Whose heart, with holy influence,
  Is upward drawn to God.

3 By cool Siloam's shady rill,
  The lily must decay;
The rose that blooms beneath the hill,
  Must shortly fade away.

223 *Remember now thy Creator in the days of thy youth.* 7s & 6s.

"REMEMBER thy Creator,"
  While youth's fair spring is bright:
Before thy cares are greater,
  Before comes age's night;
While yet the sun shines o'er thee,
  Ere night's dark pall is near;
While life is all before thee,
  Thy great Creator fear.

2 "Remember thy Creator,"
  Ere life resigns its trust,
Ere sinks dissolving nature,
  And dust returns to dust;
Before with God who gave it,
  Thy spirit shall appear;
He cries who died to save it,
  "Thy great Creator fear."

224 *Serve the Lord very early.* 7s & 6s.

GO thou, in life's fair morning;
  Go, in the bloom of youth,
And buy, for thy adorning,
  The precious pearl of truth.
Secure this heavenly treasure,
  And bind it on thy heart,
And let no worldly pleasure
  E'er cause it to depart.

2 Go while the day-star shineth,
  Go, while thy heart is light,
Go, ere thy strength declineth,
  While every sense is bright:
Sell all thou hast, and buy it,
  'T is worth all earthly things,
Rubies, and gold, and diamonds,
  Scepters, and crowns of kings.

3 Go, ere the cloud of sorrow
  Steal o'er the bloom of youth,
Defer not till to-morrow,
  Go now and buy the truth.
Go, seek thy great Creator,
  Learn early to be wise,
Go, place upon his altar,
  A morning sacrifice!

225 *Love divine, all love excelling.* 8s & 7s.

LOVE divine, all love excelling,
  Joy of heaven to earth come down !
Fix in us thy humble dwelling:
  All thy faithful mercies crown :
Jesus, thou art all compassion,
  Pure, unbounded love thou art,
Visit us with thy salvation,
  Enter ev'ry trembling heart.

2 Breathe, oh breathe thy loving Spirit
  Into ev'ry troubled breast:
Let us all in thee inherit,
  Let us find thy promised rest.
Take away the love of sinning,
  Take our load of guilt away ;
End the work of thy beginning,
  Bring us to eternal day.

3 Carry on thy new creation—
  Pure and holy may we be;
Let us see our whole salvation,
  Perfectly secured by thee :
Change from glory into glory,
  Till in heaven we take our place ;
Till we cast our crowns before thee,
  Lost in wonder, love, and praise.

226 *Missionary.* C. M.

GO, heralds of the cross, proclaim
  The wondrous word of God ;
Publish aloud, in Jesus' name,
  The gospel all abroad.

2 Broadcast upon the spacious earth,
  Sow ye the precious seed ;
Tell of the Savior's wondrous birth—
  Tell how he lived and died.

3 Tell he was buried and arose
  Triumphant from the grave,
Exalted high above his foes,
  He 's mighty still to save.

227 *Far from mortal cares retreating.* 8s & 7s, D.

FAR from mortal cares retreating,
  Sordid hopes, and vain desires,
Here our willing footsteps meeting,
  Every heart to heaven aspires,
From the Fount of glory beaming,
  Light celestial cheers our eyes,
Mercy from above proclaiming
  Peace and pardon from the skies.

2 Blessings all around bestowing,
  God withholds his care from none ;
Grace and mercy ever flowing
  From the fountain of his throne.
Lord, with favor still attend us ;
  Bless us with thy wondrous love ;
Thou, our Sun, our Shield, defend us ;
  All our hope is from above.

8

228 *Present with the Lord.* P. M.

OH think that, while you 're weeping
    here,
  His hand a golden harp is stringing ;
And with a voice serene and clear,
  His ransomed soul, without a tear,
  His Savior's praise is singing !

2 And think that all his pains are fled,
  His toils and sorrows closed forever ;
While he, whose blood for man was shed,
Has placed upon his servant's head
  A crown that fadeth never.

3 For thus, while round your lowly bier
  Surviving friends are sadly bending,
Your souls, like his, to Jesus dear,
Shall wing their flight to yonder sphere,
  Faith lightest pinions lending.

4 And thus, when to the silent tomb,
  Your lifeless dust like his is given,
Like faith shall whisper, 'midst the gloom,
That yet again in faithful bloom,
  That dust shall smile in heaven !

229 *Be baptized.* 8s & 7s.

HEAR the bless'd Redeemer call you,
  Listen to his gracious voice ;
Dread no ills that can befall you,
  While you make his ways your choice.
Jesus says, let each believer
  Be baptized in my name :
He himself in Jordan's river
  Was immersed beneath the stream.

2 Plainly here his footsteps tracing,
  Follow him without delay ;
Gladly his commands embracing,
  Lo ! your Captain leads the way :
View the rite with understanding,
  Jesus's grave before you lies ;
Be interred at his commanding,
  After his example rise.

230 *Sabbath morn.* C. M.

WHEN the worn spirit wants repose,
  And sighs her God to seek,
How sweet to hail the evening's close,
  That ends the weary week !

2 How sweet to hail the early dawn,
  That opens on the sight,
When first that soul-reviving morn
  Sheds forth new rays of light !

3 Sweet day ! thine hours too soon will
  Yet while they gently roll, [cease,
Breathe, heavenly Spirit, source of peace,
  A rest upon my soul.

4 Then, will my pilgrimage be done,
  The world's long week be o'er :
That heavenly dawn which needs no sun,
  That day, which fades no more !

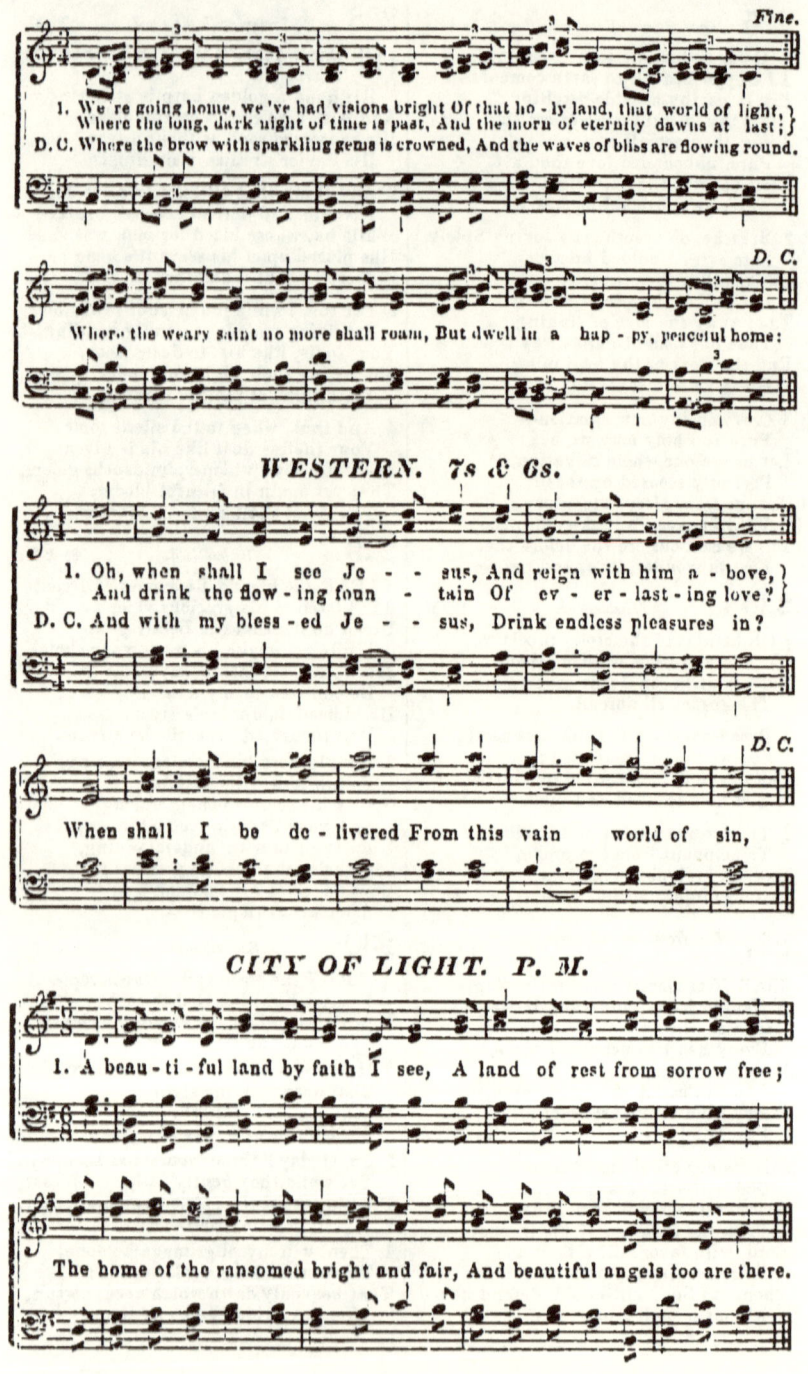

231 *It is better to depart.*

WE 'RE going home, we 've had visions
   bright
Of that holy land, that world of light,
Where the long, dark night of time is past,
And the morn of eternity dawns at last;
Where the weary saint no more shall roam,
But dwell in a happy, peaceful home;
Where the brow with sparkling gems is
   crowned,
And the waves of bliss are flowing round.

2 We 're going home, we soon shall be
Where the sky is clear, and all are free;
Where the victor's song floats o'er the
   plains,
And the seraph's anthems blend with its
   strains;
Where the sun rolls down its brilliant
   flood,
And beams on a world that is fair and
   good;
Where stars, once dimmed at nature's
   doom,
Will ever shine o'er the new earth bloom.

3 'Mid the ransomed throng, 'mid the
   seas of bliss,
'Mid the holy city's gorgeousness;
'Mid the verdant plains, 'mid angels'
   cheer,
'Mid the saints that round the throne
   appear;
Where the conqueror's song as it sounds
Is wafted on the ambrosial air;   [afar,
Through endless years we then shall
   prove,
The worth of a Savior's matchless love.

232 *We walk by faith.*   P. M.

A BEAUTIFUL land by faith I see,
   A land of rest from sorrow free;
The home of the ransomed bright and fair,
And beautiful angels too are there.

2 That land is called the City of Light.
It ne'er has known the shades of night,
For the glory of God as the light of day,
Hath driven the darkness far away.

3 In vision I see its streets of gold,
Its gates of pearl I too behold,
The river of life, the crystal sea,
The ambrosial fruit of life's fair tree.

4 The ransomed throng arrayed in white,
In rapture range the plains of light;
In one harmonious choir they praise
Their glorious Savior's matchless grace.

5 That beautiful land I mean to see,
And join in its glorious harmony;
On the mount of God through grace I 'll
   stand,   [land.
And share in the bliss of that beautiful

233 *Longing for home.*   7s & 6s.

OH, when shall I see Jesus,
   And reign with him above!
And drink the flowing fountain
   Of everlasting love,
And with my blessed Jesus,
   Drink endless pleasures in.
When shall I be delivered
   From this vain world of sin.

2 But now I am a soldier,
   My Captain 's gone before,
He 's given me my orders,
   And tells me not to fear;
And if I hold out faithful
   A crown of life he 'll give,
And all his valiant soldiers
   Eternal life shall have.

3 Through grace I am determined
   To conquer though I die,
And then away to Jesus
   On wings of love I 'll fly;
Farewell to sin and sorrow,
   I bid them both adieu,
And you, my friends, prove faithful,
   And on your way pursue.

4 And if you meet with troubles
   And trials on the way,
Then cast your care on Jesus,
   And do n't forget to pray;
Gird on the heavenly armor
   Of faith, and hope, and love,
And when your warfare 's ended
   You 'll reign with him above.

234 *The cross—the power of God.*   7s & 6s, D.

I SAW the cross of Jesus
   When burden'd with my sin;
I sought the cross of Jesus
   To give me peace within:
I brought my sins to Jesus;
   He cleansed it in his blood;
And in the cross of Jesus
   I found my peace with God.

2 I love the cross of Jesus—
   It tells me what I am:
A vile and guilty creature,
   Saved only through the Lamb.
No righteousness, no merit,
   No beauty can I plead;
Yet in the cross I glory,
   My title there I read.

3 I clasp the cross of Jesus
   In every trying hour,
My sure and certain refuge,
   My never-failing tower.
In every fear and conflict,
   I more than conqueror am;
Living I 'm safe, or dying,
   Through Christ the risen Lamb.

235   Death and the grave.   C. M.

HARK! from the tombs a doleful
    My ears attend the cry—   [sound!
" Ye living men, come view the ground
    Where you must shortly lie.

2 " Princes, this clay must be your bed,
    In spite of all your towers:
The tall, the wise, the reverend head,
    Must lie as low as ours."

3 Great God, is this our certain doom?
    And are we still secure?
Still walking downward to the tomb,
    And yet prepare no more?

4 Grant us the power of quickening grace,
    To fit our souls to fly;
Then, when we drop this dying flesh,
    We'll rise above the sky.

236   After this manner pray ye.   Cs & 5s.

OUR Father in heaven,
    We hallow thy name!
May thy kingdom holy
    On earth be the same!
Oh, give to us daily,
    Our portion of bread,
It is from thy bounty
    That all must be fed.

2 Forgive our transgressions,
    And teach us to know
That humble compassion
    That pardons each foe;
Keep us from temptation,
    From weakness and sin,
And thine be the glory,
    Forever—Amen!

237   The Lord reigneth, let the people tremble.   C. M.

HIGH as the heavens above the ground
    Reigns the Creator, God;
Wide as the whole creation's bound
    Extends his awful rod.

2 Let princes of exalted state
    To him ascribe their crown,
Render their homage at his feet,
    And cast their glories down.

3 Know that his kingdom is supreme,
    Your lofty thoughts are vain;
He calls you gods, that awful name,
    But ye must die like men.

4 Then let the sovereigns of the globe
    Not dare to vex the Just;
He puts on vengeance like a robe,
    And treads the worms to dust.

5 Ye judges of the earth, be wise,
    And think of heaven with fear;
The meanest saint that you despise
    Has an avenger there.

238   All tears shall be wiped from all eyes.   C. M.

O Thou, who dri'st the mourner's tear,
    How dark this world would be,
If, when deceived and wounded here,
    We could not fly to thee:

2 The friends who in our sunshine live,
    When winter comes, are flown;
And he who has but tears to give,
    Must weep those tears alone.

3 But thou wilt heal the broken heart,
    Which, like the plants that throw
Their fragrance from the wounded part,
    Breathes sweetness out of woe.

4 When joy no longer soothes or cheers,
    And e'en the hope that threw
A moment's sparkle o'er our tears,
    Is dimmed and vanished too.

5 Oh who could bear life's stormy doom,
    Did not thy wing of love
Come, brightly wafting through the gloom
    Our peace-branch, from above!

6 Then sorrow, touched by thee, grows
    With more than rapture's ray; [bright,
As darkness shows us worlds of light,
    We never saw by day.

239   Turn us again, O God of hosts.   C. M.

SEE, gracious God, before thy throne
    Thy mourning people bend;
'T is on thy sovereign grace alone
    Our humble hopes depend.

2 Dark, frowning judgments from thy
    Thy dreadful powers display; [hand
Yet mercy spares this guilty land,
    And still we live to pray.

3 Oh, turn us, turn us, mighty Lord,
    By thy convincing grace;
Then shall our hearts obey thy word,
    And humbly seek thy face.

240   Our land.   C. M.

LORD, while for all mankind we pray,
    Of ev'ry clime and coast,
Oh hear us for our native land—
    The land we love the most.

2 Oh guard our shores from ev'ry foe,
    With peace our borders bless,
With prosp'rous union our cities crown,
    Our fields with plenteousness.

3 Unite us in the sacred love
    Of knowledge, truth, and thee;
And let our hills and valleys shout
    The songs of liberty.

4 Lord of the nations, thus to thee
    Our country we commend;
Be thou her refuge and her trust,
    Her everlasting friend.

TOUCH NOT THE CUP. P. M.

THE WILD, DARK STORM. 14s.

241 *Not grudgingly but of a ready mind.* L. M.

TEACH us, O Lord, to keep in view
  Thy pattern, and Thy steps pursue;
Let alms bestowed, let kindness done,
Be witnessed by each rolling sun;

2 That man may last, but never lives,
Who much receives, but nothing gives;
Whom none can love, whom none can
  Creation's blot, creation's blank! [thank,

3 But he who marks, from day to day,
In generous acts his radiant way,
Treads the same path his Savior trod,
The path to glory and to God.

242 *Touch not the cup.* P. M.

TOUCH not the cup; it is death to thy
  soul;
Touch not the cup, touch not the cup!
Many I know who have quaffed from the
  bowl;
Touch not the cup, touch it not.
Then of that death-dealing bowl, oh be-
  ware! [there,
Little they thought that the demon was
Blindly they drank and were caught in
  the snare,
Touch not the cup, touch it not.

2 Touch not the cup when the wine glis-
  tens bright;
Touch not the cup, touch not the cup.
Though like the ruby it shines in the light,
Touch not the cup, touch it not.
The fangs of the serpent are hid in the
  bowl;
Deeply the poison will enter thy soul;
Soon it will plunge thee beyond thy con-
Touch not the cup, touch it not. [trol.

3 Touch not the cup; drink not a drop:
Touch not the cup, touch not the cup:
All that thou lovest entreat thee to stop;
Touch not the cup, touch it not.
Stop for the home, that to thee is so near:
Stop for thy friends, that to thee are so
  dear;
Stop for thy country, the God that you fear;
Touch not the cup, touch it not.

243 *The wild, dark storm.* 11s.

OH, tie the casement, father, dear,
  The snow falls on my bed;
Oh, tie the casement, father, dear,
It rattles on my head.
Do n't sleep so sound, my father,
I am very dumb and chill,
And I can not bear to listen,
With the room so dark and still.

2 Oh, tie the casement, father, for
The snow is falling fast,
And demons ride in fury, on
The piercing, chilling blast.

The drunkard heard no plaintive voice,
  For death enwrapt his form,
And the orphan moaned, "I 'm all alone,
  In the wild, dark storm."

3 The blast roared down the chimney
  And shook the fragile wall, [wide,
And the casement rattled louder
  At the shrill and angry call:
The child in agony uprose,
  And swayed her wasted form,
As she whispered, "I 'm all alone,
  In the wild, dark storm."

4 The light shone in upon her there,
  Her heart beat quick with fear;
She could see no form around her,
  Nor voice, nor footfall hear.
But a whisper came unto her,
  Soft as zephyr-tones might be,
And its melody breathed fairy-like,
  "My child, come home to me."

5 "There 's snow upon my bed, mamma,
  My heart is freezing fast,
And shadows from the corner dark,
  Are flitting swiftly past.
I 'll come to you, dear mother,
  If you 'll keep me very warm,
For oh! I 'm cold, and all alone,
  In the wild, dark storm."

6 The little snow-drifts softly blew,
  And silently they slept,
Upon the rugged coverlet;
  The child no longer wept.
She thought there must be warmth in
  And thrust within her hand, [them,
And drew it forth encircled,
  With a pale and icy band.

7 Death, with his icy fingers, came,
  And feeling round her heart,
Gave warning to the drunkard's child,
  From earth she must depart,
Then shrieking wild and fearfully,
  She shook the drunken form,
"I 'm dying, father, dying,
  In the wild, dark storm."

8 Poor child, her head sank backward,
  Her eyes grew dark and dim,
Her voice grew stronger in despair,
  But could not waken him;
With red and frozen fingers joined,
  She breathed in accents low,
"Where mother sleeps, where mother lies,
  'T is there I want to go."

9 The dawn came in upon her there,
  Stiff, motionless, and cold,
And the snow laid all around her head,
  And dimmed her locks of gold.
And she, beside her father, drew
  Her last, sad quivering breath;
And sire and child slept silently,
  The last, long sleep of death.

244 *God save the poor.*

LORD, from thy glorious throne,
  Drunkards look down upon—
  God save the poor!
Teach them true liberty,
Make them from custom free,
Let their homes happy be;
  God save the poor!

2 The arms of wicked men
Do thou with might restrain—
  God save the poor!
Raise thou their lowliness,
Succor thou their distress,
Thou whom the meanest bless—
  God save the poor!

3 Give them staunch honesty,
Let their pride manly be—
  God save the poor!
Help them to hold the right,
Give them both truth and might,
Lord of all life and light—
  God save the poor!

4 O God our cause maintain,
Remove the drunkard's stain—
  God save the poor!
Now, oh teetotal band,
Press forward heart and hand,
God by our side will stand—
  God save the poor!

245 *Temperance reformation.* 8s & 7s.

HAIL! the temperance reformation,
  Swiftly see it stride along!
Hail! redeemer of the nation,
  Worthy of our noblest song!
  ‖: Friends of Temperance,
  Let it echo loud and long.

2 Now the foe will quickly cower—
  From the cause of Temperance shrink:
See it, by its matchless power,
  Snatch the wretch from ruin's brink;
    Break his fetters,
    Tear asunder every link.

3 It is tens of thousands saving
  From a drunkard's grave and hell;
And our flag is proudly waving,
  Where Intemp'rance used to dwell:
    Man or Angel
    Never can its value tell.

4 Though we triumph, gracious heaven,
  Still we much assistance need;
Let thy helping hand be given,
  More the glorious work to speed:
    For the drunkard,
    For the sufferer, Lord, we plead.

246 *Meet me in heaven.* 14s.

A CHILD lay on her little couch, her
  slight form racked with pain,
She tried to smile and pleasant be, but
  tried and tried in vain;
"Mother, my lips are hot," she said,
  "give me the icy drink,
And come and sit beside me, ere to slumber's chains I sink.

2 "And try to keep me 'wake, for now
  my strength is almost gone,
I am so worn and restless, when my burning fever's on.
And lay your gentle hand upon my hot
  and throbbing brow;
Ah! that is sweet, mother!—and I am
  better—better now.

3 "You are so good and beautiful!—ah!
  mother, I half long
To linger in this happy world, although
  I know it's wrong;
You say I must not murmur, and you say
  that it is best,
Ah! mother, will you miss me, when I
  am gone unto my rest?

4 "You must not let them breathe my
  name, I know 't will make you weep
To think how coldly in the grave, all by
  myself, I sleep;
You'll miss me, too, around the hearth,
  at close of winter's ev'n,
You must not, must not weep, but think
  I'm waiting you in heaven.

5 "And when they close my eyes, and
  fold my hands so white and still,
You'll come and sit beside me then?—
  ah! yes, I know you will,
And place within my fingers, too, the
  roses sweet and pale,
They're growing wild beside the rill, far
  down this happy vale.

6 "'T is turning darker, darker now—
  you say 't is morn without,
Just midday, and the sun is bright, the
  wild birds all about;
I can not see a ray of light—how quick
  and short my breath,
Oh, tell me, mother, tell me! do you
  think that this is death?

7 "I can not bear these shadows o'er my
  closing eyelids cast,
I want to have my sight, and see your
  sweet face to the last;
I tried to hush my murmuring, oh, how
  long and hard I've striven,
And now I'm free! oh, mother, dear,
  meet me, meet me in heaven."

247 Blossom of being; seen and gone. P. M.

NO bitter tears for thee be shed,
　Blossom of being! seen and gone!
With flowers alone we strew thy bed,
　Oh blest departed one!
Whose all of life, a rosy ray,
Blushed into dawn, and passed away.

2 Yes! thou art fled, ere guilt had power
　To stain thy cherub-soul and form,
Closed in the soft ephemeral flower
　That never felt a storm!
The sunbeam's smile, the zephyr's breath,
All that it knew from birth to death.

3 Oh! hadst thou still on earth remained,
　Vision of beauty! fair as brief!
How soon thy brightness had been stained
　With passion or with grief!
Now, not a sullying breath can rise,
To dim thy glory in the skies.

248 Love. S. M.

LOVE is the strongest tie
　That can our hearts unite,
Love makes our service liberty,
　Our every burden light.

2 We run in God's commands
　When love directs the way;
With willing hearts and active hands,
　Our Maker's will obey.

3 Love softens all our toil,
　And makes our bondage blest;
The gloomy desert wears a smile
　When love inspires the breast.

4 Let love forever grow,
　And banish wrath and strife;
So shall we witness here below,
　The joys of social life.

249 I say unto all—watch. S. M.

YE servants of the Lord,
　Each in his office wait;
With joy obey his heavenly word,
　And watch before his gate.

2 Let all your lamps be bright,
　And trim the golden flame;
Gird up your loins, as in his sight,
　For awful is his name.

3 Watch!—'t is your Lord's command,
　And while we speak, he's near;
Mark every signal of his hand,
　And ready all appear.

4 Oh, happy servant he,
　In such a posture found!
He shall his Lord with rapture see,
　And be with honor crowned.

250 The rest of immortality. S. M.

OH, where shall rest be found?
　Rest to the weary soul!
'T were vain the ocean depths to sound,
　Or pierce to either pole.

2 This world can never give
　The bliss for which we sigh;
'T is not the whole of life to live,
　Nor all of death to die.

3 Beyond this vale of tears,
　There is a life above;
Unnumbered by the flight of years,
　And all that life is love.

4 There is a death, whose pang
　Outlasts the fleeting breath;
Oh, what eternal horrors hang
　Around the second death.

5 O God of truth and grace,
　Teach us that death to shun,
Lest we be driven from thy face,
　And evermore undone.

6 Here would we end our quest—
　Alone are found in thee
The life of perfect love, the rest
　Of immortality.

251 Still will we trust. P. M.

STILL will we trust, though earth seem
　dark and dreary,
And the heart faint beneath his chastening rod,
Though rough and steep our pathway,
　worn and weary,
　Still will we trust in God!

2 Our eyes see dimly till by faith anointed,
　And our blind choosing brings us grief
　　and pain;
Through him alone who hath our way
　appointed,
　We find our peace again.

3 Choose for us, God! nor let our weak
　preferring
Cheat our poor souls of good thou hast
　designed:
Choose for us, God! thy wisdom is unerr-
　And we are fools and blind. [ing,

4 So from our sky the night shall furl
　her shadows,
And day pour gladness through his
　golden gates:
Our rough path leads to flower-enameled
　meadows
　Where joy our coming waits.

5 Let us press on in patient self-denial,
　Accept the hardship, shrinking not
　　from loss—
Our guerdon lies beyond the hour of trial;
　Our crown, beyond the cross.

252 *Happy home.* 8s & 7s.

IN that world of ancient story,
  Where no storms can ever come,
Where the Savior dwells in glory,
  There remains for us a home.

Chorus.

Happy home, happy home,
  Jesus bids his foll'wers come,
To that land of bliss and glory,
  Our happy, happy home.

2 There within the heavenly mansions,
  Where life's river flows so clear,
We shall see our blessed Savior,
  If we love and serve him here.

3 There with holy angels dwelling,
  Where the ransomed wander free,
Jesus' praises ever telling,
  Sing we through eternity.

4 There amid the shining numbers,
  All our toils and labors o'er,
Where the Guardian never slumbers,
  We shall dwell for evermore.

253 *I am Alpha and Omega.* 6s & 4s, or 10s.
Rev. i. 8.

CLING to the mighty One, Ps. lxxxix.
  Cling in thy grief; Heb. xii.
Cling to the Holy One, Heb. vii. 26.
  He gives relief: Ps. cxvi. 8.
Cling to the Gracious One, Ps. cxvi. 5.
  Cling in thy pain, Ps. lv. 4.
Cling to the Faithful One, 1 Thess. v. 24.
  He will sustain. Ps. xxviii. 8.

2 Cling to the Living One, Heb. vii. 25.
  Cling in thy woe, Ps. lxxxvi. 7.
Cling to the Loving One, 1 John iv. 16.
  Through all below: Rom. viii. 38-39.
Cling to the Pardoning One, Is. lv. 7.
  He speaketh peace: John xiv. 27.
Cling to the Healing One, Exod. xv. 26.
  Anguish shall cease. Ps. cxvi. 8.

3 Cling to the Bleeding One, 1 John i. 7.
  Cling to his side; John xx. 27.
Cling to the Risen One, Rom. vi. 9.
  In him abide: John xv. 4.
Cling to the Coming One, Rev. xxii. 20.
  Hope shall arise; Titus ii. 13.
Cling to the Reigning One, Eph. i. 20-23.
  Joy lights thine eyes. Ps. xvi. 11.

254 *The rock that is higher than I.* 11s.

IN seasons of grief to my God I'll repair,
  When my heart is o'erwhelm'd with sorrow and care;
From the end of the earth unto thee will I cry,
Lead me to the Rock that is higher than I.
  Higher than I, higher than I.
Lead me to the Rock that is higher than I.

2 When Satan, the tempter, comes in like a flood
To drive my poor soul from the fountain of good,
I'll pray to the Lord who for sinners did die—
Lead me to the Rock that is higher than I.

3 And when I have finished my pilgrimage here,
Complete in Christ's righteousness I shall appear,
In the swellings of Jordan, all dangers defy,
And look to the Rock that is higher than I.

4 And when the last trumpet shall sound through the skies,
And the dead from the dust of the earth shall arise,
Transported I'll join with the ransom'd on high, [than I.
To praise the great Rock that is higher
  Higher than I, higher than I,
To praise the great Rock that is higher than I.

255 *Abide with us.* 8s & 7s.

TARRY with me, oh my Savior,
  For the day is passing by;
See, the shades of evening gather,
  And the night is drawing nigh.

2 Many friends were gathered round me
  In the bright days of the past;
But the grave has closed above them,
  And I linger here at last.

3 Deeper, deeper grows the shadows;
  Paler now the glowing west;
Swift the night of death advances;
  Shall it be night of rest?

4 Tarry with me, oh my Savior!
  Lay my head upon thy breast
Till the morning; then awake me—
  Morning of eternal rest!

256 *Night.* 8s & 7s.

HEAR my prayer, O Heavenly Father;
  Ere I lay me down to sleep;
Bid thy angels pure and holy
  Round my bed their vigil keep.

2 Great my sins are, but thy mercy
  Far outweighs them every one;
Down before thy cross I cast them,
  Trusting in thy help alone.

3 Keep me through this night of peril,
  Underneath its boundless shade;
Take me to thy rest, I pray thee,
  When my pilgrimage is made!

4 Pardon all my past transgressions;
  Give me strength for days to come;
Guide and guard me with thy blessing,
  Till thine angels bid me home!

257 Flee as a bird. P. M.

FLEE as a bird to your mountain,
  Thou who art weary of sin;
Go to the clear flowing fountain,
  Where you may wash and be clean;
Fly, th' avenger is near thee;
Call, and the Savior will hear thee,
He, on his bosom, will bear thee,
  Oh thou who art weary of sin.

2 He will protect thee forever,
  Wipe every falling tear—
He will forsake thee, oh, never,
  Sheltered so tenderly there:
Haste, then, the hours are flying,
Spend not the moments in sighing,
Cease from your sorrow and crying,
  The Savior will wipe ev'ry tear.

258 I'm going home. 6s & 4s.

I AM a stranger here;
  No home, no rest I see;
Not all earth counts most dear
  Can win a sigh from me.
    I'm going home.

2 Jesus, thy home is mine,
  And I thy Father's child,
With hopes and joys divine,
  The world's a dreary wild.
    I'm going home.

3 Home! oh! how soft and sweet,
  It thrills upon the heart!
Home! where the brethren meet
  And never, never part.
    I'm going home.

4 Home! where the Bridegroom takes
  The purchase of his love:
Home! where the Father waits
  To welcome saints above.
    I'm going home.

5 Yes! when the world looks cold,
  Which did my Lord revile,
A lamb within the fold,
  I can look up and smile.
    I'm going home.

6 When earth's delusive charms
  Would snare my pilgrim feet,
I fly to Jesus' arms,
  And yet again repeat,
    I'm going home.

7 When breaks each mortal tie
  That holds me from the goal,
This, this can satisfy
  The cravings of my soul—
    I'm going home.

8 Ah! gently, gently lead,
  Along the painful way,
Bid every word and deed,
  And every look to say,
    I'm going home.

259 The heavenly mansion. 8s & 6s.

MY heavenly home is bright and fair,
  We'll be gathered home;
No death nor sighing visit there,
  We'll be gathered home:
    Chorus.
  We'll wait till Jesus comes,
  We'll wait till Jesus comes,
  We'll wait till Jesus comes,
  And we'll be gathered home.

2 Its glittering towers the sun outshine,
  We'll be gathered home;
That heavenly mansion shall be mine,
  We'll be gathered home.

3 My Father's house is built on high,
  We'll be gathered home;
Above the arched and starry sky,
  We'll be gathered home.

4 When from this earthly prison free,
  We'll be gathered home;
That heavenly mansion mine shall be,
  We'll be gathered home.

5 While here, a stranger far from home,
  We'll be gathered home;
Affliction's waves may round me foam,
  We'll be gathered home.

6 Let others seek a home below,
  We'll be gathered home;
Which flames devour or waves o'erthrow,
  We'll be gathered home.

7 Be mine the happier lot to own,
  We'll be gathered home;
A heavenly mansion near the throne,
  We'll be gathered home.

8 Then, fail this earth, let stars decline,
  We'll be gathered home;
And sun and moon refuse to shine,
  We'll be gathered home.

9 All nature sink and cease to be,
  We'll be gathered home;
That heavenly mansion stands for me,
  We'll be gathered home.

260 Thanksgiving.

SWELL the anthem, raise the song,
  Praises to our God belong;
Saints and angels join to sing
Praises to the Heavenly King.

2 Blessings from his liberal hand
Flow around this happy land:
Kept by him, no foes annoy;
Peace and freedom we enjoy.

3 Here, beneath a virtuous sway,
May we cheerfully obey—
Never feel oppression's rod—
Ever own and worship God.

261 *There yet is room.* 6s & 8s.

YOU dying sons of men,
Immerged in sin and woe,
The gospel's voice attend,
Which Jesus sends to you.
You perishing and guilty, come,
In Jesus' arms there is yet room.

2 No longer now delay,
Nor vain excuses frame,
He bids you come to-day,
Though poor, and blind, and lame:
All things are ready, sinner, come,
For every trembling soul there's room.

3 Believe the heavenly word,
His messengers proclaim:
He is a gracious Lord,
And faithful is his name:
Repenting souls, return and come;
Cast off despair, there yet is room.

4 Compelled by bleeding love,
You wandering souls, draw near;
Christ calls you from above,
His charming accents hear!
Let whosoever will, now come:
In mercy's breast there still is room.

262 *Declare among the people his doings.* H. M.

COME, ev'ry pious heart
That loves the Savior's name,
Your noblest pow'rs exert
To celebrate his fame:
Tell all above, and all below,
The debt of love to him you owe.

2 Such was his zeal for God,
And such his love for you,
He nobly undertook
What angels could not do:
His ev'ry deed of love and grace
All words exceed, all thoughts surpass.

3 He left his starry crown,
And laid his robes aside;
On wings of love came down,
And wept, and bled, and died:
What he endur'd, oh who can tell,
To save our souls from death and hell

4 From the dark grave he rose,
The mansion of the dead;
And thence his mighty foes
In glorious triumph led:
Up through the sky the Conq'ror rode,
And reigns on high the Son of God.

5 From thence he'll quickly come,
His chariot will not stay,
And bear our spirits home
To realms of endless day:
There shall we see his lovely face,
And ever be in his embrace.

263 *Fountain of life.* 9s & 8s.

ALL you that are weary and sad—come!
And you that are cheerful and glad—come!
In robes of humility clad—come!
The Savior invites you to-day.
Let youth in its freshness and bloom—come!
Let man in the pride of his noon—come!
Let age on the verge of the tomb—come!
Let none in his pride stay away.

2 Let the halt, and the maimed, and the blind—come!
Let all who are freely inclined—come!
With an humble and peaceable mind—come!
Away from the waters of strife.
The Spirit and Bride freely say—come!
And let him that heareth it, say—come!
And let him that thirsteth to-day—come!
And drink of the fountain of life.

264 *Christ's resurrection.* 7s, D.

MARY to the Savior's tomb,
Hasted at the early dawn,
Spice she brought and rich perfume,
But the Lord she loved had gone;
For awhile she lingering stood,
Filled with sorrow and surprise;
Trembling, while a crystal flood
Issued from her weeping eyes.

2 But her sorrows quickly fled,
When she heard his welcome voice;
Christ had risen from the dead—
Now he bids her heart rejoice.
What a change his word can make,
Turning darkness into day;
Ye who weep for Jesus' sake,
He will wipe your tears away.

3 He who came to comfort her,
When she thought her all was lost,
Will for your relief appear,
Though you now are tempest tost.
On his arm your burden cast;
On his love your thoughts employ;
Weeping for awhile may last,
But the morning brings the joy.

265 *Spread the tidings.* 7s.

WEEPING sinners, dry your tears;
Jesus on the throne appears;
Mercy comes with balmy wing,
Bids you his salvation sing.

2 Peace he brings you by his death,
Peace he speaks with ev'ry breath;
Can you slight such heav'nly charms?
Flee, oh flee to Jesus' arms.

266 *Suffer little children to come unto me.* P. M.

I THINK when I read that sweet story of old,
When Jesus was here among men,
How he called little children as lambs to his fold,
I should like to have been with them then.
I wish that his hands had been placed on my head, [me,
That his arm had been thrown around
And that I might have seen his kind look when he said,
" Let the little ones come unto me."

2 Yet still to his footstool in prayer I may
And ask for a share in his love; [go,
And if I thus earnestly seek him below,
I shall see him and hear him above,
In that beautiful place he has gone to prepare
For all who are washed and forgiven;
And many dear children are gathering there,
" For of such is the kingdom of heaven."

3 But thousands and thousands who wander and fall,
Never heard of that heavenly home;
I should like them to know there is room for them all,
And that Jesus has bid them to come;
I long for the joy of that glorious time,
The sweetest, and brightest, and best,
When the dear little children of every clime
Shall crowd to his arms and be blessed.

267 *Precious promises.* 11s.

HOW firm a foundation, you saints of the Lord,
Is laid for your faith in his excellent word!
What more can he say than to you he has said,
You who unto Jesus for refuge have fled?

2 In ev'ry condition, in sickness, in health,
In poverty's vale, or abounding in wealth;
At home and abroad, on the land, on the sea,
As your days may demand, so your succor shall be.

3 Fear not—I am with you: oh be not dismay'd!
I, I am your God, and will still give you aid;
I'll strengthen you, help you, and cause you to stand,
Upheld by my righteous, omnipotent hand.

4 When through the deep waters I cause you to go,
The rivers of sorrow shall not you o'erflow;
For I will be with you your troubles to bless,
And sanctify to you your deepest distress.

5 When through fiery trials your pathway shall lie,
My grace, all-sufficient, shall be your supply:
The flame shall not hurt you: I only design
Your dross to consume, and your gold to refine.

268 *Remember thy Creator, etc.* C. M.

YE joyous ones, upon whose brow
The light of youth is shed,
O'er whose glad path life's early flowers
In glowing beauty spread:
Forget not him whose love hath poured
Around that golden light,
And tinged those opening buds of hope
With hues so softly bright.

2 Thou tempted one, just entering
Upon enchanted ground,
Ten thousand snares are spread for thee,
Ten thousand foes surround:
A dark and a deceitful band,
Upon thy pathway lower;
Trust not thine own unaided strength
To save thee from their power.

3 Thou whose yet bright and joyous eye
May soon be dimmed with tears,
To whom the hours of bitterness
Must come in coming years;
Teach early thy confiding eye
To pierce the cloudy screen,
To look above the storms, where all
Is holy and serene.

269 *A child's prayer.* C. M.

DEAR Jesus, ever at my side,
How loving must thou be,
To leave thy home in heaven to guard
A little child like me.

2 Thy beautiful and shining face
I see not, though so near;
The sweetness of thy soft, low voice
I am too deaf to hear.

3 But I have felt thee in my thoughts,
Fighting with sin for me;
And when my heart loves God, I know
The sweetness is from thee.

4 And when, dear Savior, I kneel down,
Morning and night, to prayer,
Something there is within my heart
Which tells me thou art there.

270   *Life is onward flowing.*   7s & 6s.

AS flows the rapid river,
   With channel broad and free,
Its waters rippling ever,
   And hastening to the sea.
So life is onward flowing,
   And days of offered peace,
And man is swiftly going,
   Where calls of mercy cease.

2 As moons are ever waning,
   As hastes the sun away,
As stormy winds, complaining,
   Bring on the wintry day;
So fast the night comes o'er us—
   The darkness of the grave—
And death is just before us:
   God takes the life he gave.

271   *Gladly we hear thy gentle voice.*   P. M.

SAVIOR! thy gentle voice
   Gladly we hear;
Author of all our joys
   Be ever near;
Our souls would cling to thee,
Let us thy fullness see,
   Our life to cheer.

2 Fountain of life divine!
   Thee we adore;
We would be wholly thine
   For evermore;
Freely forgive our sin,
Grant heavenly peace within,
   Thy light restore.

3 Though to our faith unseen,
   While darkness reigns,
On thee alone we lean
   While life remains;
By thy free grace restored,
Our souls shall bless the Lord
   In joyful strains!

272   *Sunday-school celebration.*   7s & 6s.

TO thee, O blessed Savior,
   Our grateful songs we raise;
Oh, tune our hearts and voices
   Thy holy name to praise;
'T is by thy sovereign mercy
   We 're here allowed to meet;
To join with friends and teachers,
   Thy blessing to entreat.

2 Lord, guide and bless our teachers,
   Who labor for our good,
And may the holy Scriptures
   By us be understood;
Oh, may our hearts be given
   To thee, our glorious King;
That we may meet in heaven,
   Thy praises there to sing.

3 And may the precious gospel
   Be published all abroad,
Till the benighted heathen
   Shall know and serve the Lord;
Till o'er the wide creation
   The rays of truth shall shine,
And nations now in darkness
   Arise to light divine.

273   *Grieve not the Spirit.*   8s & 6s.

OH Savior, lend a listening ear,
   And answer my request!
Forgive, and wipe the falling tear,
Now with thy love my spirit cheer,
   And set my heart at rest.

2 I mourn the hidings of thy face;
   The absence of that smile,
Which led me to a throne of grace,
And gave my soul a resting-place
   From earthly care and toil.

3 'T is sin that separates from thee
   This poor benighted soul;
My folly and my guilt I see,
And now upon the bended knee,
   I yield to thy control.

4 Up to the place of thine abode
   I lift my waiting eye;
To thee, O holy Lamb of God!
Whose blood for me so freely flowed,
   I raise my ardent cry.

274   *The beautiful of lands.*   7s & 6s, D.

THERE is a land immortal,
   The beautiful of lands;
Beside its ancient portal
   A silent sentry stands;
He only can undo it,
   And open wide the door;
And mortals who pass through it,
   Are mortals nevermore.

2 Though dark and drear the passage
   That leadeth to the gate,
Yet grace comes with the message,
   To souls that watch and wait;
And at the time appointed
   A messenger comes down,
And leads the Lord's anointed
   From cross to glory's crown.

3 Their sighs are lost in singing,
   They 're blessed in their tears;
Their journey heavenward winging,
   They leave on earth their fears;
Death like an angel seemeth;
   "We welcome thee," they cry;
Their face with glory beameth—
   'T is life for them to die!

275   *Praise to God.*   C. M.

O GOD, my heart is fully bent
  To magnify thy name;
My tongue, with cheerful songs of praise,
  Shall celebrate thy fame.
Be thou, O God, exalted high
  Above the starry frame;
And let the world, with one consent,
  Confess thy glorious name.

276   *The year of jubilee.*   H. M.

FAIR shines the morning star,
  The silver trumpets sound,
Their notes re-echoing far,
  While dawns the day around:
Joy to the slave; the slave is free;
It is the year of jubilee.

2 Prisoners of hope, in gloom
  And silence left to die,
With Christ's unfolding tomb,
  Your portals open fly;
Rise with your Lord; he sets you free;
It is the year of jubilee.

3 Ye, who yourselves have sold
  For debts to justice due,
Ransomed, but not with gold,
  He gave himself for you!
The blood of Christ hath made you free;
It is the year of jubilee.

4 Captives of sin and shame,
  O'er earth and ocean, hear
An angel's voice proclaim
  The Lord's accepted year;
Let Jacob rise, be Israel free;
It is the year of jubilee.

277   *Omnipotent Creator.*   C. M.

ETERNAL Wisdom! thee we praise!
  Thee the creation sings:
With thy loved name, rocks, hills, and
And heaven's high palace rings. [seas,

2 Infinite strength and equal skill
  Shine through thy works abroad,
Our souls with vast amazement fill,
  And speak the builder God.

3 Thy hand, how wide it spreads the sky,
  How glorious to behold!
Tinged with a blue of heavenly dye,
  And starred with sparkling gold.

4 There thou hast bade the globes of light
  Their endless circuits run:
There the pale planet rules the night,
  The day obeys the sun.

5 On the thin air, without a prop,
  Hang fruitful showers around:
At thy command they freely drop
  Their fatness on the ground.

6 There, like a trumpet, loud and strong,
  Thy thunder shakes our coast;
While the red lightnings wave along
  The banners of thy host.

7 Thy glories blaze all nature round,
  And strike the wondering sight,
Through skies, and seas, and solid ground,
  With terror and delight.

8 But the mild glories of thy grace
  Our softer passions move;
Pity divine in Jesus' face
  We see, adore, and love.

9 The Savior calls—let every ear
  Attend the heavenly sound;
Ye doubting souls, dismiss your fear,
  Hope smiles reviving round.

10 For every thirsty, longing heart,
  Here streams of bounty flow,
And life, and health, and bliss impart,
  To banish mortal woe.

278   *Weep not for me.*   8s & 4s.

WHEN the spark of life is waning,
  Weep not for me;
When the languid eye is streaming,
  Weep not for me;
When the feeble pulse is ceasing,
  Start not at its swift decreasing;
'T is the fettered soul's releasing;
  Weep not for me.

2 When the pangs of death assail me,
  Weep not for me;
Christ is mine, he can not fail me,
  Weep not for me;
Yes, though sin and doubt endeavor,
From his love my soul to sever,
Jesus is my strength forever;
  Weep not for me.

279   *They that sow in tears shall reap in joy.*   C. M.

THERE is an hour of hallow'd peace
  For those with care oppress'd,
When sighs and sorrowing tears shall
  And all be hush'd to rest. [cease,

2 'T is then the soul is freed from fears
  And doubts which here annoy;
Then they that oft had sown in tears
  Shall reap again in joy.

3 There is a home of sweet repose,
  Where storms assail no more;
The stream of endless pleasure flows
  On that celestial shore.

4 There purity with love appears,
  And bliss without alloy;
There they that oft had sown in tears
  Shall reap again in joy.

MISCELLANEOUS. 113

280 *Shout the tidings of salvation.* 8s & 7s.

SHOUT the tidings of salvation,
To the aged and the young;
Till the precious invitation
Waken every heart and tongue.
Chorus.
Send the sound
The earth around,
From the rising to the setting of the sun,
Till each gathering crowd
Shall proclaim aloud,
The glorious work is done.

2 Shout the tidings of salvation
O'er the prairies of the west;
Till each gathering congregation,
With the gospel sound is blest.

3 Shout the tidings of salvation,
Mingling with the ocean's roar;
Till the ships of every nation,
Bear the news from shore to shore.

4 Shout the tidings of salvation
O'er the islands of the sea;
Till, in humble adoration,
All to Christ shall bow the knee.

281 *The Lord God is a Sun.* 7s & 3.

JESUS, Sun of Righteousness,
Brightest beam of love divine,
With the early morning rays
Do thou on our darkness shine,
And dispel with purest light
All our night!

2 Like the sun's reviving ray,
May thy love, with tender glow,
All our coldness melt away,
Warm and cheer us forth to go,
Gladly serve thee and obey
All the day!

3 Thou our only Life and Guide!
Never leave us nor forsake:
In thy light may we abide
Till th' eternal morning break;
Moving on to Zion's hill
Homeward still!

282 *It is finished.* 8s, 7s & 4.

HARK! the voice of love and mercy
Sounds aloud from Calvary;
See! it rends the rocks asunder,
Shakes the earth, and vails the sky!
It is finish'd!
Hear the dying Savior cry.

2 It is finish'd! Oh what pleasure
Do these precious words afford:
Heavenly blessings without measure
Flow to us from Christ the Lord;
It is finish'd!
Saints, the dying words record.

3 Finish'd all the types and shadows
Of the ceremonial law!
Finish'd all that God had promis'd;
Death and hell no more shall awe;
It is finish'd!
Saints, from this your comfort draw.

4 Tune your harps anew, you seraphs,
Join to sing the pleasing theme;
All on earth and all in heaven,
Join to praise Immanuel's name:
Hallelujah!
Glory to the bleeding Lamb!

283 *Love of God, all love excelling.* 8s, 7s & 4.

LOVE of God, all love excelling!
How can I its wonders tell?
Now, my troubled spirit quelling,
Now, it breaks the powers of hell:
Oh what mercies
Start beneath its magic spell.

2 Love of God, all love embracing
In its wide extended arms;
All our doubts and fears displacing,
Saves our souls from death's alarms!
Oh what sweetness
Dwells within its blissful charms!

3 Love of God, all love possessing,
Filling all our souls with joy;
Pouring on each heart a blessing,
Which no time can e'er destroy.
Now may praises
All our hearts and tongues employ.

4 Love of God, all love extending,
Far o'er sea and ocean strands;
Thou art on the breezes sending
Joyful news to distant lands:
May thy triumphs
Bind the world within thy bands.

284 *Honor the Lord.* 8s, 7s & 6s.

WITH my substance I will honor
My Redeemer and my Lord;
Were ten thousand worlds my manor,
All were nothing to his word.
Hallelujah—
Now we offer to the Lord.

2 While the heralds of salvation,
His abounding grace proclaim;
Let his saints of every station,
Gladly join to spread his fame.
Hallelujah—
Gifts we offer to his name.

3 May his kingdom be promoted;
May the world the Savior know;
Be to him these gifts devoted,
For to him my all I owe.
Hallelujah—
Run ye heralds to and fro.

285 *Christ's amazing love.* C. M.

PLUNGED in a gulf of dark despair,
  We wretched sinners lay,
Without one cheering beam of hope,
  Or spark of glimmering day.

2 With pitying eyes the Prince of grace
  Beheld our helpless grief;
He saw, and—oh! amazing love—
  He ran to our relief.

3 Down from the shining seats above,
  With joyful haste he fled,
Entered the grave in mortal flesh,
  And dwelt among the dead.

4 Oh, for this love let rocks and hills
  Their lasting silence break;
And all harmonious human tongues
  The Savior's praises speak.

5 Angels! assist our mighty joys;
  Strike all your harps of gold:
But when you raise your highest notes,
  His love can ne'er be told.

286 *A fountain for sin.* C. M.

THERE is a fountain filled with blood
  Drawn from Immanuel's veins;
And sinners, plunged beneath that flood,
  Lose all their guilty stains.

2 The dying thief rejoiced to see
  That fountain in his day;
And there have I, as vile as he,
  Washed all my sins away.

3 O Lamb of God, thy precious blood
  Shall never lose its power,
Till all the ransomed Church of God
  Be saved to sin no more.

4 E'er since, by faith, I saw the stream
  Thy flowing wounds supply,
Redeeming love has been my theme,
  And shall be till I die.

5 And when this lisping, stammering
  Lies silent in the grave, [tongue
Then, in a nobler, sweeter song,
  I'll sing thy power to save.

287 *Come, sound his praise abroad.* S. M.

COME, sound his praise abroad,
  And hymns of glory sing;
Jehovah is the sovereign God,
  The universal King.

2 He formed the deeps unknown;
  He gave the seas their bound;
The watery worlds are all his own,
  And all the solid ground.

3 Come, worship at his throne;
  Come, bow before the Lord;
We are his works, and not our own;
  He formed us by his word.

288 *Ever-green Mountains.* P. M.

THERE'S a land far away, 'mid the
  stars, we are told, [time,
Where they know not the sorrows of
Where the pure waters wander through
  valleys of gold,
And where life is a treasure sublime;
'T is the land of our God—'tis the home
  of the soul, [roll;
Where the ages of splendor eternally
Where the way-weary traveler reaches
  his goal,
On the ever-green mountains of life.

2 Here our gaze can not soar to that beau-
  tiful land,
But our visions have told of its bliss,
And our souls by the gale from its gar-
  dens are fanned,
When we faint in the deserts of this;
And we sometimes have longed for its
  holy repose,
When our spirits were torn with temp-
  tation and woes,
And we've drank from the tide of the
  river that flows
From the ever-green mountains of life.

3 Oh, the stars never tread the blue
  heavens by night,
But we think where the ransomed
  have trod,
And the day never smiles from his pal-
  ace of light,
But we feel the bright smiles of our God.
We are traveling homeward through
  changes and gloom,
To a kingdom where pleasures un-
  changingly bloom;
And our guide is the glory that shines
  through the tomb
From the ever-green mountains of life.

289 *Come, we that love the Lord.* S. M.

COME, we that love the Lord,
  And let our joys be known;
Join in a song with sweet accord,
  And thus surround the throne.

2 The sorrows of the mind
  Be banished from this place!
Religion never was designed
  To make our pleasures less.

3 Let those refuse to sing
  Who never knew our God;
But children of the heavenly King
  May speak their joys abroad.

4 The men of grace have found
  Glory begun below;
Celestial fruits on earthly ground
  From hope and faith may grow.

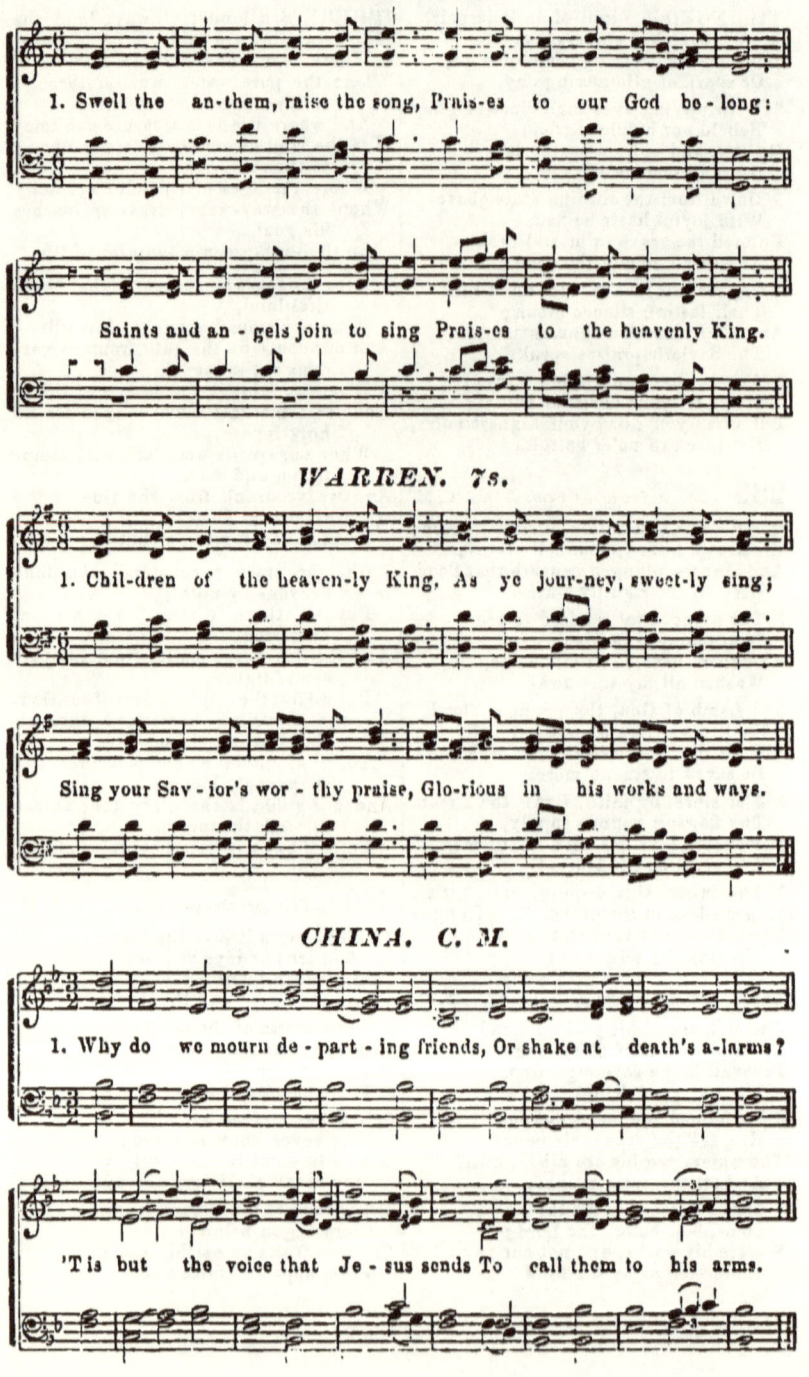

290 *Praise to God.* 7s.

SWELL the anthem, raise the song,
Praises to our God belong:
Saints and angels join to sing
Praises to the heavenly King.

2 Guarded by his watchful eye,
We still stand securely high.
Blessings from his liberal hand,
Flow around this happy land.

3 Here, beneath bright freedom's ray,
We enjoy a glorious sway—
Never feel oppression's rod—
Always have the smile of God.

4 Hark! the voice of nature sings
Praises to the King of kings;
Let us join the choral song,
And the grateful notes prolong.

291 *Children of the heavenly King.* 7s.

CHILDREN of the heavenly King
As ye journey sweetly sing;
Sing your Savior's worthy praise,
Glorious in his works and ways.

2 We are traveling home to God,
In the way the fathers trod;
They are happy now, and we
Soon their happiness shall see.

3 Shout, ye little flock, and blest;
You near Jesus' throne shall rest;
There your seats are now prepared,
There your kingdom and reward.

4 Fear not, brethren, joyful stand
On the borders of our land;
Jesus Christ, our Father's Son,
Bids you undismayed go on.

5 Oh, ye banished seed, be glad!
Christ our Advocate is made;
Us to save, our flesh assumes,
Brother to our souls becomes.

6 Lord! obediently we'll go,
Gladly leaving all below;
Only thou our leader be,
And we still will follow thee.

292 *Why do we mourn departing friends.* C. M.

WHY do we mourn departing friends,
Or shake at death's alarms?
'T is but the voice that Jesus sent
To call them to his arms.

2 Are we not tending upward, too,
As fast as time can move?
Nor would we wish the time more slow
To keep us from our Love.

3 Why should we tremble to convey
Their bodies to the tomb?
'T was there the flesh of Jesus lay,
Amid its silent gloom.

4 The graves of all the saints he blest,
And soften'd ev'ry bed;
Where should the dying members rest
But with their dying Head?

5 Thence he arose, ascending high,
And show'd our feet the way;
Up to the Lord our souls shall fly,
At the great rising day.

6 Then let the last loud trumpet sound,
And bid our kindred rise:
Awake, ye nations under ground;
Ye saints, ascend the skies.

293 *Earnest entreaty.* 7s.

HASTE, oh sinner! to be wise,
Stay not for the morrow's sun;
Wisdom warns thee from the skies
All the paths of death to shun.

2 Haste, and mercy now implore;
Stay not for the morrow's sun;
Thy probation may be o'er
Ere this evening's work is done.

3 Haste, oh sinner! now return;
Stay not for the morrow's sun,
Lest thy lamp should cease to burn
Ere salvation's work is done.

4 Haste, while yet thou canst be blest;
Stay not for the morrow's sun,
Death may thy poor soul arrest
Ere the morrow is begun.

294 *My voice shalt thou hear in the morning.* 7s.

NOW the shades of night are gone;
Now the morning light is come;
Lord, may I be thine to-day—
Drive the shades of sin away.

2 Fill my soul with heav'nly light,
Banish doubt and cleanse my sight;
In thy service, Lord, to-day,
Help me labor, help me pray.

3 Keep my haughty passions bound
Save me from my foes around;
Going out and coming in,
Keep me safe from ev'ry sin.

4 When my work of life is past,
Oh! receive me then at last!
When I reach the heavenly shore,
Night of sin will be no more.

295 *Psalm iii: 5.* 7s.

THOU that dost my life prolong
Kindly aid my morning song;
Thankful let my offerings rise
To the God that rules the skies.

2 Gently, with the dawning ray,
On my soul thy beams display;
Sweeter than the smiling morn,
Let thy cheering light return.

296   Forward.   7s.

WHEN we can not see our way,
  Let us trust and still obey;
He who bids us forward go,
Can not fail the way to show.

2 Though the sea be deep and wide,
Though a passage seem denied;
Fearless let us still proceed,
Since the Lord vouchsafes to lead.

3 Though it seems the gloom of night,
Though we see no ray of light:
Since the Lord himself is there,
'T is not meet that we should fear.

4 Night with him is never night,
Where he is, there all is light;
When he calls us, why delay?
They are happy who obey.

5 Be it ours, then, while we 're here,
Him to follow without fear:
Where he calls us, there to go,
What he bids us, that to do.

297   At the hour of prayer.   8s & 6s.

BLEST is the hour when cares depart,
  And earthly scenes are far—
When tears of woe forget to start,
And gently dawns upon the heart
Devotion's holy star.

2 Blest is the place where angels bend
To hear our worship rise,
Where kindred hearts their musings blend,
And all the soul's affections tend
Beyond the vailing skies.

3 Blest are the hallowed vows that bind
Man to his work of love—
Bind him to cheer the humble mind,
Console the weeping, lead the blind,
And guide to joys above.

4 Sweet shall the song of glory swell,
Savior divine, to thee,
When they whose work is finished well
In thy own courts of rest shall dwell,
Blest through eternity.

298   Time speeds away.   L. M.

TIME speeds away, away, away,
  Another hour, another day,
Another month, another year,
Drop from our lives like leaflets sere:
Drop like the life-blood from our hearts,
The rose-bloom from our cheek departs,
The tresses from our temples fall,
The eye grows dim and strange to all.

2 Time speeds away, away, away,
Like torrent in a stormy day;
He undermines the stately tower,
Uproots the tree and snaps the flower,
And sweeps from our distracted breast,
The friends that loved, the friends that blessed,
And leaves us weeping on the shore,
To which they can return no more.

3 Time speeds away, away, away,
No eagle through the sky of day,
No wind along the hills can flee,
So swiftly or so smooth as he;
Like fiery steed, from stage to stage,
He bears us on from youth to age,
Then plunges in the fearful sea
Of fathomless eternity.

299   Christ the Way, the Truth, and the Life.   L. M.

THOU art the Way; and he who sighs,
  Amid this starless waste of woe,
To find a pathway to the skies,
A light from heaven's eternal glow,
By thee must come, thou Gate of love,
Through which the saints undoubting
Till faith discovers, like the dove, [trod,
An ark, a resting-place in God.

2 Thou art the Truth, whose steady day
Shines on through earthly blight and
The pure, the everlasting ray,   [bloom;
The Lamp that shines e'en in the tomb;
The Light that out of darkness springs,
And guideth those that blindly go;
The Word whose precious radiance flings
Its luster upon all below.

3 Thou art the Life, the blessed Well
With living waters gushing o'er,
Which those that drink shall ever dwell
Where sin and thirst are known no more.
Thou art the mystic Pillar given,
Our Lamp by night, our Light by day;
Thou art the sacred bread from heaven;
Thou art the Life, the Truth, the Way.

300   That they go forward.   7s.

OFT in sorrow, oft in woe,
  Onward, Christian, onward go;
Fight the fight, maintain the strife,
Strengthened with the bread of life.

2 Onward, Christian, onward go;
Join the war, and face the foe;
Will you flee in danger's hour?
Know you not your Captain's power?

3 Let your drooping heart be glad;
March, in heavenly armor clad;
Fight, nor think the battle long;
Soon shall victory tune your song.

4 Onward, then, to battle move;
More than conqueror you shall prove;
Though opposed by many a foe,
Christian soldier, onward go.

301   The shining shore.   8s & 7s.

MY days are gliding swiftly by,
And I a pilgrim stranger,
Would not detain them as they fly—
Those hours of toil and danger.

Chorus.

For oh! we stand on Jordan's strand,
Our friends are passing over;
And just before, the shining shore
We may almost discover.

2 We 'll gird our loins, my brethren dear,
Our distant home discerning;
Our absent Lord has left us word,
Let every lamp be burning.

3 Should coming days be cold and dark,
We need not cease our singing;
That perfect rest naught can molest
Where golden harps are ringing.

4 Let sorrow's rudest tempest blow,
Each cord on earth to sever;
Our King says, "Come," and there's our
Forever, oh! forever.   [home,

302   All my springs are in thee.   P. M.

AS down in the sunless retreats of the ocean,
Sweet flowers are springing no mortal can see,
So deep in my heart, the still prayer of devotion,
Unheard by the world, rises silent to thee.
My God! silent to thee—
Pure, warm, silent to thee.

2 As still to the star of its worship, though clouded,
The needle points faithfully o'er the dim sea,
So, dark as I roam, through this wint'ry world shrouded,
The hope of my spirit turns trembling to thee.
My God! trembling to thee—
True, fond, trembling to thee

303   My peace I give unto you.   7s.

YE who in his courts are found
List'ning to the joyful sound,
Lost and hopeless as ye are,
Sons of sorrow, sin, and care,
Glorify the King of kings;
Take the peace the gospel brings.

2 Turn to Christ your longing eyes;
View his bleeding sacrifice:
See in him your sins forgiv'n,
Pardon, holiness, and heav'n;
Glorify the King of kings;
Take the peace the gospel brings.

304   He is our peace.   7s.

WEARY souls, that wander wide
From the central point of bliss,
Turn to Jesus crucified;
Fly to those dear wounds of his;
Sink into the purple flood,
Rise into the life of God.

2 Find in Christ the way of peace,
Peace unspeakable, unknown;
By his pain he gives you ease,
Life, by his expiring groan;
Rise, exalted by his fall;
Find in Christ your all in all.

3 Oh believe the record true,
God to you his Son hath given!
You may now be happy, too;
Find on earth the life of heaven;
Live the life of heaven above,
All the life of glorious love.

305   Come and welcome.   7s.

FROM the cross uplifted high,
Where the Savior deigns to die,
What melodious sounds we hear,
Bursting on the ravish'd ear!
"Love's redeeming work is done;
Come and welcome, sinner, come.

2 "Sprinkled now with blood the throne,
Why beneath thy burdens groan?
On my pierced body laid,
Justice owns the ransom paid;
Bow the knee, embrace the Son;
Come and welcome, sinner, come.

3 "Spread for thee, the festal board,
See with richest dainties stor'd;
To thy Father's bosom press'd,
Yet again a child confess'd,
Never from his house to roam,
Come and welcome, sinner, come.

4 "Soon the days of life shall end;
Lo, I come, your Savior, Friend,
Safe your spirits to convey
To the realms of endless day,
Up to my eternal home;
Come and welcome, sinner, come.

306   A new creature.   8s & 7s.

SINCE first thy word awaked my heart
Like light new dawning o'er me,
Where'er I turn my eyes, thou art
All light and love before me.

2 Naught else I feel, or hear, or see,
All bonds of earth I sever;
Thee, O my Lord, and only thee,
I live for, now, and ever.

3 Like him whose fetters dropped away
When light shone o'er his prison,
My soul, now touch'd by mercy's ray,
Hath from its chains arisen.

11

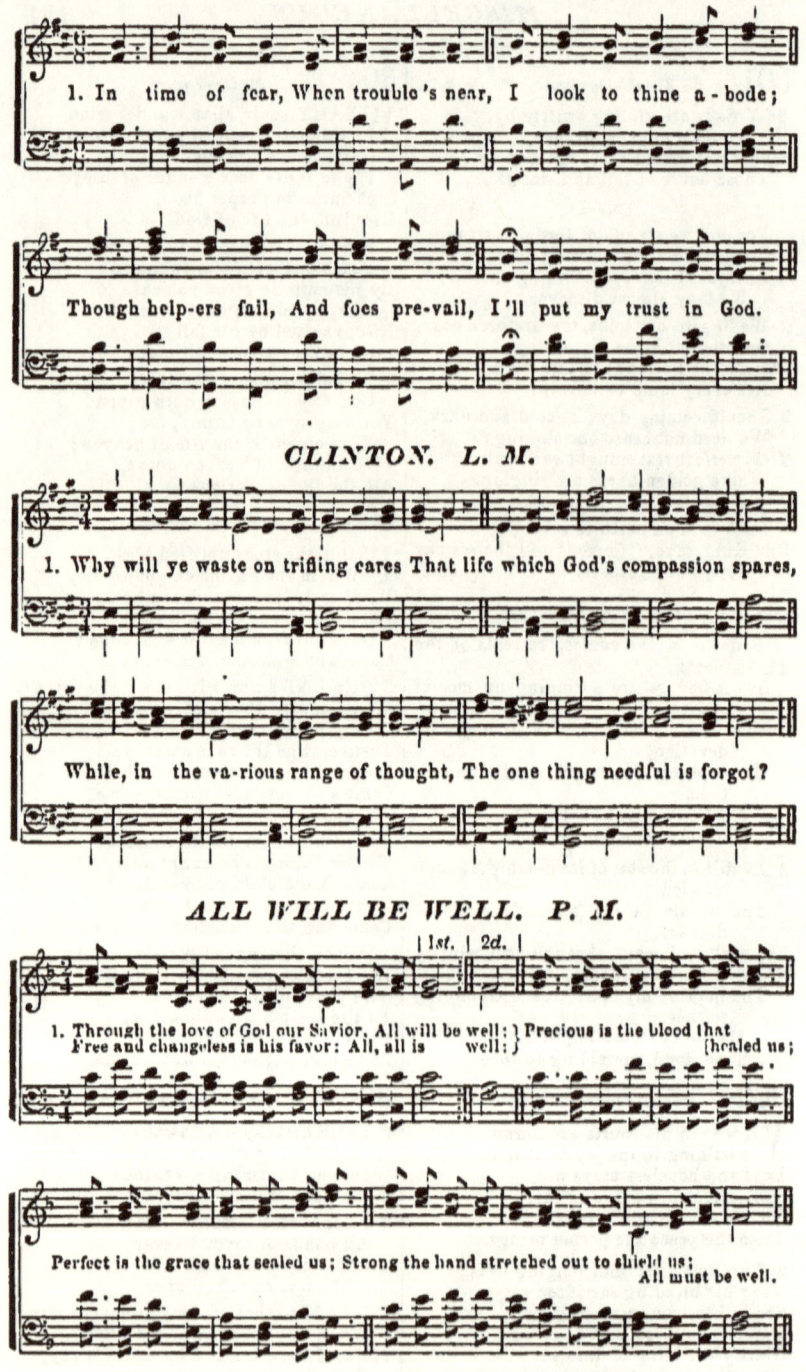

307 *Trust in God amid perils.* 4s & 6s.

IN time of fear,
When trouble's near,
I look to thine abode;
Though helpers fail,
And foes prevail,
I'll put my trust in God.

2 And what is life
But toil and strife?
What terror has the grave?
Thine arm of power,
In peril's hour,
The trembling soul will save.

3 In darkest skies,
Though some storms arise,
I will not be dismayed;
O God of light,
And boundless might,
My soul on thee is stayed!

308 *One thing needful.* L. M.

WHY will ye waste on trifling cares
That life which God's compassion spares;
While, in the various range of thought,
The one thing needful is forgot?

2 Shall God invite you from above?
Shall Jesus urge his dying love?
Shall troubled conscience give you pain?
And all these pleas unite in vain?

3 Not so your eyes will always view
Those objects which you now pursue:
Not so will heaven and hell appear,
When death's decisive hour is near.

4 Almighty God! thy grace impart;
Fix deep conviction on each heart;
Nor let us waste on trifling cares
That life which thy compassion spares.

309 *Make me to know mine end.* L. M.

O GOD, thy grace and blessing give
To us, who on thy name attend,
That we this mortal life may live
Regardful of our journey's end.

2 Teach us to know that Jesus died,
And rose again, our souls to save;
Teach us to take him as our Guide,
Our Help from childhood to the grave.

3 Then shall not death with terror come,
But welcome as a bidden guest,
The herald of a better home,
The messenger of peace and rest.

4 And, when the awful signs appear
Of judgment, and the throne above,
Our hearts still fixed, we shall not fear,
God is our trust, and God is Love.

310 *It is well.* P. M.

THROUGH the love of God our Savior,
All will be well:
Free and changeless is his favor;
All, all is well:
Precious is the blood that healed us;
Perfect is the grace that sealed us;
Strong the hand stretched out to shield us;
All must be well.

2 Though we pass through tribulation,
All will be well;
Ours is such a full salvation;
All, all is well:
Happy, still in God confiding,
Fruitful, if in Christ abiding,
Holy, through the Spirit's guiding,
All must be well.

3 We expect a bright to-morrow;
All will be well:
Faith can sing, through days of sorrow,
All, all is well:
On our Father's love relying,
Jesus every need supplying,
Or in living, or in dying,
All must be well.

311 *He called the name of that place Bethel.* L. M.

OH, bow thine ear, eternal One,
On thee our heart adoring calls;
To thee the followers of thy Son [walls.
Have raised, and now devote these

2 Here let thy holy days be kept;
And be this place to worship given,
Like that bright spot where Jacob slept,
The house of God, the gate of heaven.

3 Here may thine honor dwell; and here,
As incense, let thy children's prayer,
From contrite hearts and lips sincere,
Rise on the still and holy air.

4 Here be thy praise devoutly sung;
Here let thy truth beam forth to save,
As when, of old, thy Spirit hung,
On wings of light, o'er Jordan's wave.

5 And when the lips, that with thy name
Are vocal now, to dust shall turn,
On others may devotion's flame
Be kindled here, and purely burn!

312 *His mercy endureth forever.* L. M.

OH render thanks to God above,
The fountain of eternal love;
Whose mercy firm through ages past
Has stood, and shall forever last.

2 Who can his mighty deeds express,
Not only vast, but numberless!
What mortal eloquence can raise
His tribute of immortal praise!

313   *Jesus is mine.*   6s & 4s.

NOW I have found a friend,
  Jesus is mine;
His love shall never end,
  Jesus is mine.
Though earthly joys decrease;
Though human friendships cease,
Now I have lasting peace;
  Jesus is mine.

2 Though I grow poor and old,
  Jesus is mine;
He will my faith uphold,
  Jesus is mine;
He shall my wants supply,
His precious blood is nigh,
Naught can my hope destroy,
  Jesus is mine!

3 When earth shall pass away,
  Jesus is mine.
In the great Judgment-day,
  Jesus is mine.
Oh! what a glorious thing,
Then to behold my King,
On tuneful harp to sing,
  Jesus is mine.

4 Farewell mortality!
  Jesus is mine.
Welcome eternity!
  Jesus is mine.
He my Redemption is,
Wisdom and Righteousness,
Life, Light, and Holiness,
  Jesus is mine.

314   *Arise and depart, for this is not your rest.*   6s.

GO up, go up, my heart,
  Dwell with thy God above;
For here thou canst not rest,
  Nor here give out thy love.

2 Go up, go up, my heart,
  Be not a trifler here;
Ascend above these clouds,
  Dwell in a higher sphere.

3 Let not thy love flow out
  To things so soiled and dim;
Go up to heaven and God,
  Take up thy love to him.

4 Waste not thy precious stores
  On creature-love below;
To God that wealth belongs,
  On him that wealth bestow.

5 Go up, reluctant heart,
  Take up thy rest above;
Arise, earth-clinging thoughts;
  Ascend, my lingering love!

315   *A parting hymn.*

PEACEFULLY, tenderly,
  Here, as we part,
The farewell that lingers
  Be breathed from the heart;
No place more fitting,
  Oh house of the Lord—
Here be it spoken,
  That last prayerful word.

2 Thoughtfully, carefully,
  Solemn and slow!
Tears are bedewing
  The path that we go.
Perils before us
  We know not to-day—
Kindly and safely,
  O Lord, lead the way.

3 Upwardly, steadfastly
  Gaze on that brow:
Jesus, our Leader,
  Reigns conqueror now.
His steps let us follow,
  His sufferings dare,
Go up to glory,
  His blessedness share.

4 Patiently, cheerfully,
  Up, and depart
To labor and duty
  With gladness of heart;
The ransomed, with triumph,
  To Zion we'll bring,
Shouting salvation
  To Jesus, our King.

316   *My spirit longs for thee.*   6s.

MY spirit longs for thee
  Within my troubled breast,
Though I unworthy be
  Of so divine a Guest.

2 Of so divine a Guest
  Unworthy though I be,
Yet has my heart no rest
  Unless it come from thee.

3 Unless it come from thee,
  In vain I look around;
In all that I can see,
  No rest is to be found.

4 No rest is to be found
  But in thy blessed love:
Oh let my wish be crowned,
  And send it from above!

317 *The accepted time.* S. M.

NOW is th' accepted time,
  Now is the day of grace;
Now sinners come without delay,
  And seek the Savior's face.

2 Now is th' accepted time,
  The Savior calls to-day;
To-morrow it may be too late—
  Then why should you delay?

3 Now is th' accepted time,
  The gospel bids you come;
And every promise in his word,
  Declares there yet is room.

318 *Praise to God.* S. M.

OUR Father and our God,
  Who art in heaven above;
Thy name be praised, by all adored,
  In sweetest strains of love.

2 Thy kingdom spread as leaven,
  And every heart control;
Thy will be done on earth as heaven
  By every living soul.

3 Give us our daily bread—
  Forgive, as we forgive;
Oh may we not in sin be led,
  But humbly with thee live.

4 Free us from every ill—
  Our trembling souls defend,
For thine's the kingdom, power, and will,
  For evermore—Amen.

319 *Virtue and grace.* S. M.

GREAT God, at thy command,
  Seasons in order rise;
Thy power and love in concert reign,
  Through earth, and seas, and skies.

2 With grateful gifts we own,
  Thy providential hand;
While grass for kine, and herb, and corn
  For men, enrich the land.

3 But greater still the gift
  Of thy beloved Son:
By him forgiveness, peace, and joy,
  Through endless ages run.

320 *Praise to the Lord.* S. M.

OH bless the Lord, my soul—
  His grace to thee proclaim;
And all that is within me join
  To bless his holy name.

2 He will not always chide;
  He will with patience wait;
His wrath is ever slow to rise,
  And ready to abate.

3 He pardons all thy sins,
  Prolongs thy feeble breath;
He healeth thy infirmities,
  And ransoms thee from death.

321 *Joyfully, onward I move.* Cs.

JOYFULLY, joyfully onward I move,
  Bound for the land of bright spirits
Angelic choristers sing as I come, [above;
  Joyfully, joyfully haste to thy home.

2 Soon, with my pilgrimage ended below,
  Home, to that land of delight will I go;
Pilgrim and stranger no more shall I
  Joyfully, joyfully resting at home. [roam,

3 Friends fondly cherished have passed
      on before,   [shore;
  Waiting they watch me approaching the
Singing to cheer me through death's chilling gloom,
  Joyfully, joyfully haste to thy home.

4 Sounds of sweet melody fall on my ear;
  Harps of the blessed, your voices I hear;
Rings with the harmony heaven's high dome,
  Joyfully, joyfully haste to thy home.

5 Death, with thy weapons of war lay me
      low;   [blow!
  Strike, king of terrors, I fear not the
Jesus hath broken the bars of the tomb,
  Joyfully, joyfully will I go home.

6 Bright will the morn of eternity dawn,
  Death shall be banished, his scepter be gone;
Joyfully then shall I witness his doom,
  Joyfully, joyfully, safely at home.

322 *Make our calling and election sure.* S. M.

A CHARGE to keep I have,
  A God to glorify;
A never-dying soul to save,
  And fit it for the sky.

2 To serve the present age,
  My calling to fulfill;
Oh, may it all my powers engage,
  To do my Master's will.

3 Arm me with jealous care,
  As in thy sight to live;
And thy poor servant, Lord, prepare,
  A strict account to give!

4 Help me to watch and pray,
  And on thyself rely;
Assured if I my trust betray,
  I shall forever die.

323 *Baptism.* S. M.

HERE, Savior, we would come,
  In thine appointed way;
Obedient to thy high commands,
  Our solemn vows to pay.

2 Oh bless this sacred rite,
  To bring us near to thee;
And may we find that as our day,
  Our strength shall also be.

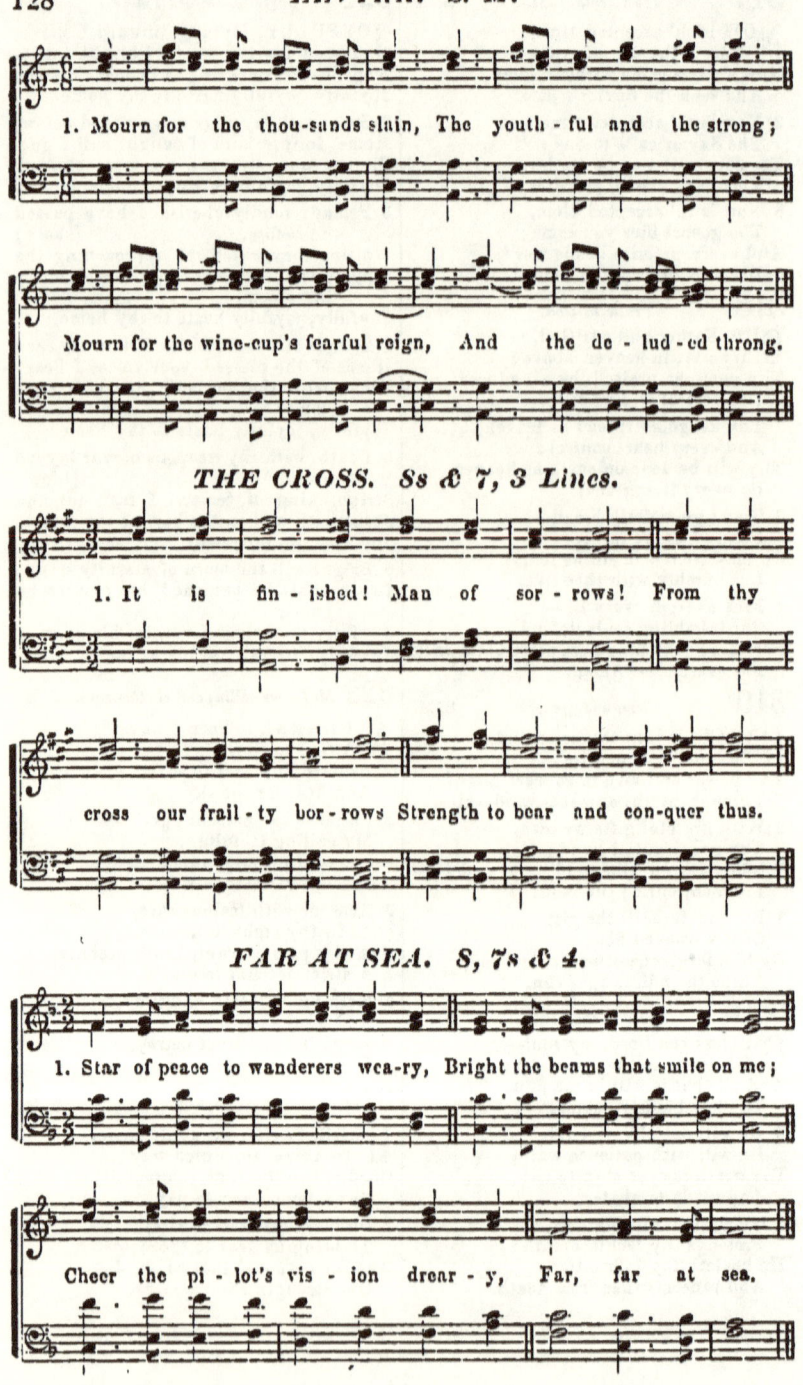

324 Temperance. S. M.

MOURN for the thousands slain,
The youthful and the strong;
Mourn for the wine-cup's fearful reign,
And the deluded throng.

2 Mourn for the tarnished gem—
For reason's light divine,
Quenched from the soul's bright diadem,
Where God had bid it shine.

3 Mourn for the ruined soul—
Eternal life and light
Lost by the fiery, maddening bowl,
And turned to hopeless night.

4 Mourn for the lost—but call,
Call to the strong, the free;
Rouse them to shun that dreadful fall,
And to the refuge flee.

5 Mourn for the lost—but pray,
Pray to our God above,
To break the fell destroyer's sway,
And show his saving love.

325 I will draw all men unto me. 8s & 7s.

IT is finished! Man of Sorrows!
From thy cross our frailty borrows
Strength to bear and conquer thus.

2 While extended there we view thee,
Mighty Sufferer! draw us to thee;
Sufferer victorious!

3 Not in vain for us uplifted,
Man of Sorrows, wonder-gifted!
May that sacred emblem be;

4 Lifted high amid the ages,
Guide of heroes, saints, and sages;
May it guide us still to thee!

326 Far, far at sea. 8s, 7s & 4.

STAR of Peace, to wanderers weary,
Bright the beams that smile on me;
Cheer the pilot's vision dreary,
Far, far at sea.

2 Star of Hope, gleam on the billow,
Bless the soul that sighs for thee;
Bless the sailor's lonely pillow,
Far, far at sea.

3 Star of Faith, when winds are mocking
All his toil, he flies to thee;
Save him, on the billows rocking,
Far, far at sea.

4 Star Divine! oh, safely guide him—
Bring the wanderer home to thee;
Sore temptations long have tried him,
Far, far at sea.

327 Perfect peace in Christ. S. M.

THOU very present aid
In suffering and distress,
The soul which still on thee is stayed,
Is kept in perfect peace.

2 The soul, by faith reclined
On the Redeemer's breast,
'Mid raging storms exults to find
An everlasting rest.

3 Sorrow and fear are gone
Whene'er thy face appears:
It stills the sighing orphan's moan,
And dries the widow's tears:

4 It hallows every cross;
It sweetly comforts me;
Makes me forget my every loss,
And find my all in thee.

5 Jesus, to whom I fly,
Doth all my wishes fill;
What though created streams are dry,
I have the fountain still.

6 Stripped of my earthly friends,
I find them all in One;
And peace and joy that never ends,
And heaven in Christ begun.

328 It shall stand forever. S. M.

THY kingdom, gracious Lord,
Shall never pass away;
Firm as thy truth it still shall stand,
When earthly thrones decay.

2 Thy people here have found,
Through many weary years,
The sweet communion, joy, and peace,
To banish all their fears.

3 And now while in thy courts,
Do thou our love increase;
Give us the food our spirits need,
And fill our hearts with peace.

329 Praise the Lord. 8s, 7s & 4.

PRAISE the Lord, ye saints adore him,
All unite with one accord;
Bring your offerings, come before him—
Oh praise the Lord.

2 Praise the Lord! who every blessing
On our heads hath richly poured;
Sing aloud, his love confessing—
Oh praise the Lord.

3 Praise the Lord! who would not praise
He hath us to grace restored: [him?
To the highest honors raise him—
Oh praise the Lord.

4 Praise the Lord! your songs excelling
Worldly music's richest chord;
Sing—your Savior's glory telling—
Oh praise the Lord.

330
Am I only born to die? P. M.

AND am I only born to die?
And must I suddenly comply
With nature's stern decree?
What after death for me remains?
Celestial joys, or hellish pains,
To all eternity.

331
Evening aspiration. P. M.

GOD that madest earth and heaven,
Darkness and light!
Who the day for toil has given,
For rest the night!
May thine angel guards defend us,
Slumber sweet thy mercy send us,
Holy dreams and hopes attend us,
This livelong night!

332
Book of grace. 8s, 7 & 4.

BOOK of grace, and book of glory!
Gift of God to age and youth;
Wondrous in thy sacred story,
Bright, bright with truth.

2 Book of love! in accents tender,
Speaking unto such as we;
May it lead us, Lord, to render
All, all to thee.

3 Book of hope! the spirit sighing,
Consolation finds in thee;
As it hears the Savior crying—
"Come, come to me."

4 Book of life! when we, reposing,
Bid farewell to friends we love,
Give us for the life then closing,
Life, life above.

333
The precious word. 8s & 6s.

HOW precious, Lord, thy sacred word,
What life and joy those leaves afford,
To thine in their distress!
Thy precepts guide their doubtful way,
Thy voice forbids their feet to stray,
Thy promise leads to rest.

2 Thy threat'nings wake our slumbering eyes,
And warn us where our danger lies;
But 'tis thy gospel, Lord,
That makes our guilty conscience clean,
Converts the soul and conquers sin,
And freedom full affords.

3 We thank thee for thy precious word,
And all thy mercies, gracious Lord,
Oh crown us with thy love;
Then joy shall tune our constant songs
Till we shall join immortal tongues
In nobler praise above.

334
Glorious hope of perfect love. 8s & 6s.

OH glorious hope of perfect love!
It lifts me up to things above;
It bears on eagles' wings;
It gives my ravished soul a taste,
And makes me for some moments feast
With Jesus, priests, and kings.

2 Rejoicing now in earnest hope,
I stand, and from the mountain top
See all the land below:
Rivers of milk and honey rise,
And all the fruits of paradise
In endless plenty grow.

3 A land of corn, and wine, and oil,
Favored with God's peculiar smile,
With every blessing blest;
There dwells the Lord our righteousness,
And keeps his own in perfect peace,
And everlasting rest.

4 Oh, that I might at once go up!
No more on this side Jordan stop,
But now the land possess!
This moment end my legal years;
Sorrows, and sins, and doubts, and fears,
A howling wilderness.

335
The corner-stone. 8s & 6s.

HAD I ten thousand gifts beside,
I'd cleave to Jesus crucified,
And build on him alone;
For no foundation is there given,
On which I'd place my hopes of heaven,
But Christ, the corner-stone.

2 There is no path to heavenly bliss,
To solid joy, or lasting peace,
But Christ th' appointed road;
Oh may we tread the sacred way!
By faith rejoice, and praise and pray,
Till we sit down with God.

336
Death of a sister. 8s & 7s.

SISTER, thou wast mild and lovely,
Gentle as the summer's breeze,
Pleasant as the air of evening,
When it floats among the trees.

2 Peaceful be thy silent slumber,
Peaceful in the grave so low;
Thou no more will join our number,
Thou no more our songs shall know.

3 Dearest sister, thou hast left us,
Here thy loss we deeply feel;
But 'tis God that hath bereft us,
He can all our sorrows heal.

4 Yet again we hope to meet thee,
When the day of life is fled;
Then in heaven with joy to greet thee,
Where no farewell tear is shed.

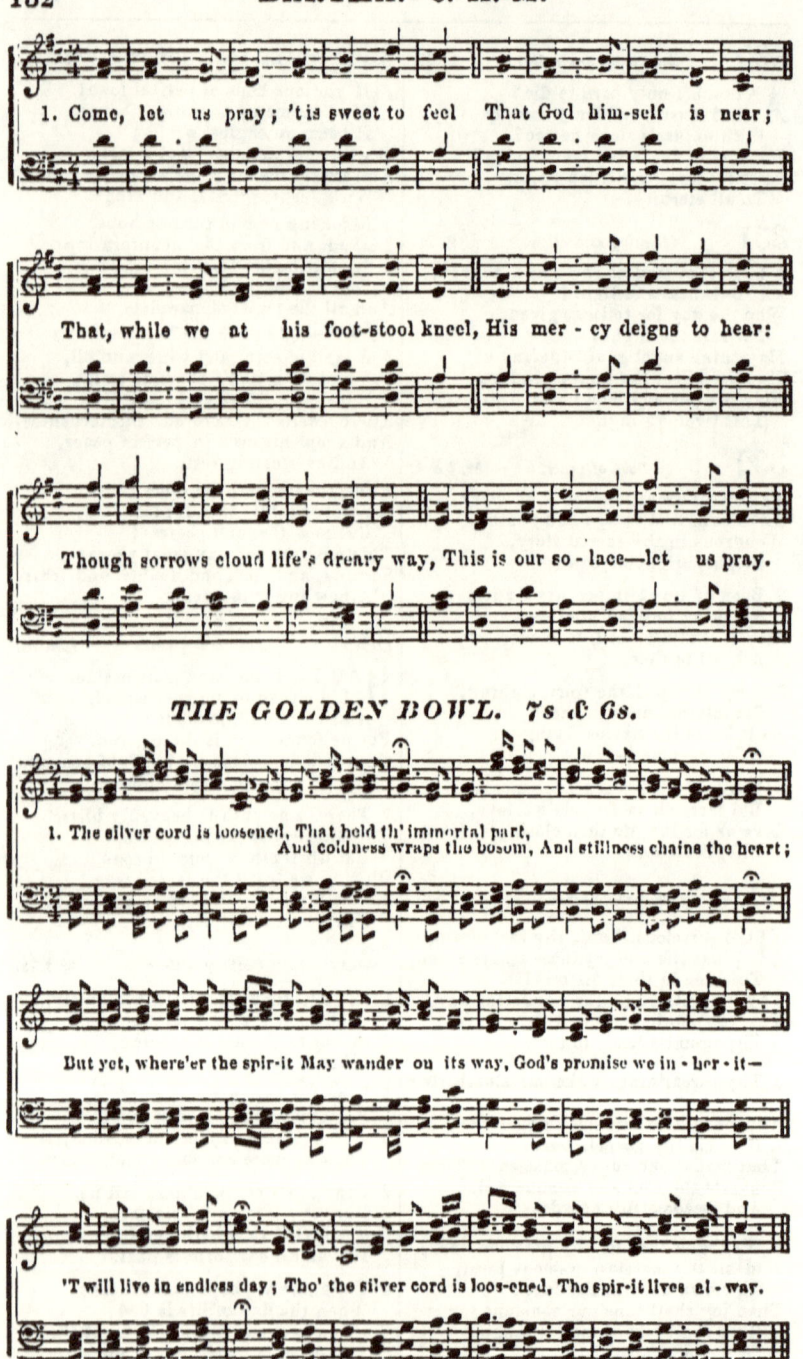

337 *Come, let us pray.* C. H. M.

COME, let us pray: 't is sweet to feel
That God himself is near;
That, while we at his footstool kneel,
His mercy deigns to hear:
Though sorrows cloud life's dreary way,
This is our solace—let us pray.

2 Come, let us pray: the burning brow,
The heart oppressed with care,
And all the woes that throng us now,
Will be relieved by prayer:
Jesus will smile our griefs away;
Oh, glorious thought!—come, let us pray.

3 Come, let us pray: the mercy-seat
Invites the fervent prayer,
And Jesus ready stands to greet
The contrite spirit there:
Oh, loiter not, nor longer stay
From him who loves us—let us pray.

338 *They looked at him and were lightened.* C. L. M.

I LOOK to thee in every need,
And never look in vain;
I feel thy strong and tender love,
And all is well again:
The thought of thee is mightier far
Than sin and pain and sorrow are.

2 Discouraged in the work of life,
Disheartened by its load,
Shamed by its failures or its fears,
I sink beside the road:
But let me only think of thee,
And then new heart springs up in me.

3 Thy calmness bends serene above,
My restlessness to still;
Around me flows thy quickening life,
To nerve my faltering will:
Thy presence fills my solitude;
Thy providence turns all to good.

4 Embosomed in thy cov'nant love,
Held in thy law, I stand;
Thy hand in all things I behold,
And all things in thy hand:
Thou leadest me by unsought ways,
And turn'st my mourning into praise.

339 *The silver cord.* 7s & 6s.

THE silver cord is loosened,
That held the immortal part,
And coldness wraps the bosom,
And stillness chains the heart;
But yet, where'er the spirit
May wander on its way,
God's promise we inherit,
'T will live in endless day:
Tho' the silver cord is loosened,
The spirit lives alway.

2 The golden bowl is broken,
That held the vital spark,
The lips, which oft have spoken,
Are still, the eyes are dark:
The soul, to God who gave it,
Has winged its rapid way,
With him who died to save it,
To dwell in light for aye:
Though the golden bowl is broken,
The spirit lives alway.

3 The cistern wheel is broken,
Checked is the fount of life,
Silent is every token
Of nature's jarring strife.
The promise we inherit,
That there will come a day,
When each immortal spirit
Shall seek its kindred clay:
Though the cistern wheel be broken,
Yet man shall live for aye.

340 *There is no night in heaven.* 7s & 6s.

THERE is no night in heaven:
In that blest world above
Work never can bring weariness,
For work itself is love.
There is no night in heaven:
Yet nightly round the bed
Of every Christian wanderer
Faith has an angel tread.

2 There is no grief in heaven:
For life is one glad day,
And tears are of those former things
Which all have passed away.
There is no grief in heaven:
Yet angels from on high,
On golden pinions earthward glide,
The Christian's tears to dry.

3 There is no want in heaven:
The Lamb of God supplies
Life's tree of twelvefold fruitage still,
Life's spring which never dries.
There is no want in heaven:
Yet in a desert land
The fainting prophet was sustained
And fed by angel's hand.

4 There is no sin in heaven:
Behold that blessed throng;
All holy in their spotless robes,
All holy is their song.
There is no sin in heaven:
Here who from sin is free?
Yet angels aid us in our strife
For Christ's true liberty.

5 There is no death in heaven:
For they who gain that shore
Have won their immortality,
And they can die no more.
There is no death in heaven:
But, when the Christian dies,
The angels wait his parting soul,
And waft it to the skies.

341. *Loving kindness.* L. M.

AWAKE, my soul, in joyful lays,
And sing thy great Redeemer's praise;
He justly claims a song from me,
His loving kindness, oh how free!

2 When trouble, like a gloomy cloud,
Has gather'd thick and thunder'd loud,
He near my soul has always stood,
His loving kindness, oh how good!

3 Often I feel my sinful heart
Prone from my Jesus to depart;
But though I have him oft forgot,
His loving kindness changes not.

4 Soon shall I pass the gloomy vale,
Soon all my mortal powers must fail;
Oh may my last expiring breath,
His loving kindness sing in death.

5 Then let me mount and soar away
To the bright world of endless day;
And sing, with rapture and surprise,
His loving kindness in the skies.

342. *The Christian banner.* L. M.

THE Christian banner! dread no loss
Where that broad ensign floats unrolled,
But let the fair and sacred cross
 Blaze out from every radiant fold:
Stern foes arise, a countless throng,
 Loud as the storms of Kara's sea,
But though the strife be fierce and long,
 That cross shall wave in victory.

2 Sound the shrill trumpet, sound, and
 The people of the mighty King, [call
And bid them keep that standard all
 In martial thousands gathering;
Let them come forth from every clime,
 That lies beneath the circling sun,
Various, as flowers in that sweet clime,
 Where flowers are, in heart, but one.

3 Soldiers of heaven! take sword and
 shield,
 Look up to him who rules on high,
And forward to the glorious field,
 Where noble martyrs bleed and die;
Press onward, scorning flight or fear,
 As deep waves burst on Norway's coast,
And let the startled nations hear
 The war-shout of the Christian host.

4 Lift up the banner—rest no more,
Nor let this righteous warfare cease,
Till man's last tribe shall bow before
 The Lord of lords—the Prince of Peace:
Go! bear it forth, ye strong and brave;
 Let not those bright folds once be furled,
Till that high sun shall see them wave
 Above a blest but conquered world.

343. *The power of God unto salvation.* L. M.

GOD, in the gospel of his Son,
Makes his eternal counsels known;
'T is here his richest mercy shines,
And truth is drawn in fairest lines.

2 Here sinners of an humble frame
May taste his grace and learn his name;
'T is writ in characters of blood,
Severely just—immensely good.

3 Here Jesus, in ten thousand ways,
His soul-attracting charms displays;
Recounts his poverty and pains,
And tells his love in melting strains.

4 May this blest volume ever lie
Close to my heart, and near my eye—
Till life's last hour my soul engage,
And be my chosen heritage!

344. *The Spirit of the Lord, etc.* L. M.

FLING out the banner! let it float
 Sky-ward and sea-ward, high and
 wide;
The sun, that lights its shining folds,
 The cross, on which the Savior died.

2 Fling out the banner! angels bend,
 In anxious silence o'er the sign;
And vainly seek to comprehend
 The wonder of the love divine.

3 Fling out the banner! heathen lands
 Shall see, from far, the glorious sight,
And nations, crowding to be born,
 Baptize their spirits in its light.

4 Fling out the banner! sin-sick souls,
 That sink and perish in the strife,
Shall touch in faith its radiant hem,
 And spring immortal into life.

5 Fling out the banner! let it float
 Sky-ward and sea-ward, high and wide;
Our glory, only in the cross;
 Our only hope the Crucified.

6 Fling out the banner! wide and high,
 Sea-ward and sky-ward, let it shine;
Nor skill, nor might, nor merit, ours;
 We conquer only in that sign.

345. *Wherewithal shall a young man, etc.* C. M.

HOW shall the young secure their hearts,
 And guard their lives from sin?
Thy word the choicest rules imparts
 To keep the conscience clean.

2 'T is like the sun, a heavenly light,
 That guides us all the day,
And through the dangers of the night
 A lamp to lead our way.

NEWTON. P. M.

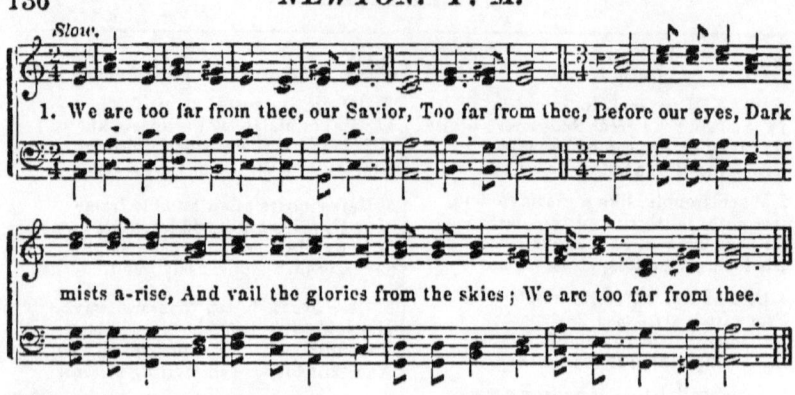

1. We are too far from thee, our Savior, Too far from thee, Before our eyes, Dark mists a-rise, And vail the glories from the skies; We are too far from thee.

346   *Nearer.*   P. M.

WE are too far from thee, our Savior,
   Too far from thee.
Before our eyes, Dark mists arise,
And vail the glories from the skies;
   We are too far from thee.

2 We are too far from thee, our Savior,
   Too far from thee.
Fierce pains oppress, Dark cares distress,
Made darker by our loneliness;
   We are too far from thee.

3 We are too far from thee, our Savior,
   Too far from thee.
Dark waters roll Above the soul,
Striving to reach the heavenly goal;
   We are too far from thee.

4 We are too far from thee, our Savior,
   Too far from thee.
Alone, afraid, Our path is laid
In darkness; send thy heavenly aid;
   We are too far from thee.

5 We are too far from thee, our Savior,
   Too far from thee.
E'en if thy rod Bring us to God,
In meekness be the pathway trod,
   If it but lead to God.

6 Draw us more close to thee, our Savior,
   More close to thee.
Let come what will Of good or ill,
'T is one to us, we knowing still
   Thou drawest us to thee.

INVITATION. 11s & 10s.

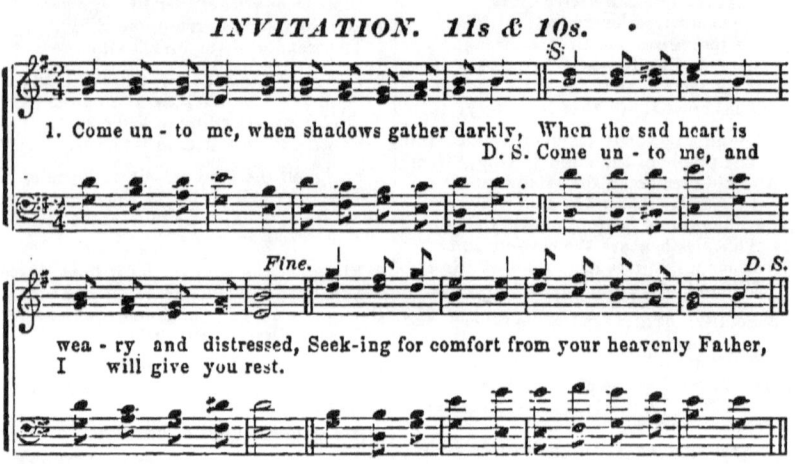

1. Come un-to me, when shadows gather darkly, When the sad heart is weary and distressed, Seek-ing for comfort from your heavenly Father, I will give you rest.
D. S. Come un-to me, and

347   *Come unto me.*   11s & 10s.

COME unto me, when shadows darkly gather,
   When the sad heart is weary and distressed,
Seeking for comfort from your heav'nly Father,
   Come unto me, and I will give you rest.

2 Ye who have mourned when the spring flowers were taken,
   When the ripe fruit fell richly to the ground,
When the loved slept, in brighter homes to waken,
   Where their pale brows with spirit-wreaths are crowned.

3 Large are the mansions in thy Father's dwelling,
   Glad are the homes that sorrows never dim;
Sweet are the harps in holy music swelling,
   Soft are the tones which raise the heavenly hymn.

4 There, like an Eden blossoming in gladness,
   Bloom the fair flowers the earth too rudely pressed;
Come unto me, all ye who droop in sadness,
   Come unto me, and I will give you rest.

MANUAL OF ROUND NOTE MUSIC.

LESSON I.

THE elements of music may be classed under four heads, or distinctions. Under the first head, sounds are *long* or *short*. (TIME.)
Under the second, they are *high* or *low*. (MELODY.)
Under the third, they are *loud* or *soft*. (EXPRESSION.)
Combinations of sounds, or HARMONY, forms the fourth distinction.

REMARK.—These distinctions should be practiced separately, until each is thoroughly understood, both theoretically and practically, by the beginner.

Perpendicular lines, with the spaces between them, are termed *bars* and *measures*, thus:

| Bar. | Bar. | Bar. | Bar. |
| Measure. | Measure. | Measure. |

In order to give variety to the time in music, the measures are divided into parts usually denoted by figures, thus:*

2. Double Measure.   3. Triple Measure.

4. Quadruple Measure.

6. Sextuple Measure.

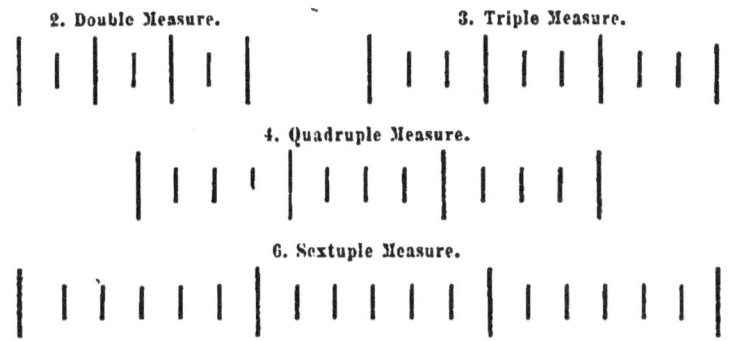

NOTE.—Let the teacher turn to different pieces of music, and request the pupils to name the kind of time of each piece, until ready answers are obtained.

QUESTIONS—1. Into how many distinctions do we divide the elements of music? 2. Name the first distinction; the second; the third; the fourth. 3. Name these perpendicular lines (pointing to them in the book or on the blackboard). 4. What are the spaces between the bars called? 5. How many varieties of measure have we? 6. What figures indicate the first variety? What the second? What the third? What the fourth? 7. Give the name of each variety. 8. Into how many parts is double measure divided? triple? etc. 9. How many bars and measures have we, in each of these examples?

Sing a few tunes by rote from the commencement of the class.

* Some writers designate double measure by the letter C, with a bar across, thus, ₵; and quadruple by the letter C, thus C. (137)

LESSON II.

In order to perform music with accuracy, a motion of the hand is necessary, called beating time. Double measure has two beats in a measure, thus:

2. | Down, | Up, | Down, | Up, | Down, | Up. |

Triple measure has three beats, thus:

3. | Down, | Left, | Up, | Down, | Left, | Up, | Down, | Left, | Up |

Quadruple measure has four beats, thus:

4. | Down, | Left, | Right, | Up, | Down, | Left, | Right, | Up, | Down, | Left, | Right, | Up. |

Sextuple measure, six, thus:

6. | Down, | Down, | Down, | Up, | Up, | Up, | Down, | Down, | Down, | Up, | Up, | Up, |

Or two, thus:

6. | Down, Up, | Down, Up, |
    1, 2, 3, 4, 5, 6, 1, 2, 3, 4, 5, 6,

when rapidity in execution is necessary.

NOTE.—The pupil should be careful to move the hand promptly in beating time, as this is indispensable to a correct performance. He should, also, from the commencement, make it an *invariable* rule to *beat the time*, notwithstanding the effort which may be required to acquire this *most important* requisite to correct mechanical execution. Some beginners may find it necessary to omit singing for awhile, in order to devote all their attention to the manner of beating time.

No teacher can expect to be successful, unless he insists upon the observance of the above instructions. Let the right hand of every pupil be made to move with accuracy and ease, the motion proceeding from the wrist, with the arm immovable, in all the varieties of measure, before attempting the voice.

Exercises, something like the following, should now be practiced, pronouncing one word or syllable to each beat:

2. Down, up, | one, two, | loud, soft, | roam-ing, | flow-ing, | etc.
3. Down, left, up, | one, two, three, | loud, soft, soft, | wil-ling-ly, | etc.
4. Down, left, right, up, | one, two, three, four, | loud, soft, loud, soft, | gen-tle-man-ly, | rep-u-ta-bly, | etc.
6. Down, down, down, up, up, up, | one, two, three, four, five, six, | loud, soft, loud, soft, loud, soft, | in-stru-men-tal-i-ty, | etc.

QUESTIONS.—1. What do we mean by "beating time"? 2. What is its use? 3. How many beats has double measure? how many triple? quadruple? sextuple? 4. What distinguishes the different varieties of measure? 5. Should the pupil find difficulty in singing and beating time together, what course should be pursued? 6. What should never be omitted, in order to execute music in time? 7. Which hand should be used in beating time? 8. Whence should the motion proceed? 9. A word of how many syllables represents double measure? triple? quadruple? sextuple?

LESSON III.

Of Accent, or Loud and Soft Sounds. (Expression.)

IN order to give more expression to music, certain sounds should be sung louder than others. This is usually termed *accent*, and corresponds to the accent of the words which are set to the music. The accent should be laid on the *first* beat in double and triple measures; the first and third in quadruple; and first and fourth in sextuple. All these rules are subject to exceptions, as will be shown hereafter.

Let the pupil practice all the varieties of measure, using the word *loud* on the accented, and *soft* on the unaccented, parts of the measure.

Of the Characters used to Denote the Length of Sounds.

Long and short sounds are represented by characters called notes, thus:

The whole note (Semibreve), represented by the figure 1,*

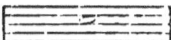

is equal to two halves (Minim), represented by the figure 2;*

or four quarters (Crotchet), represented by the figure 4;*

or eight eighths (Quaver), represented by the figure 8;*

or sixteen sixteenths (Semiquaver), represented by the figure 16;*

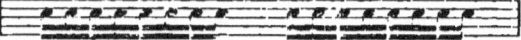

or thirty-two thirty-seconds (Demisemiquaver), represented by the figure 32.*

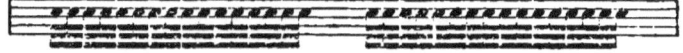

Rests and Dotted notes.

Characters indicating silence in music are termed rests, and each note has a corresponding rest, thus:

Whole rest.   Half rest.   Quarter rest.   Eighth rest.   Sixteenth rest.   Thirty-second rest.

---

*The pupil will take notice that the lower figure at the commencement of a piece of music, represents the kind of notes, or rather their value in a measure, and the upper, the kind of measure.

A dot after a note or rest adds one-half to its value; thus, 𝅗𝅥. a dotted whole note is equal to three halves 𝅗𝅥 𝅗𝅥 𝅗𝅥; a 𝅗𝅥· equal to three 𝅘𝅥 𝅘𝅥 𝅘𝅥; a dotted rest, thus, ▬. is equal to three half rests, thus, ▬ ▬ ▬; a ▬. equal to 𝄽 𝄽 𝄽, etc.

A second dot adds one-half to the first dot; thus, 𝅗𝅥·· is equal to 𝅘𝅥 𝅘𝅥 𝅘𝅥 𝅘𝅥; 𝅘𝅥·· is equal to 𝅘𝅥𝅮 𝅘𝅥𝅮 𝅘𝅥𝅮 𝅘𝅥𝅮, etc.

Exercises in Long and Short Sounds and Rests.

Sing one La to each note.

REMARK.—The stems of notes may turn up or down, and be connected, thus, 𝅘𝅥 𝅘𝅥𝅮𝅘𝅥𝅮𝅘𝅥𝅮𝅘𝅥𝅮 and their value is not changed. A whole rest in a measure alone indicates that it is to be counted in silence; hence, the whole rest is also called a whole measure rest.

QUESTIONS.—1. What is accent? 2. Which beat is accented in double measure? triple? quadruple? sextuple? 3. What are those characters termed which represent the length of sounds? 4. What name is given to the longest note? the next? the next? the next? etc. 5. How many half notes to a whole? how many quarters? how many eighths? etc. 6. How many quarters to one half? how many eighths? how many sixteenths? etc. 7. How many eighths to one quarter? how many sixteenths? how many thirty-seconds? 8. How many sixteenths to one eighth? how many thirty-seconds? 9. What are characters indicating silence called? 10. On which side of the line is the whole rest? half? etc. 11. Which way does the quarter rest turn? eighth? etc. 12. How much does a dot add to the value of a rest or note? 13. A dotted whole is equal to what three notes? a dotted half? quarter? etc.

NOTE.—The ingenious and careful teacher will vary these, as well as other questions, in many ways, to afford variety and instruction.

LESSON IV.

Second Distinction—High and Low Sounds, or Melody.

A REGULAR series of eight notes, all differing in pitch, is termed *the diatonic scale.* The numerals one, two, three, etc., are used to designate these eight sounds. The first seven letters of the alphabet are also used: C being applied to one, D to two, E to three, F to four, G to five, A to six, B to seven, and C again to eight. There are also seven syllables, namely, *Do, ra, mi, fa, sol, la, si.*

Five lines and four spaces, thus, constitute what is called the staff,

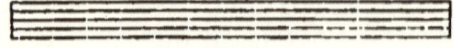

MANUAL OF ROUND NOTE MUSIC. 141

and it determines the pitch of sounds. Each line or space in the staff is called a degree, making nine in all; and as the compass of voices and instruments is much greater than the staff of five lines will allow, added lines below and above are used to any extent which may be necessary. The diatonic scale is placed on the staff thus:

Characters called *clefs* are used to denote where one of the scale is written, thus:

NOTE.—The order of intervals of the diatonic scale may be introduced here, or in Lesson VI, at the option of the teacher.

The scale with the G clef, together with numerals, letters, and syllables, is written thus:

1	2	3	4	5	6	7	8	8	7	6	5	4	3	2	1
C	D	E	F	G	A	B	C	C	B	A	G	F	E	D	C
Do,	re,	mi,	fa,	sol,	la,	si,	do.	Do,	si,	la,	sol,	fa,	mi,	re,	do.

Pronounced. Do, re, me, fah, saul, lah, se, do.   Do, se, lah, saul, fah, me, ra, do.

The F clef is written thus:

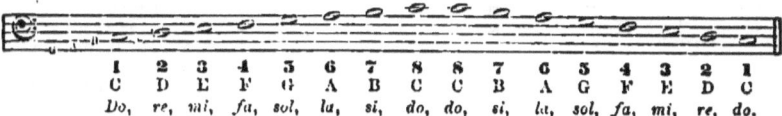

1	2	3	4	5	6	7	8	8	7	6	5	4	3	2	1
C	D	E	F	G	A	B	C	C	B	A	G	F	E	D	C
Do,	re,	mi,	fa,	sol,	la,	si,	do,	do,	si,	la,	sol,	fa,	mi,	re,	do.

Sing the scale with the numerals, letters, and syllables, in all the varieties of measure, being careful to accent correctly.

QUESTIONS.—1. What is the second distinction? 2. How many sounds have we in the diatonic scale? 3. What numerals are used to designate the scale? what letters? what syllables? 4. How many lines and spaces has the staff? 5. What is the use of the staff? It determines the pitch of sounds. 6. How many degrees in the staff? 7. How are other ones acquired? 8. What characters are used to determine where one is written? 9. Where is one written with the G clef? with the base? 10. What letter to the first line, G clef? first space? second line? etc. 11. What letter to the first line, base clef? first space? etc.

Question the pupils something like the following, on the succeeding exercises, before singing them:*

What is the first character used? A Clef. Which clef? The treble. What do the figures indicate? The kind of measure and notes. What kind of measure in No. 1? Double. No. 2? Triple, etc. What are the perpendicular lines called? Bars. The spaces between the bars? Measures. How many beats to a measure in No. 1? Two. No. 2? Three, etc. What one note comes to a beat in No. 1? A half. No. 2? A quarter, etc. What are the five lines and spaces called? A

---

*In some classes, perhaps the majority, Lesson VI should be studied before singing these exercises.

MANUAL OF ROUND NOTE MUSIC.

Staff. What does the staff indicate? The pitch of sounds. What characters determine where *one* of the scale is written? The clefs. What is the last character to every piece of music? A close, thus:

Question all the exercises, as above, and sing the numerals and letters, as well as syllables.

The following exercise is more difficult than the above, and the teacher will first sing it to the class, letting them beat the time.

A piece of music may commence on any degree of the scale.

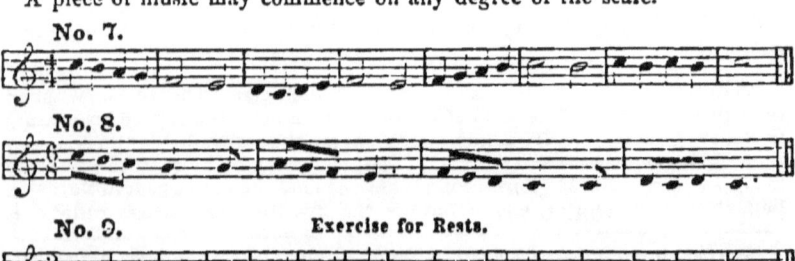

Exercise for Rests.

LESSON V.

Difficult Exercises in Long and Short Sounds and Rests.

REMARK.—Every school or class can spend not merely one evening, but several, on such exercises as below, and the result will show itself most prominently in the future excellence of the pupils.

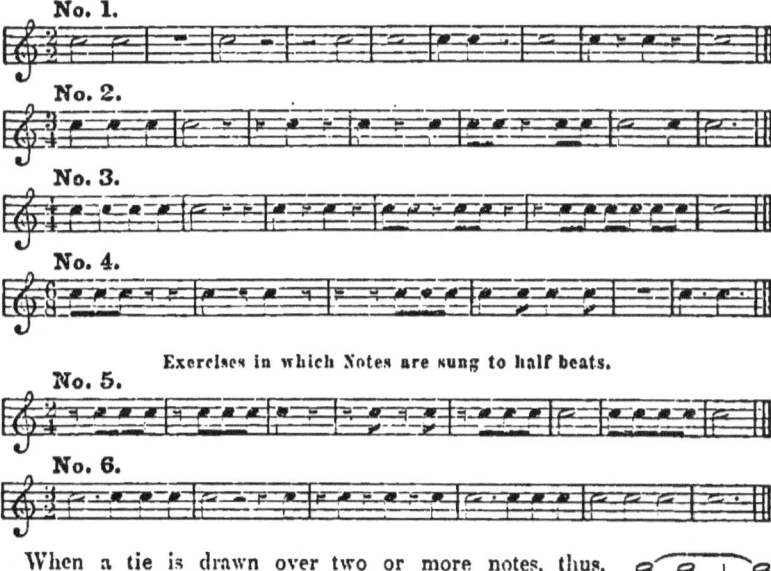

When a tie is drawn over two or more notes, thus, it shows the sound is to be continued even over the bar, thus:

A piece of music may commence on any beat of the measure. This is peculiarly necessary in vocal music, in order that the accent of the poetry may agree with that of the music; thus,

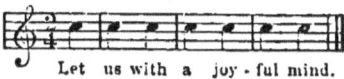
Let us with a joy - ful mind.

is wrong, as the accented words of the poetry come to the unaccented port of the measure. It should have been thus:

Let us with a joy - ful mind.

But in many meters the words commence with an unaccented word, thus:

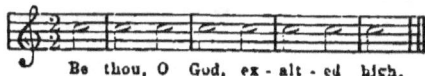
Be thou, O God, ex - alt - ed high.

MANUAL OF ROUND NOTE MUSIC.

Exercises commencing on Different Parts of the Measure.

NOTE.—The pupil may practice tunes, singing them without reference to the key or pitch, i. e., all the notes to a given sound, using the syllable *La*, or words, thus:

Such exercises will afford great variety in the practice of long and short sounds (Time), and is certainly one of the most useful exercises for classes. The teacher may with propriety write tunes on the blackboard, as above.

LESSON VI.

Continuation of High and Low Sounds, or Melody.

IN analyzing the diatonic scale, there are seven intervals, viz., five major and two minor seconds.

From one to two is a major, two to three major, three to four minor, four to five major, five to six major, six to seven major, seven to eight minor seconds. This order of intervals must be strictly enforced, or false intonations will arise, a habit that every singer should carefully avoid.

REMARK.—The terms *whole* and *half tones* are deservedly discontinued by many of our best teachers, and the more correct terms of *major* and *minor seconds* substituted. A whole tone is a *sound*, and not an *interval* or *distance* from one sound to another. Besides the above-named intervals, we have thirds, fourths,

MANUAL OF ROUND NOTE MUSIC. 145

fifths, etc. Let the teacher exercise the pupils in the intervals something as follows: Teacher says (pointing to them on the blackboard), Sing one. The pupils sing Do. *Teacher*, Sing three. *Pupils*, Mi. *Teacher*, Sing five. *Pupils*, Sol, etc. When the pupils have acquired readiness in the intervals of one, three, five, eight, others may be gradually introduced: the fourth first, then the second and fourth; second, fourth, and sixth; second, fourth, sixth, and seventh; and, finally, all the intervals.

Here we have a series of progressive intervals, from the most simple to the most difficult:

No. 1. Intervals of the Third, Fifth, and Eighth.

No. 2. Intervals of the Fourth.

No. 3. Intervals of the Sixth, Seventh, and Others.

No. 4. Intervals, in Difficult Time.

Two or more sounds, heard at the same time form a CHORD, and a succession of chords constitutes harmony.

Let the two sections of the school sing the following chords:

First sec. sing 1,   Second sec. sing 3.   First sec. sing 8,   Second sec. sing 5.
"   "   " 3,   "   "   " 5.   "   "   " 5,   "   "   " 3.
"   "   " 3,   "   "   " 8.   "   "   " 3,   "   "   " 1.
"   "   " 5,   "   "   " 3.

NOTE.—Divide the school also into three or four sections, and practice together the numerals 1, 3, 5, 8.

This combination of sounds is called the COMMON CHORD.

In harmony, the notes that are to be sung together are written over or under each other on separate staves, or on the same staff.

LESSON VII.

Bass Clef.

As has been shown in Lesson IV, we have an F or bass clef which is used for male voices. One of the scale with this clef is written on the second space.

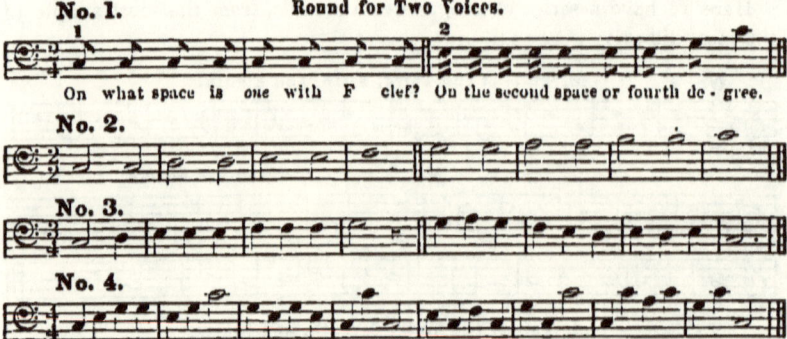

No. 1. Round for Two Voices.

On what space is one with F clef? On the second space or fourth de-gree.

Here we have an exercise in two parts; the male voices will sing the bass, and the females the upper, staff.

LESSON VIII.

Extension of the Scale.

In addition to the scale of eight sounds with which we are now acquainted, we can form other scales above and below, thus:

Or with the bass clef, thus:

REMARK.—Although the base clef is not used for female voices, yet a knowledge of it can not but be beneficial to female as well as male singers.

These extended scales are but a repetition of the one we have been using;

MANUAL OF ROUND NOTE MUSIC. 147

i. e., the intervals are precisely the same, if we take *eight* of the old scale as *one* of the extended; and the letters and numerals are the same also.

No. 3. Exercises for the Practice of the Extended Scales.

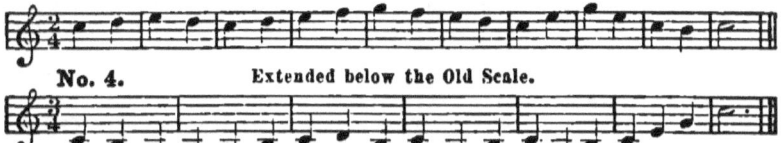

No. 4. Extended below the Old Scale.

No. 5. Extension of the Scale in the Bass Clef Above and Below the Old Scale.

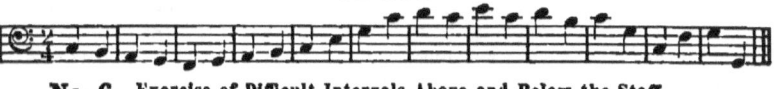

No. 6. Exercise of Difficult Intervals Above and Below the Staff.

NOTE TO THE TEACHER.—All tunes in the key of C that have no accidentals in them may now be practiced, and the class should not be allowed to go farther until some readiness has been acquired in reading simple tunes at sight. The Bass by male, and the Soprano by female, voices, may now be employed together, after having been practiced separately. A Brace, thus, { shows how many parts are to be sung together.

LESSON IX.

Classification of Voices.

ALTHOUGH the male and female voices may be employed together, yet, strictly speaking, they are not in unison. The female voice is eight sounds, or an octave, higher than the male voice. To prove this, the teacher should request the female portion of the class to sustain some given sound, while the teacher, commencing an octave lower, should sing up the scale (using the falsetto voice, if necessary), until he is strictly in unison with the female voices. The class will not fail to perceive the difference, a knowledge of which will be of great importance to them as singers and musicians. After this is thoroughly understood, the following scale should be practiced, the male voices commencing it, and the females joining when they can reach the pitch, say about G, fourth space bass clef:

No. 1.

* Middle C—both the same pitch.

The teacher will remark to the class that as the male and female voices differ in pitch, they can not sing the same part without creating what is termed false harmony and faulty progressions; *i. e.*, consecutive octaves, etc. The female voices are divided into high and low, or Soprano and Alto. A good soprano will sing up to A above the staff, and an alto should be able to sing to A below. A tenor voice (the highest male voice) should be able to sing F or G above the bass clef, and the bass voice should sing G, first line bass clef. See the foregoing exercise, in which the voices are illustrated, and about the compass of each is shown. Another rule, which will enable the pupil to decide which is the legitimate part for him or her, is this: If the high notes generally can be sung easier than the low, then tenor for male and soprano for female voices, although they may not be able to reach G above. If, on the contrary, the low notes are sung with greater ease, then base for male and alto for female voices. A faithful teacher will also try each voice separately, and give suitable instructions as to quality of tone, and manner of producing it (for all voices differ in this respect). Also, its formation on the high and low notes should be very particularly attended to. Here we have, at one view, the manner in which the parts are usually arranged:

Although the G clef is generally used in this country for the tenor, yet it is not correct, for instead of the music being performed where written, it is in reality sung eight notes lower.

The C clef, which is in common use in Europe, would remedy this difficulty, but as it requires some time to acquire a knowledge of it, by common consent the G clef has been substituted for it in this country. Sometimes the soprano and alto are written on one staff, and the tenor and bass on another, making but two staffs in a brace, instead of four, as in No. 2. This way of writing music saves room, and other important advantages are derived from it. See exercise No. 3.

The highest notes in the G clef are for the soprano, and the highest in the bass for the tenor. Continue to practice tunes as variety and profit require.

LESSON X.

Loud and Soft Tones, or Expression.

A TONE produced by no unusual vocal exertion, is a *medium* or *middle* tone; it is marked *m*, and called *mezzo*.

A tone produced by some vocal restraint, is a *soft* tone; it is marked *p*, and called *piano*.

A tone produced by considerable vocal exertion is a *loud* tone; it is marked *f*, and called *forte*.

A tone produced by the greatest vocal restraint, is marked *pp*, and called *pianissimo*.

A tone produced by the greatest vocal exertion, but not so loud as to injure the quality, is marked *ff*, and called *fortissimo*.

A modification of *forte* and *piano*, is marked *fp*. Of *mezzo* and *piano*, *mp*. Of *mezzo* and *forte*, *mf*, etc.

When an *unaccented* note is connected with the following accented note, it is said to be SYNCOPATED.

A TIE [⌒] connects notes on the same degree, which are performed as one. See exercise following.

MANUAL OF ROUND NOTE MUSIC. 149

No. 1.

Join now with me in this mel-o-dy,   Sing with firm accent, and slur the notes.

A tone begun, continued, and ended with the same power, is called an ORGAN TONE [=====].

A tone begun *soft* and gradually increased in power, is called a CRESCENDO [*Cres.* or <].

An inversion of the Crescendo is called a DIMINUENDO [*Dim.* or >].

A union of the Crescendo and Diminuendo is called a SWELL [<>].

A sudden Swell is called a PRESSURE TONE [< or <>].

A very short tone, produced with force and immediately diminished, is called an EXPLOSIVE TONE, sometimes FORZANDO, or SFORZANDO [*sf.*, *fz.*, or >].

STACCATO marks [' ' ' '] denote that a passage is to be performed in a short, distinct manner.

LEGATO means smooth and connected, the opposite of Staccato.

A SLUR [⌒] indicates that certain notes are sung to one syllable. See exercise above, and tune *Siloam*.

No. 2.   **Explosive Tone and Staccato.**

The TURN [∼] consists of a principal sound, with the sounds next above and below it. It should be performed with care and neatness, but not too quick; thus:

No. 3.
Written.   Performed.   Or.   Or.   Or.

Ornamental or grace notes are often introduced into a melody, that do not essentially belong to it; they are commonly written in smaller characters, and are called PASSING NOTES.

When a passing note precedes an essential note, on an *accented* part of the measure, it is called an APPOGGIATURA.

When a passing note follows an essential note on an *unaccented* part of the measure it is called an AFTER NOTE.

No. 4.   Appoggiatura.
Written.

Performed.

No. 5.   After Note.
Written.   Performed.

The SHAKE [*tr.*] consists of a rapid alternation of two sounds. It should be much cultivated by those who would acquire smoothness and flexibility of voice.

No. 6.

Miscellaneous Characters in Music.

A figure 3 placed over three notes, thus, 𝅗𝅥 𝅗𝅥 𝅗𝅥, shows that they are to be sung in the time of two of the same kind; for example, thus:

A double bar, thus, ‖, denotes the end of a strain or line in poetry.

The figure 6, thus, ♩♩♩♩♩♩, placed over six notes, shows that they are to be sung in the time of four of the same kind.

Dots placed in a piece of music, thus, 𝄇 𝄆, denote that it is to be repeated, and they are called REPEATS.

A PAUSE or HOLD over a note or rest, thus, 𝄐 𝄐, denotes a suspension of the time, during which the hand should remain stationary.

LESSON XI.

Chromatic Scale.

OUT of every major second of the diatonic scale, two intervals can be procured by the use of a sharp [♯] or flat [♭]. The sharp elevates a sound before which it is placed a *chromatic* interval, and a flat depresses it a *chromatic* interval. A series of twelve intervals is called the CHROMATIC SCALE, thus:

The following Letters, Numerals, and Syllables are applied to the Chromatic Scale:

NOTE.—When naming the chromatic intervals by numerals, say, Sharp one, sharp two, flat six, flat seven, etc.; but when naming them by letters, C sharp, D flat, E flat, etc.

The pupil will observe that from any letter to the same made flat or sharp, the interval is a chromatic one; and from any letter to the next above or below in the chromatic scale, the interval is a minor second.

QUESTIONS.—What is the interval from C to C♯ (sharp)? C♯ to D? etc. C to B, in descending? B to B♭ (flat)? B♭ to A? A to A♭? etc.

MANUAL OF ROUND NOTE MUSIC. 151

Commence the practice of the chromatic scale something in the following manner: The class sings one, after which the teacher sings sharp one, the class imitating him. Then two, sharp two, etc. For the future, the class should devote a short time, each lesson, to the practice of this scale.

The influence of a sharp or flat extends from measure to measure, until a note intervenes which is on a different degree from that before which it is placed.*

A NATURAL [♮] is used to contradict or take away the power of a flat or a sharp.

No. 1. Example.

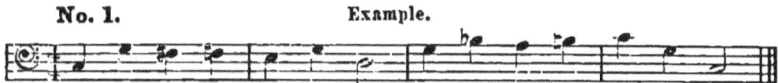

After a *sharped* tone the ear naturally expects the next above; but after a *flatted* tone, the next below.

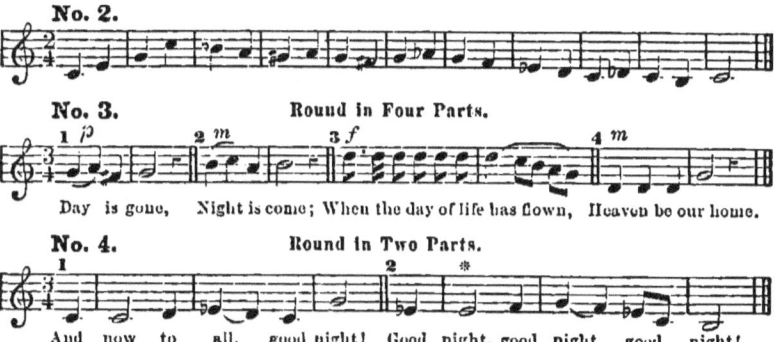

No. 2.

No. 3. Round in Four Parts.

1 *p* 2 *m* 3 *f* 4 *m*

Day is gone, Night is come; When the day of life has flown, Heaven be our home.

No. 4. Round in Two Parts.

1 2

And now to all, good night! Good night, good night, good night!

LESSON XII.

Minor Scale.

THERE is yet a third scale in music, called the *Minor* or *soft* mode. It consists of seven intervals, and has two forms of progression; thus,

No. 1.

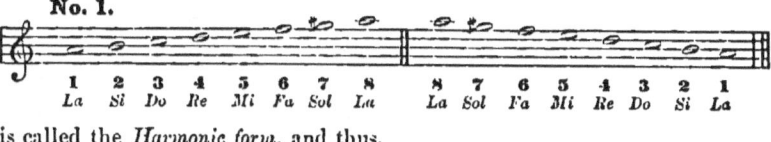

| 1 | 2 | 3 | 4 | 5 | 6 | 7 | 8 | 8 | 7 | 6 | 5 | 4 | 3 | 2 | 1 |
| La | Si | Do | Re | Mi | Fa | Sol | La | La | Sol | Fa | Mi | Re | Do | Si | La |

is called the *Harmonic form*, and thus,

No. 2.

---

* When a note succeeds one that has been made flat or sharp, *without a note intervening* on another degree of the staff, the effect of the accidental continues, although in another measure.

is termed the *Melodic form*. The seconds are as follows in the *Harmonic* form: From one to two, a major second; from two to three, minor; three to four and four to five, major seconds; five to six, minor second; six to seven, an extended second; and seven to eight, a minor second. The same progression is observed in descending.

In the *Melodic* form of the minor scale, the intervals occur as follows, viz.: From one to two, a major second; two to three, a minor second; three to four, four to five, five to six, and six to seven, all major seconds; and seven to eight, a minor second. The descending scale in the melodic form differs, viz.: eight to seven and seven to six, major seconds; six to five, a minor second; five to four and four to three, major seconds; three to two, minor second; two to one, major second. Question as follows on the harmonic form:

How many major seconds has the harmonic form, and between which numerals do they occur? How many minors? Between which numerals does the extended second occur? Is the form the same descending as ascending? etc.

Question as follows on the melodic form:

How many major and minor seconds has the melodic form of the minor scale ascending, and between which numerals do they occur? Name the seconds descending. In what respect does this form of the scale differ from the *harmonic form?* How does it differ from the major scale? etc.

The scale of A minor has the same signature that C major has, hence some guide is necessary in order to distinguish between the two. When the signature is natural, and any part commences on A, it is generally in the minor mode. When sharp five occurs often, the piece of music is generally in A minor. After hearing some minor music, the ear will enable one to decide whether it is in the major or minor mode. But as the key or mode is constantly varying in most pieces of music, it is impossible to decide with certainty in relation to the key, without some knowledge of modulation, etc.

LESSON XIII.

Transposition of the Scale.

WHEN a scale of eight sounds occurs founded on any letter—the order of intervals being from one to two and two to three, major seconds; three to four, a minor; four to five, five to six, and six to seven, major seconds; and seven to eight, a minor second—it is named after the letter on which one is written. Thus, if one is written on C, it is called the scale of C; if on D, the scale of D; if on E, the scale of E, etc. When a piece of music commences in the key of C (although other keys may be introduced in the course of the piece by means of accidentals), the signature is said to be natural; or, in other words, there are no flats or sharps used at the commencement. But when a piece of music has sharps or flats placed at the commencement, it is said to be transposed. The signature (or number of flats or sharps) placed at the commencement of a piece of music will decide the key. The pupil will take notice, in transposing the scale, that the same order of

MANUAL OF ROUND NOTE MUSIC. 153

intervals as in the key of C must be preserved, *i. e.*, from three to four and seven to eight must be minor seconds, and all the rest major seconds. In the first regular transposition of the scale by fifths, G becomes one of the new scale, thus:

No. 1. Scale in the Key of G Imperfect.

The above example is not, strictly speaking, in the key of G, although we take G as one. When F sharp is introduced, then, *and then only*, the transposition takes place, thus:

No. 2. Scale in the Key of G Perfect.

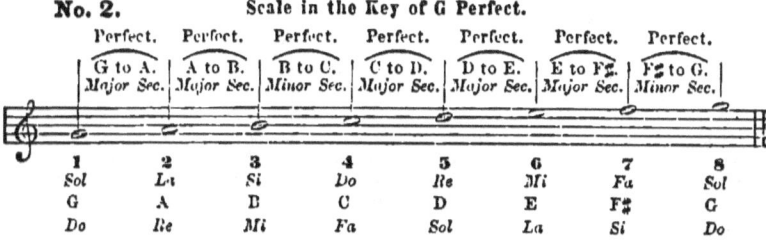

The same method is followed in all the transpositions by sharps viz., the fifth above or fourth below is taken as one of a new key, in every succeeding transposition, and an additional sharp will be required also in every succeeding transposition. Question as follows:

What do you understand by the transposition of the scale? *Ans.* When any other letter besides C is taken as one of a new scale, and accidentals are introduced. When is the scale said to be in its natural position? What letter is used to designate the natural key? What is the signature to C? In transposing the scale, what order of intervals should always be preserved? What is the first transposition? *Ans.* To G, the fifth of C. What is the signature to G? If F is not sharped, how many intervals would be wrong? What would be the interval from six to seven without the F sharp? What should it be? etc.

No. 3.

No. 4.

Practice tunes in the key of G. Question on each tune something as follows:

What is the signature? *Ans.* One sharp. What letter is sharped? *Ans.* F. Why do we sharp F? *Ans.* To regulate the order of the intervals. What is the order of intervals in all the transpositions? *Ans.* Between three and four and seven and eight are minor seconds; all the rest are major seconds. Name the letters to the scale of G. *Ans.* G is one, A is two, B is three, C is four, D is five, E is six, F sharp is seven, and G is eight.

154   MANUAL OF ROUND NOTE MUSIC.

REMARK.—Most classes will be able to understand the theory, and, to a certain extent, the practical part of the art that we have been over, in about twelve or thirteen lessons, *if the teacher has been faithful.* Of course, in our division of the elements into lessons, it is not intended that they shall be followed out to the letter, but changes should be made as the interest of the class may require. Many classes will require twenty-four, or even more, lessons, to acquire what we have been over in these few lessons. *There is but little danger of going too slow* in teaching the elements of music. The rest of the transpositions may be taken up as the class may require, but let it be impressed on the mind, that if the first transposition is well understood, all the rest will come easy, and but little time will be required in teaching them.

Second transposition by sharps (Key of D).—One is written on D, the fifth to G, and in order to preserve the order of intervals, two sharps are used, viz., C♯ (new sharp) and F♯, thus:

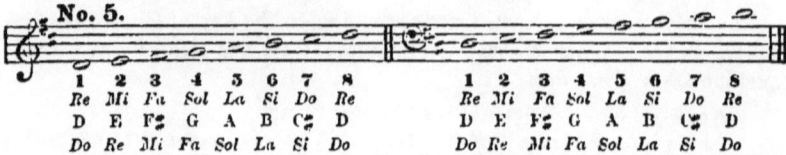

No. 5.

1	2	3	4	5	6	7	8		1	2	3	4	5	6	7	8
Re	Mi	Fa	Sol	La	Si	Do	Re		Re	Mi	Fa	Sol	La	Si	Do	Re
D	E	F♯	G	A	B	C♯	D		D	E	F♯	G	A	B	C♯	D
Do	Re	Mi	Fa	Sol	La	Si	Do		Do	Re	Mi	Fa	Sol	La	Si	Do

QUESTIONS.—In what key is this scale? *Ans.* D. How do you know it to be in the key of D? *Ans.* By the signature. What is the signature? *Ans.* Two sharps. What letters are sharp? *Ans.* F and C. Why do we sharp F and C? *Ans.* To preserve the order of intervals. What numerals of the new scale are sharped? *Ans.* Three and seven. In order to transpose a scale to its next affinity in sharps, what numeral of it must we sharp? *Ans.* The fourth. What was the fourth to C? *Ans.* F. By sharping F, into what key do we modulate or transpose the scale? *Ans.* G. By sharping the fourth to G (which is C), into what key do we modulate? *Ans.* D, etc.

Practice tunes in D.

Third transposition by sharps (Key of A).—One is written on A, the fifth to D, and, in order to preserve the order of intervals, three sharps are found necessary, viz., G♯ (the new sharp), F♯, and C♯, thus:

No. 6.

1	2	3	4	5	6	7	8		1	2	3	4	5	6	7	8
La	Si	Do	Re	Mi	Fa	Sol	La		La	Si	Do	Re	Mi	Fa	Sol	La
A	B	C♯	D	E	F♯	G♯	A		A	B	C♯	D	E	F♯	G♯	A
Do	Re	Mi	Fa	Sol	La	Si	Do		Do	Re	Mi	Fa	Sol	La	Si	Do

Question as in the key of D. Sing tunes in the key of A, and exercises in the keys of D and A.

Fourth transposition by sharps (Key of E).—One of this key is written on E, the fifth of A, and the new sharp is D♯, making four sharps, viz., F♯, C♯, G♯, and D♯; thus:

No. 7.

1	2	3	4	5	6	7	8		1	2	3	4	5	6	7	8
Mi	Fa	Sol	La	Si	Do	Re	Mi		Mi	Fa	Sol	La	Si	Do	Re	Mi
E	F♯	G♯	A	B	C♯	D♯	E		E	F♯	G♯	A	B	C♯	D♯	E
Do	Re	Mi	Fa	Sol	La	Si	Do		Do	Re	Mi	Fa	Sol	La	Si	Do

Question as in the other keys, and practice tunes in the key of E.

MANUAL OF ROUND NOTE MUSIC. 155

Fifth and sixth transpositions by sharps (Keys of B and F#).—Seldom used. Thus:

In the above example we pass to the key of E, and back again, progressively, through the intermediate keys of G, D, A. The pupil should be questioned and instructed on it, until he can tell readily where the modulation takes place from one key to another.

First transposition of the scale by fourths.—To transpose the scale by flats, we take the fourth (instead of the fifth) of every new scale. F is the fourth of C, hence it is one of the new scale (key of F), thus:

No. 10.
Imperfect, because B is not Flat.   Perfect, because B is Flat.

1	2	3	4	5	6	7	8	1	2	3	4	5	6	7	8
Fa	Sol	La	Si	Do	Re	Mi	Fa	Fa	Sol	La	Si	Do	Re	Mi	Fa
F	G	A	B	C	D	E	F	F	G	A	B♭	C	D	E	F
Do	Re	Mi	Fa	Sol	La	Si	Do	Do	Re	Mi	Fa	Sol	La	Si	Do

The order of intervals must be the same in the flat keys as in the sharps. By analyzing the perfect example above, we find that from F to G is a major; G to A, a major; A to B♭ (three to four), a minor; B♭ to C, a major; C to D, a major; D to E, a major; E to F, a minor second. Question something as follows:

What is the signature to the key of F? *Ans.* One flat. What letter is flat? *Ans.* B. Why do we flat? *Ans.* To regulate the order of intervals. Name the letters as they occur in this scale.

The flat keys are transposed a fourth instead of a fifth, and flats are used instead of sharps to regulate the order of intervals—the fourth of each new scale being flatted instead of the seventh being sharped, as in the sharp keys, etc.

Second, third, and fourth transpositions by flats stand thus:

No. 11.   Key of B♭—Signature, Two Flats.

1	2	3	4	5	6	7	8	1	2	3	4	5	6	7	8
Si	Do	Re	Mi	Fa	Sol	La	Si	Si	Do	Re	Mi	Fa	Sol	La	Si
B♭	C	D	E♭	F	G	A	B♭	B♭	C	D	E♭	F	G	A	B♭
Do	Re	Mi	Fa	Sol	La	Si	Do	Do	Re	Mi	Fa	Sol	La	Si	Do

MANUAL OF ROUND NOTE MUSIC.

It will be perceived that in each succeeding new scale, the fourth of the old scale is taken as one of the new, and that an additional flat is used to each.

Other modulations may be procured by continuing to use additional flats, but as they would not be of any practical use, we omit them here. Questions should be proposed on all the scales, as in the key of F, and the practice of tunes should be introduced in all these keys, in the order of the transpositions as above.

Every major has its relative minor scale, founded on the third letter below, *i. e.*, the relative minor to C is A; to D, B, etc. The order of intervals in the minor scale is the same, as shown in Lesson XII, in all cases. Question the class as follows:

What is the relative minor scale to G major? *Ans.* E. What is the signature of the relative minor to any major scale? *Ans.* The same as its major. What is the signature to E minor? *Ans.* One sharp. Is it necessary to introduce any accidentals in the minor scale? *Ans.* Yes; the seventh is always sharped both in ascending and descending in the harmonic form (for example, see Lesson XII); but in the melodic form only in ascending. Which form of the minor scale is now generally used? *Ans.* The harmonic. Why? *Ans.* Because every note of the scale is susceptible of natural harmonics. What is the relative minor to A major? *Ans.* F sharp minor. To E major? *Ans.* C sharp minor. To F major? *Ans.* D minor. B flat major? *Ans.* G minor. E flat major? *Ans.* C minor. A flat major? *Ans.* F minor.

Here we have all the minor scales at one view:

Practice tunes in all the minor scales.

INDEX OF TUNES.

	PAGE.
Abba	40
Aldwinkle	22
Alva	108
All will be well	122
Amazing grace	58
Amboy	116
America. S. M.	126
America. P. M.	96
Antioch	34
Antwerp	48
Arlington	18
Ascension	42
Ashley	134
Aspiration	18
Aylesbury	48
Balerma	14
Baltimore	78
Barby	110
Bavaria	26
Bealoth	36
Beautiful World	90
Berlin	110
Bertha	132
Biblos	130
Boylston	16
Breast the wave, Christian	78
Bridgewater	10
Buford	76
Calvary	60
Carolans	118
Charity	124
Chester	10
China	116
City of Light	90
Clarington	42
Clinton	122
Come to Jesus	64
Confidence	100
Consolation	14
Coronation	28
Cowper	114
Darkness and Light	130
Day Spring	62
Delight	104
Devizes	50
Devotion	5
Dundee	36
Dunlap's Creek	14
Effingham	31
Elvira	128
Eltham	84
Emotion	108
Enterprise	58
Far, far at sea	128
Favorite	36
Fidelity	106
Fiducia	92
Florence	114

	PAGE.
Forgiveness	58
Fountain	102
Fountain of Life	104
Geer	24
Germany	38
Going home	102
Golden Hill	18
Gorham	72
Good News	48
Gratitude	12
Greenville	96
Hallowed be thy Name	8
Happy Day	38
Happy Home	100
Harwell	80
Heavenly Home	102
Hebron	6
Hedding	130
Holiness	124
Homeward bound	76
Honor	70
Hope	68
Hunter	106
Idumea	126
Illinois	86
I'm on my journey home	62
Innocence	106
Invitation	136
Ives	38
Joyfulness	126
Kingsley	72
Know ye that Better Land	74
Lenox	40
Light	44
Lilly	124
Love	72
Lovest thou me	32
Loving-kindness	134
Luton	10
Marion	88
Marsden	98
Mary	80
Martyn	104
Meet me in heaven	96
Mear	44
Mercy	66
Mercy-seat	68
Mortality	44
Nettleton	32
New	30
New Geneva	98
New Richmond, L. M.	12
New Richmond, D. C. M.	28
Newton	136
Northfield	28

(157)

INDEX OF FIRST LINES.

	PAGE.
Nothing but leaves	76
No. 300	54
No. 373	56
No. 374	56
No. 400	52
No. 600	52
No. 700	50
No. 710	88
No. 788	122
No. 800	40
No. 801	98
No. 900	34
No. 1000	20
No. 1400	54
Ocean	26
Old Hundred	8
On	108
Only waiting	82
Ortonville	30
Ottumwa	120
Palmyra	114
Paris	110
Passing away	62
Penitence	52
Peterboro'	70
Pilesgrove	6
Portugal	12
Praise	26
Prayer	66
Primrose	30
Pulaski	84
Resolution	56
Rest for the weary	74
Richview	120
Righteousness	112
Rock of Ages	82
Salvation	60
Schenectady	22
Simeon	68
Simplicity	54
Shall we sing	84
Solace	92
Sonnet	82

	PAGE.
Soon and forever	80
St. Thomas	46
Suffield	16
Sunbury	22
Supplication	92
Sweet hour of prayer	66
Tallis	20
Temperance	94
Tidings	112
Time speeds away	118
The Agony	42
The Banner	134
The Cross	128
The Golden Bowl	132
The Heavenly Region	78
The Hour of Prayer	118
The Rock	100
The Shining Shore	120
The Wild, Dark Storm	94
Tonti	86
Touch not the cup	94
Truro	70
Trust	112
Turn, sinner, turn	60
Uxbridge	24
Vernon	40
Virginia	88
Wakefield	24
Warning	64
Warren	116
Wells	8
Western	90
Where is my home	50
Wilmot	32
Will you go	64
Windham	6
Windsor	20
Winchester	16
White	86
Woodstock	74
Zion	46

INDEX OF FIRST LINES.

	PAGE.
A beautiful land I see, by faith	91
A child lay in her little couch	97
A charge to keep I have	127
Again, indulgent Lord, return	31
Ah! whither should I go	53
All-powerful, self-existent God	5
All hail the power of Jesus' name	29
All nature feels attractive power	73
All you that are weary and sad, come	105
Amazing grace, how sweet the sound	59
Amid the splendors of the sun	73
And can my heart aspire so high	21
And must I be to judgment brought	77

	PAGE.
Angels! roll the rock away	39
And is the gospel peace and love	49
And am I only born to die	131
Approach, my soul, the mercy-seat	69
As flows the rapid river	109
As down in the sunless retreat of the ocean	121
Awake, Jerusalem, awake	7
Awake, my soul, in joyful lays	135
Before Jehovah's awful throne	9
Behold, the bright morning appears	43
Behold the glories of the Lamb	45
Behold! the lofty sky	47

INDEX OF FIRST LINES.

First Line	PAGE
Behold the sure foundation stone	31
Be thou, O God, exalted high	9
Bless, oh my soul, the living God	23
Blow ye the trumpet, blow	41
Blest is the hour when cares depart	119
Book of grace, and book of glory	131
Borne on the ocean's stormy wave	35
Breast the wave, Christian	79
Brother, hast thou wandered far	55
By cool Siloam's shady rill	87
By faith in Christ I walk with God	51
Children of the Heavenly King	117
Cling to the mighty One	101
Come, let us with a joyful heart	13
Come ye saints, come and adore him	27
Come, thou fount of every blessing	33
Come you that love the Lord	37
Come all who would to glory go	39
Come, humble sinner, in whose breast	61
Come to the glorious gospel feast	61
Come, poor sinners, seek salvation	61
Come, you sinners, come to Jesus	63
Come ye sinners, poor and needy	65
Come, let us with a joyful heart	71
Come, every pious heart	105
Como, sound his praise abroad	115
Come we that love the Lord	115
Come, let us pray ; 't is sweet to feel	133
Come unto me, when shadows darkly	136
Compared with Christ, in all beside	15
Courage, my soul, thy heavy cross	59
Dear Refuge of my weary soul	75
Dear Jesus, ever at my side	107
Dread Sovereign, let my evening song	19
Earth has a joy unknown in heaven	59
Ere mountains reared their forms sublime	7
Eternal power, whose high abode	5
Eternal Wisdom, thee we praise	111
Faith is the brightest evidence	51
Faith adds new charms to earthly bliss	51
Fair shines the morning star	100
Far from mortal cares retreating	89
Father of mercies, in thy Word	47
Father, I long, I faint to see	17
Flee as a bird to your mountain	103
Fling out the banner, let it float	135
For me, oh did my Savior bleed	37
From the cross uplifted high	121
From all that 's mortal, all that 's vain	71
From every stormy wind that blows	69
From thee, O God, our joys shall rise	15
From all that dwell below the skies	17
Give to our God immortal praise	13
Give thanks to God, he reigns above	11
Glory to thee, whose powerful word	9
God is the refuge of his saints	13
God of all created wonder	27
God of mercy ! God of love	15
God, that madest earth and heaven	131
God, in the gospel of his Son	135
Go thou in life's fair morning	87
Go, heralds of the cross, proclaim	89
Go up, go up, my heart	125
Grace! 't is a charming sound	49
Greatest of beings, source of life	11
Great God, with wonder and with praise	15
Great God, how infinite art thou	15
Great God, where'er we pitch our tents	19
Great source of life and light	45
Great God, at thy command	127
Had I the tongues of Greeks and Jews	13
Had I ten thousand gifts besides	131
Hail the blest day the Lord has made	35
Hail, sacred truth ! when piercing rays	47
Hail! the temperance reformation	97
Hark, my soul—it is the Lord	33
Hark ! from the tombs a doleful sound	93
Hark ! from the tombs a doleful sound	93
Hark ! the voice of love and mercy	113
Hark ! ten thousand harps and voices	81
Haste, oh sinner, to be wise	117
Hasten, Lord, the glorious time	85

First Line	PAGE
Haste, oh sinner—now be wise	61
Heavenly Father, sovereign Lord	33
He dies, the friend of sinners dies	43
Hear the bless'd Redeemer calls you	89
Hear my prayer, oh heavenly Father	101
Here will we meet the Savior's poor	71
Here, Savior, we would come	127
High as the heavens above the ground	93
Holy and reverend is the name	29
Hosanna to the Prince of Light	19
How sweet to be allowed to pray	25
How happy every child of grace	59
How sweet to be allowed to pray	69
How charming is the place	69
How sweet the melting lay	69
How blest the sacred tie that binds	71
How sweet, how heavenly is the sight	73
How firm a foundation, you saints	107
How shall the young secure their hearts	135
How precious, Lord, thy sacred word	131
How sweet, how heavenly is the sight	73
I am a stranger here	103
I did thee wrong, my God	55
I love thy kingdom, Lord	27
I love to steal awhile away	25
I love to steal awhile away	75
I look to thee in every need	133
In duties, and in sufferings, too	57
In one fraternal bond of love	71
In the Christian's home in glory	75
In that world of ancient story	101
In seasons of grief to my God I 'll repair	101
In time of fear	123
In all my Lord's appointed ways	57
Is this the kind return	17
I send the joys of earth away	35
I saw the cross of Jesus	91
I think when I read that sweet story of old	107
It is finished, man of sorrows	129
I will extol thee, Lord, on high	21
Jehovah reigns ; he dwells in light	11
Jesus, thou source of calm repose	41
Jesus, let thy pitying eye	53
Jesus, and shall it ever be	57
Jesus, lover of my soul	67
Jesus Christ, my Lord and Savior	87
Jesus, Sun of Righteousness	113
Jesus says that we must love him	87
Joy to the world, the Lord is come	35
Joyfully, joyfully, onward I move	127
Just as I am, without one plea	51
Keep silence—all created things	29
Kind Father, look with pity now	55
Kind Lord, before thy face	41
Know ye the better land	75
Let not despair, nor fell revenge	37
Let thy kingdom, blessed Savior	83
Light of the lonely pilgrim's heart	23
List to the dreamy tone that dwells	9
Like morning—when her early breeze	112
Lord, thou hast searched and seen me	7
Lord, my weak thoughts in vain would	7
Lord, in whose might the Savior trod	45
Lord, let thy Spirit penetrate	45
Lord, to us thy Word is precious	47
Lord, I have made thy word my choice	47
Lord, at thy temple we appear	69
Lord, while for all mankind we pray	93
Lord, from thy glorious throne	97
Love is the strongest tie	99
Love of God, all love excelling	113
Love divine, all love excelling	89
Love divine, all love excelling	33
Majestic sweetness sits enthroned	31
Mary to the Savior's tomb	105
Mourn for the thousands slain	129
Mortals awake, with angels join	35
My helper, God, I bless his name	5
My God, how excellent thy grace	13
My God was with me all the night	19
My God, thy service well demands	21
My spirit looks to God alone	21

INDEX OF FIRST LINES.

	PAGE.
My God, my life, my love	23
My God, my Father, while I stray	35
My heavenly home is bright and fair	103
My days are gliding swiftly by	121
My spirit longs for thee	125
Nature, with all her power, shall sing	9
Nature, with all her power, shall sing	25
Night, with ebon pinion	43
No bitter tears for thee be shed	99
Nothing but leaves! the Spirit grieves	77
Now in a song of grateful praise	31
Now is the accepted time	127
Now I have found a friend	125
Now the shades of night are gone	117
Now be the gospel banner	49
Oft in sorrow, oft in woe	119
Oh thou who didst uphold my way	15
Oh thou from whom all goodness flows	23
Oh happy day that fixed my choice	39
Oh thou that hearest prayer	41
Oh thou that hearest when sinners cry	43
Oh for a faith that will not shrink	51
Oh who would remain in this prison of clay	53
Oh! let me sins of sins forgiven	59
Oh love divine, how sweet thou art	73
Oh how the hearts of those revive	75
Oh! sing to me of heaven	79
Oh think that while you're weeping here	89
Oh when shall I see Jesus	91
Oh thou who dry'st the mourner's tear	93
Oh tie the casement, father, dear	95
Oh where shall rest be found	99
Oh, bow thine ear, eternal One	123
Oh render thanks to God above	123
Oh glorious hope of perfect love	131
Oh bless the Lord, my soul	127
O God, our help in ages past	15
O God, with humble heart and voice	19
O God, my heart is fully bent	111
O God, thy grace and blessing give	123
O Jesus, I have come to thee	57
O Lord, how full of sweet content	13
O Lord, thy perfect Word	47
O Lord, our heavenly King	17
O Lord, and shall thy Spirit rest	45
Only waiting till the shadows	83
O Savior, lend a listening ear	109
Our Father, God, who art in heaven	17
Our Father in heaven	93
Our Father and our God	127
Ont on an ocean—all boundless we ride	77
Our life is like an idle dream	55
Peacefully, tenderly	125
Plunged in a gulf of dark despair	115
Praise the Lord, 'tis good to raise	7
Praise waits in Zion, Lord, for thee	11
Praise the Lord, ye heavens adore him	27
Praise the Lord, ye saints adore him	129
Prayer is appointed to convey	67
Prayer is the soul's sincere desire	67
Quick as the spark inspires	47
Remark, my soul, the narrow bounds	63
Remember thy Creator	87
Rock of Ages, cleft for me	83
Rocked in the cradle of the deep	13
Savior! though my rebellious will	21
Savior, thy gentle voice	109
Saved ourselves by Jesus' blood	83
See, gracious God, before thy throne	93
Shall we sing in heaven forever	85
Shout the tidings of salvation	113
Since all the varying scenes of time	25
Since God is mine, then present things	29
Sinners, will you scorn the message	63
Sinner, go; will you go	79
Sinners, are you still secure	61
Since first thy word awaked my heart	121
Sister, thou wast mild and lovely	131
Songs of praise awoke the morn	33

	PAGE.
Soon and forever the breaking of day	81
Stand up and bless the Lord	17
Star of peace, to wanderer weary	129
Still will we trust, though earth seem	99
Sweet is the friendly voice	53
Sweet hour of prayer	67
Swell the anthem, raise the song	117
Swell the anthem, raise the song	103
Tarry with me, oh my Savior	101
Teach us, O Lord, to keep in view	95
The heavens declare thy glory, Lord	11
The Lord of Sabbaoth let us praise	31
The Savior risen to-day we praise	37
The Lord my pasture shall prepare	41
The angels that watched round the tomb	43
The God who dwells above the skies	49
The morning light is breaking	49
The sinner who confesseth me	55
The turf shall be my fragrant shrine	67
The silver cord is loosened	133
The Christian banner, dread no loss	135
Thee we adore, eternal name	77
There seems a voice in every gale	11
There comes a day, a fearful day	25
There's a region above	79
There is a land immortal	109
There is an hour of hallowed peace	111
There is a fountain filled with blood	115
There's a land far away	115
There is no night in heaven	133
They who on the Lord rely	61
Thou that dost my life prolong	117
Thou art the Way; and he who sighs	119
Thou very present aid	129
Through the love of God our Savior	123
Through tribulation deep	41
Thus far the Lord has led me on	7
Thy kingdom, gracious Lord	129
Time speeds away, away, away	119
To the hall of the feast came the sinful	81
To thee, oh blessed Savior	87
To thee, oh blessed Savior	109
Touch not the cup, it is death to thy soul	95
'T was the commission of our Lord	57
We are too far from thee, our Savior	136
We love thy name, we love thy laws	57
We have heard of that bright, that holy	85
Weary souls, that wander wide	121
We're traveling to an heavenly home	63
We're passing from the earth away	63
We're traveling home to heaven	65
We're going home, we've had visions	91
Weeping sinners, dry your tears	105
What could your Redeemer do	39
What wondrous, mighty work is this	73
When languor and disease invade	21
When morning reviveth her beams	27
When the orb of morn enlightens	27
Where countless throngs in spirit one	51
When for eternal worlds we steer	83
When the worn spirit wants repose	89
When the spark of life is waning	111
When we can not see our way	119
While Theo I seek, protecting Power	25
Who are these in bright array	39
Why do we mourn departing friends	117
Why will ye waste on trifling cares	123
With joy we hail the sacred day	29
With my substance I will honor	71
With my substance I will honor	113
With Israel's God, who can compare	9
Within thy house, O Lord our God	31
Ye nations round the earth rejoice	23
Ye joyous ones, upon whose brow	107
Ye servants of the Lord	99
Ye who in his courts are found	14
You may sing of the beasts of the mountain	53
You dying sons of men	105
Young people, all attention give	65
Your harps, ye trembling saints	121

www.ingramcontent.com/pod-product-compliance
Lightning Source LLC
Chambersburg PA
CBHW022120160426
43197CB00009B/1099